This collection of innovative, powerful case studies tells us that epistemic justice is fundamentally about the work of creative academics in designing new and exciting learning adventures for their students. They remind us that addressing decolonisation is not about flicking a switch; it is the interweaving of creativity and commitment to transformation.

– Ahmed Bawa, Professor of Higher Education, Johannesburg Business School; former Chief Executive Officer of Universities South Africa

Ten stimulating essays offer valuable contextualisation for decolonisation, Africanisation, and epistemic justice struggles in contemporary South Africa ... this book enables questions of transformation, reconciliation and justice to be approached anew.

– Su-ming Khoo, Professor, School of Political Science and Sociology, University of Galway, Ireland

This provocative book engages meaningfully with epistemic (in)justice by invoking a critical-social imaginary for curriculum change ... the editors have curated an outstanding collection that turns to our entangled past to reimagine our present and future.

– Kasturi Behari-Leak, Dean, Centre for Higher Education Development, and co-chair, Curriculum Change Working Group, University of Cape Town

If, like me, you're interested in how universities actually work ... you will be drawn to the discussion about the University of Cape Town's (UCT) innards around the question of decolonisation. I thoroughly enjoyed the multiple insightful analyses of how teaching and learning happens in some of UCT's classrooms.

– Crain Soudien, Professor, School of Education, University of Cape Town

This is brave, honest and deeply reflexive collection, which illuminates both personal and political struggles in engaging with curriculum change. It makes a significant contribution to decolonial scholarship in an African context.

– Harsha Kathard, Professor and acting Deputy Vice-Chancellor, Teaching and Learning, University of Cape Town, and Research Director, Inclusive Practices Africa

EPISTEMIC JUSTICE AND THE POSTCOLONIAL UNIVERSITY

EDITED BY AMRITA PANDE, RUCHI CHATURVEDI
AND SHARI DAYA

WITS UNIVERSITY PRESS

Published in South Africa by:
Wits University Press
1 Jan Smuts Avenue
Johannesburg 2001

www.witspress.co.za

First published 2023

http://dx.doi.org.10.18772/22023087847

978-1-77614-784-7 (Paperback)
978-1-77614-785-4 (Hardback)
978-1-77614-786-1 (Web PDF)
978-1-77614-787-8 (EPUB)

This publication is peer reviewed following international best practice standards for
academic and scholarly books.

Project manager: Catherine Damerell
Copy editor: Catherine Damerell
Proofreaders: Koliswa Moropa, Lee Smith
Indexer: Margaret Ramsay
Cover design: Hothouse
Typeset in 10 point Garamond Pro

CONTENTS

FIGURES AND TABLES

ABBREVIATIONS AND ACRONYMS

ACC	African Centre for Cities (UCT)
ACDI	African Climate and Development Initiative (UCT)
AGI	African Gender Institute (UCT)
AMCU	Association of Mineworkers and Construction Union
ANC	African National Congress
AU	African Union
AZAPO	Azanian People's Organisation
BAC	Black Academic Caucus (UCT)
BACCC	Black Academic Caucus Curriculum Committee (UCT)
BRICS	Brazil, Russia, India, China, South Africa
CARICOM	Caribbean Community (Antigua and Barbuda, Bahamas, Barbados, Belize, Dominica, Grenada, Guyana, Haiti, Jamaica, Montserrat, Saint Kitts and Nevis, Saint Lucia, Saint Vincent and the Grenadines, Suriname, and Trinidad and Tobago)
CAS	Centre for African Studies (UCT)
CCA	Centre for Contemporary Art (Lagos)
CCWG	Curriculum Change Working Group (UCT)
CODESRIA	Council for the Development of Social Science Research in Africa
FAWE	Forum for African Women Educationalists
FMF	Fees Must Fall
IFP	Inkatha Freedom Party
NGO	non-governmental organisation
NUM	National Union of Mineworkers
RDP	Reconstruction and Development Programme
RMF	Rhodes Must Fall
SACP	South African Communist Party
SADC	Southern African Development Community
SANCO	South African National Civic Organisation
SAPS	South African Police Service

SASO	South African Students, Organisation
SJC	Social Justice Coalition
SOGIESC	sexual orientation, gender identity, gender expression and sex characteristics
TNC	transnational corporation
TRC	Truth and Reconciliation Commission
UDF	United Democratic Front
UNESCO	United Nations Educational, Scientific and Cultural Organization
WTO	World Trade Organization

ACKNOWLEDGEMENTS

This book grew out of a University of Cape Town (UCT) teaching grant awarded to the volume editors as members of the Black Academic Caucus Curriculum Committee (BACCC) in 2016. Seeking to bring vital conversations around decolonisation and epistemic justice into the university space, we used this funding to run a two-part workshop and host a dialogue with Gayatri Chakravorty Spivak, together with partners at the UCT Institute for Creative Arts. Spivak subsequently delivered a UCT public lecture, entitled 'Still Hoping for a Revolution', as part of our programme of events. Our thanks go to Jay Pather and Catherine Boulle at the Institute for Creative Arts (ICA), and Mignonne Breier and Judith Rix at the University Research Office, for co-hosting these critical conversations.

In 2018, participants from the earlier workshops came together again in an open forum on interdisciplinary and transdisciplinary methodologies. In 2019, presenters met in a more focused session to workshop their papers for this publication. Alongside the contributors and editors of this volume, the 2016, 2018 and 2019 workshop presenters included Kristen Abrahams, Denisha Anand, Ihsaan Bassier, Victoria Collis-Buthelezi, Sumangala Damodaran, Brian Kamanzi, Harsha Kathard, Trevor McArthur, Camalita Naicker, Siyabonga Njica, Ayanda Nombila, Teni Ntoi, Zarina Patel, Mershen Pillay, António Tómas and Leslie Witz. Their incisive insights inspired us to take this collection forward. We hope that their rich contributions to these sessions will be shared in other publication spaces.

The 2018 and 2019 events took place under the aegis of the MPhil in Theories of Justice and Inequality programme housed in the Department of Sociology at UCT. We would especially like to thank Sepideh Azari, Kirsty Button, Rutendo Hadebe and Rhoda Isaacs for invaluable administrative support. Our treasured colleagues Trevor McArthur and Bianca Tame played a crucial role in organising these workshops. Emma Daitz has been a rigorous and thoughtful editorial assistant throughout this project and helped to bring it to fruition. Project findings were presented at UCT's 2019 Teaching and Learning Conference on 'Reimagining Higher Education'.

Additional financial support for this book project was provided by National Research Foundation (NRF) of South Africa grants (Grant numbers 118573 and 103712); the UCT Research Support Services; a University Capacity Development Grant (UCT sub-project code 1003); and the University Cape Town HUB of the Andrew W. Mellon-funded Other Universals, a supra-national consortium, convened by the Centre for Humanities Research, University of the Western Cape.

INTRODUCTION

EPISTEMIC JUSTICE AND THE UNIVERSITY OF CAPE TOWN: THINKING ACROSS DISCIPLINES

Ruchi Chaturvedi, Shari Daya and Amrita Pande

Cape Town is often referred to as the last colonial outpost in Africa. Driving into the city via the N2 highway, one cannot miss the red-roofed, ivy-covered buildings forming the Upper Campus of the University of Cape Town (UCT), poised on the slopes of Devil's Peak and overlooking the suburbs. From the highway, the campus appears leafy, staid and serene, but this image belies a tumultuous history that stretches from the colonial era into the present. This book takes UCT's history as a point of departure to explore urgent questions of legacies, violence and justice in the dynamic landscape of South African higher education. It does not provide a social history of the institution, nor does it pretend to deliver a comprehensive account of the many forms of resistance, struggle and, indeed, transformation that have played out on UCT campuses. Rather, building on Gayatri Chakravorty Spivak's (1988) seminal work on epistemic violence, the volume as a whole – and we as the authors of this introduction – seek to take seriously the systemic and still-pervasive othering of certain bodies in the academy, while actively seeking to build an understanding of what epistemic *justice* looks like in particular spaces of teaching, learning and research at this institution.

Anyone familiar with South African university politics in recent years will be well aware that on 8 March 2015, student activist Chumani Maxwele emptied a bucket of human faeces on a statue of Cecil John Rhodes which had been prominently positioned at the entrance to UCT's Upper Campus since 1934. This attack on South Africa's 'last Rhodesian landscape' (Nick Shepherd, cited in Knudsen and Andersen 2019, 241) was a protest against the 'resilient colonialism' (Nyamnjoh 2016) and the ongoing celebration of imperial and colonial figures at universities in South Africa. It ignited a worldwide student movement which came to be known as Fallism, in the form of Rhodes Must Fall (RMF) and the subsequent Fees Must Fall (FMF).

In no small measure, Maxwele's catalytic shit-throwing positioned UCT as a leader in the global quest for decolonising knowledge. The story of this event and the consequent rise of the Fallist movements has become for many the 'origin story' of decolonisation in South African higher education as we move later into the twenty-first century. In this volume, however, we seek to shift and expand this story both in *time*, by historicising the colonial and decolonial narratives with which many scholars are now working in South Africa, and in *space*, by exploring the specific sites from which transformation has been emerging for many years through struggles, contestations and experiments. Insofar as they relate to the African continent, these stories are little-known, yet as far back as the 1960s, after political independence, many African countries confronted the challenges of transforming higher education by initiating conversations around 'Afrocentricity' (Cheikh Anta Diop University, Dakar, Senegal), 'Africanising' their universities as a national project (University of Nigeria, Nsukka), recovering and rewriting African agency in history and archives (Ibadan School in Nigeria), emphasising pan-Africanism (Al Akhawayn University in Ifrane, Morocco) and, just as importantly, by admitting African students. These processes began much later in South Africa, and South African institutions demonstrate little awareness of our other African colleagues' journeys along the road of decolonial transformation.

Of course, South Africa stands among the very last of the world's postcolonial regions to achieve political equality for all its citizens. Nearly 30 years after the first democratic election in 1994, the ways in which the country continues to grapple with its colonial (including apartheid) legacies is well documented and highlighted in accounts of spatial segregation, massive social and economic inequalities, systemic racism, and visceral interpersonal hurt, hate and bias. South Africa also continues to reckon with the epistemic injustices that colonialism as a system of knowledge and representation left in its wake.

UCT, and the nation more broadly, thus inhabits a 'post-colonial time' (Hall 1996, 242) – an era that is neither cleanly separated from the past nor mired in it. This is an era of 'liquid modernity', as Zygmunt Bauman (2013) has put it, where relations of power and knowledge are not the same as they were even just a few years ago, and where many struggle to locate themselves or narrate the meaning of events. In our institutions of higher education, a paradigm shift is under way. That shift is signalled through renewed calls for decolonisation on many campuses of the country, drawing attention to the need to rethink curricula and pedagogies, as well as the material spaces of the lecture theatres, classrooms, corridors, meeting rooms and living areas that staff and students inhabit. In the realms of scholarship and activism, it is abundantly clear that we – that is, the entire academic community – must interrogate historical inequalities and their persistence and transformation into the present if we are to reshape our institutions of higher learning as spaces of justice.

The inequalities in our institutions run deep, creating boundaries between those who count as credible producers of knowledge and those who are 'known' or the objects of such knowledge (Fricker 2007; Shilliam 2016). These inequalities rest on historical legacies but are simultaneously taking on new forms in the present. The essays in this collection hold the past and the present, and their complex events and discourses, in productive tension. As the editors of this volume, we are acutely aware of the backdrop of collusion, oppression and epistemic violence that characterises UCT and other institutions. At the same time, we seek to emphasise that in this time of new forms of power and new resistance, academics have much to learn from the efforts of past generations who strove to transform higher education at UCT, and in South Africa more broadly. Their efforts opened pathways for the emergence of what Stuart Hall terms a new episteme in formation (1996, 255). The work of deconstruction and critique, of tracing the relations of power-knowledge and epistemic violence, has been ongoing for decades, as has the work of 'reconstructing' our fields, modes and spaces of study. As Hall (1996, 254) observes, even as the 'after-effects' of colonialism cast a long shadow, it is important to not only confront them but also go beyond them. This book is precisely about the concrete work of going beyond the legacy of systemic oppression in order to explore efforts to achieve epistemic justice in the academy.

The often contradictory and discomfiting histories of UCT have informed the analyses in this volume. Like the editors, the majority of the contributors are womxn. Most of us joined the university in the first decade of the 2000s and were soon grappling with questions of what it meant to teach and learn in South African higher education before, during and after the Fallist years. This volume was conceptualised under the aegis of the Black Academic Caucus Curriculum Committee (BACCC) in 2016, during the Fallist movements. Collectively, we sought to deconstruct and reconstruct a wide range of

disciplines and areas of study. As a curriculum committee, we wanted to articulate answers to incisive questions raised by the student movements about the
epistemic orientations of the UCT curriculum, and the ethics of research in
the institution (Kessi, Marks and Ramugondo 2020).

Passion as well as reflexivity were in the air. Students' questions propelled
us. Shared camaraderie, songs sung together in mass meetings, the energies
and support of university workers and staff sustained us. That solidarity was
vital when we met again some days and weeks after the rape and murder of
UCT student Uyinene Mrwetyana in 2019. Fundamental lessons of feminist
scholarship and activism became vivid in that instance amidst meetings and
demonstrations to protest her slaying and celebrate her life: namely, to interrogate and challenge all forms of violence – structural, symbolic, epistemic
and physical – and to do so together in ways that brought solace and generated strength, through tears and smiles. We have, in the course of making this
book, sought to abide by those lessons.

SITUATING UCT

We locate this collection at a university that has campuses in some of the
wealthiest and lushest areas of the city of Cape Town, not because UCT is
exemplary in its transformative practices – far from it. Rather, our UCT
starting point is a deliberate attempt to trouble and deepen the South
African decolonisation narratives that in some sense arose from this site
and have taken hold around this institution, albeit in variegated and uneven ways. UCT is both the birthplace of Fallism and a space of pervasive
racism and structural violence (IRTC [Institutional Reconciliation and
Transformation Commission] 2019), one that regularly celebrates its position as the top-ranking university in Africa, yet struggles to retain Black
staff. What can epistemic justice and decolonisation mean in an institution
that has colluded with colonialism and apartheid even while resisting them?

We can start at the beginning: UCT was established in 1829 as the South
African College, a high school for boys from wealthy white English - and
Dutch-speaking families. Fifty-seven years later, in 1886, the college admitted
womxn for the first time. As described on UCT's official website, funding
from mining companies with interests in gold and diamonds, and a substantial grant from the colonial state, led to its establishment as a university in
1918 – complete with not only departments of mineralogy and geology 'to

meet the need for skilled personnel in the country's emerging diamond and gold-mining industries' but also a medical school, an education department, and courses in engineering.[1]

UCT's autobiographical narrative proceeds from commemorative statements about its initial founding to a celebratory section about the resistance mounted by its students and staff against the apartheid state from the 1960s to the 1990s. The way that the institution tells its own history and its jump from one moment to the other – from UCT's establishment under the aegis of the colonial state to its defiance of the state – is rapid, and rather awkward. In one paragraph, visitors to UCT's official website learn that the university received a substantial grant from the erstwhile colonial state, as well as land bequeathed by Cecil John Rhodes, and in the next instance, we see the institution's anti-apartheid struggle credentials proudly displayed. Between these moments sits a loud silence around UCT's long history of complicity with the colonial and apartheid state.

Complicity is a theme that some of UCT's luminaries – from former vice-chancellor Njabulo S. Ndebele (1986, 2007), to former students such as literary theorist Mark Sanders (2002) and novelist J. M. Coetzee (1974, 1982) – have explored in their works. Recognition of complicity in the institution and maintenance of settler colonialism and apartheid must underpin ethical, intellectual, social and political engagements with UCT (Sanders 2002; Clingman 2005). The charge sheet against the university is long. Teresa Barnes' (2015, 2019) research on how the legitimacy of apartheid was reproduced in public higher education grounds our understanding of much of this complicity, as does Lungisile Ntsebeza's (2012, 2014, and this volume) ongoing research on the history of the Centre for African Studies and the 'dis-appointment' of the eminent anthropologist Archie Mafeje.

Mahmood Mamdani's (1998) searing critique of the humanities faculty's 'foundation course', delivered at a 1998 public seminar, pushes us to revisit not only the ways in which Africa has been taught at UCT, and the premise of Bantu education reproduced, but also to recall how the university was constituted as a site of segregationist practices, how it sought to facilitate the work of 'native' administrations, and led by people who consigned the 'native' to the 'waiting room of history' (Chakrabarty 2000, 8–9). Mafeje (cited in Hendricks 2008, 426) described his time as a student at UCT in the 1950s in this way:

... we were not allowed to use any of the facilities at the university, including things like dining halls and residences for students ... then there was a swimming pool down near the College of Music ... out of bloody-mindedness one day I jumped into the whites-only pool ... as soon as I got in they all screamed and got out of the pool.

In the meantime, J. P. Duminy, the vice-chancellor of the university from 1958–1967, lamented that the '10 million Africans ... far outnumbered the Whites and Cape Coloured folk' in the country. In reference to African communities, he wrote:

> The small group of the 'elite' (the upper crust) find themselves in a no-man's land full of uncertainties and frustrations; the semi-Westernized (the middle layer) have been cut adrift from their tribal sanctions and customs, and live in conditions which leave a lot to be desired ... the lower layer (the primitive majority), backward, superstitious, ignorant, eke out an uncertain existence ... We have suffered criticism and contempt from all quarters of the world for refusing to entertain the idea of granting universal franchise to these people, but it should be obvious that such an idea is quite unreasonable and altogether untenable (cited in Hendricks 2008, 424).

UCT's own mission, as its much celebrated vice-chancellor during the war years and champion of academic freedom T. B. Davie noted, was to contribute towards 'intellectual and spiritual salvation' of the African, otherwise deemed 'primitive and barbaric', through contact with the 'superior culture of the white man' (cited in Barnes 2015, 13). That was the reasoning for the limited forms of social integration that UCT offered to its Black students in the early years of apartheid. In the 1960s, the UCT administration and council dispensed with principles of academic freedom at the behest of the education ministry and rescinded its appointment of its own alumnus Archie Mafeje on account of his race. Mafeje's 'dis-appointment' provoked a nine-day student sit-in of the university's key administrative building in August 1968 (Phillips 2019, 318–324). An apology from the university followed four decades later in 2008. In the intervening years, Mafeje went on to earn a PhD in anthropology from Cambridge University, became the head of the Sociology Department at the University of Dar-es-Salaam, Queen Juliana professor of anthropology and sociology of development at the Institute of Social Studies in The Hague, and director of the Multidisciplinary Research Centre at the University of Namibia. At UCT, meanwhile, Andrew Murray, the chair of philosophy and ethics from 1937–1970, an avowed anti-communist and supporter of apartheid, testified for the state in the 1956 Treason Trial, gave opinions and witness statements against several anti-apartheid activists until the 1980s leading to their imprisonment, while also actively working as a member of the South African censorship board (Barnes 2015, 24–25; 2019, 70–82).

Through these decades of colonial and apartheid rule, there are many other questions that arise: what was happening in lecture theatres, classrooms, seminars and boardrooms at the time? What was happening in university curricula in the disciplines of psychology, history, biology and criminal law? What was happening in faculty and committee meetings? We know from Howard Phillips' book *UCT under Apartheid* (2019, 268 -270), covering the period 1948–1968, that UCT accepted racially segregated ward rounds and post-mortems in its famous medical school, that the Michaelis School of Fine Art conducted racially segregated life-drawing classes, that the Zoology Department organised 'whites-only' field trips, that sports teams were similarly segregated and so was seating at intervarsity games. To paraphrase Phillips (2019, 551), UCT was after all cut from the same cloth as apartheid South Africa.

If that was the case, then how else did UCT's entanglement with colonialism and apartheid reproduce racist thinking even as sections of its staff and student body were mobilising against it? In what ways did the university's curricula and classrooms, and the research and pedagogical labours of its staff reflect, repeat and authorise racialised and ethnicised identities while endeavouring to civilise them? The university's self-narratives do not guide us here, but old and new scholarship tells future researchers where to look. They might for instance look in social anthropologist Alfred Radcliffe-Brown's ethnological files which he compiled during his time at UCT as a 'specialist on the native question' (Phillips 1993, 24). Studies may be conducted on 'adaptive bourgeois theories of social control' that university academics produced in the service of colonial administration (Mafeje 1976, 318). Researchers might also comb the archives of economics departments that taught students to measure the success of the colour bar policy, or question papers of anatomy courses that grappled with eugenics even as they taught students to measure craniums, noses and femurs for racial differences.[2] Equally, they could study the history of English literary studies (Collis-Buthelezi 2016, 73), and examine the details of the 'disadvantaged curriculum' on African studies that the university continued to produce for 'disadvantaged students' even in the post-apartheid era (Mamdani 1998, 72).

Mamdani, newly appointed as professor of African studies in the late 1990s, developed a curriculum for a course entitled 'Problematising Africa', which sought to displace essentialist frameworks of interpreting African society, polity and economy. In their place Mamdani argued for a historical sociology anchored in the work of scholars writing from the continent that gave meaningful historical depth to African experience. The course he sought to institute at UCT (but was barred from doing) revolved around debates on history, political economy and gendered life of the continent, drawing on the writings of scholars such as Cheikh Anta Diop, Wamba dia Wamba, Ifi Amadiume and Issa Shivji. Mamdani's view was that their different understandings of the African continent produced a complex, multilayered picture of the continent. It contained lessons for the newly democratic South Africa as it sought to understand itself and its relationship with the rest of Africa. The programme resulted in much contestation within the university from administrators and staff who had refuted that relationship and who, Mamdani noted, offered a racialised periodisation of African history through disciplines that centred 'White experience as a universal, human, experience' (1998, 63–64). Existing teaching practices, argued Mamdani (1998), failed to combine pedagogical challenges and the needs of a historically disadvantaged student body with an excellent curriculum. In 1999, Mamdani left UCT altogether, and it was some time before genuine evidence of meaningful Africanisation and decolonisation was visible in UCT curricula.

Between the Mamdani affair and the early 2020s, however, much has changed at UCT, including in (some) curricula. Hedley Twidle, a professor in the Department of English Literary Studies, remarks that the books of J. M. Coetzee were inescapable in that department just a few years before, and 'are now barely taught' (2017, 106). Instead, contemporary writing from Black Africa and the global South features prominently, and modernity and coloniality are directly interrogated. At the Centre for African Studies, a course entitled 'Problematising the Study of Africa: Interrogating the

Disciplines', inspired by Mamdani's work, is offered at the postgraduate level. This volume shows how the current cohort of academic staff are engaging with curriculum debates and ongoing attempts to challenge epistemic canons within their disciplines – art history and visual culture, history, law, psychology, geography and urban studies. Despite these positive examples, deep and crosscutting interventions into the established curriculum are difficult to achieve, more so in certain disciplines whose paradigms are often seen as value-neutral, stable or natural. This was illustrated in some of the intense debates around the UCT Curriculum Change Working Group Framework, a document produced by the Curriculum Change Working Group (CCWG), established in 2016 to 'facilitate dialogue across the university over a period of 18 months ... in order to shape strategies for meaningful curriculum change' (CCWG 2018, 4).[3]

The old and new research about the Mafeje 'dis-appointment' and the Mamdani affair has allowed us to chronicle the institution's complicity in pushing back against previous attempts at Africanisation and decolonisation. In the archives we find much less written about the institution's refusal to acknowledge and support feminist and pan-African spaces and energies. This was illustrated in the vigorous discussions, which started as early as 1995, about whether there was any need to establish a gender institute at UCT. In 1995, as Mamphela Ramphele stepped into the role of deputy vice-chancellor, the founding of such an institute became a way to take employment equity seriously.

Initially, a gender institute was understood quite narrowly as a space of opportunity that could bring together soft-funded English-speaking womxn scholars from across the continent. Although from its inception the African Gender Institute (AGI) attempted to be pan-African, this aim was realised more fully in 1999, when Amina Mama, based in Nigeria at that time, took over as the chair of gender studies. Mama's deepest commitment was to create a relationship with African feminist thought, and policymaking on the continent. UCT, however, did very little to support this deep commitment. In effect, it was made clear to the AGI that, in order to survive and to have any institutional standing, it needed to focus its energies on a fee-generating undergraduate teaching programme and not on pan-African feminist work. Given the historical trajectory, it is no surprise that in 2012, Amina Mama 'chose' to leave UCT. In this volume, Kealeboga Mase Ramaru provides a multigenerational analysis of AGI's 'placemaking' as a producer of feminist knowledge and networks. The importance of this placemaking, despite and within this legacy of institutional politics and barriers, was brought into sharp relief during the Fallist movement when Black womxn at UCT ensured that feminism remained a guiding principle of the student movement (Ramaru 2017, and this volume).

In the wake of rising student resistance over the past five years, universities within South Africa have embraced the 'decolonial turn' in a range of ways: through assemblies, curriculum change, equity programmes, and more. Yet decoloniality itself is not always conceptualised with the requisite care in writing and practice within the South African academy. In the following section, we explore the decolonial school of thought as it has emerged in contemporary writings, situating these debates within the South African context and exploring how a focus on epistemic justice may enrich and expand them.

DECOLONIAL THINKING FROM SOUTH AFRICA

Decolonial thinking, broadly viewed, borrows heavily from the writings and philosophies of Latin American scholars Aníbal Quijano (2007), Ramón Grosfoguel (2007, 2008), Walter Mignolo (2011) and Nelson Maldonado-Torres (2007). For these scholars, colonisation affirms the process of colonialism, and the unequal relations between colonised and coloniser. Even as colonisation is brought to an end, the project of colonialism continues, in the form of economic exploitation or 'neo-colonialism' (Nkrumah 1965), and as an epistemic project – colonisation of the mind and psyche. In Ngũgĩ wa Thiong'o's (1986, 9) poetic lament: '... the night of the sword and the bullet was followed by the morning of the chalk and blackboard'. The scholars make a critical distinction between 'colonialism' and 'coloniality', and hence, 'decolonisation' and 'decoloniality'. Decoloniality, then, becomes an epistemic project that can delink Southern imaginations from the tenacious webs of Western knowledge systems. Struggles for epistemic freedom flourish across all countries which have a legacy of slavery, racism and colonialism – though nomenclatures may vary (Ndlovu-Gatsheni 2018).

Unarguably, a planetary and interconnected struggle requires a close South–South dialogue. Theories do travel, at least to a certain extent. However, if scholars who are sympathetic to the decolonial theories emerging from Latin America are truly committed to making local conditions the basis of theory formulations, they need to pay keen attention to historicising local conditions within southern Africa (Ndlovu-Gatsheni 2018; Pillay 2021). Struggles for epistemic freedom must vary depending on the past and present of these various geopolitical sites, and to analyse them as one will be detrimental to the struggle as well as any endeavour to understand that struggle. The decolonial turn, in any university, nation or continent, cannot be one that is divorced from historical experience and/or lifted out of context. How do we tread this delicate line, and historicise and problematise this concept of decoloniality, without conflating 'state boundaries with epistemic boundaries' and falling into the trap of nativism, exceptionalism or 'intellectual claustrophobia' (Mamdani 2001, xiii)?

The Latin American call for decoloniality is not limited to Latin America, yet when this concept is applied, however productively, to African or southern African realities, it needs to be reframed in ways that make sense for our particular histories and problems. The purpose here is not for theorists in Africa to compete with analytical thrusts in Latin America, but to be mindful of comparable yet disparate histories, and caution against any theoretical application based solely on the camaraderie of a shared colonial wound (Pillay 2018, 2021). The African continent not only has distinct precolonial societies but also its own precolonial genealogies of education which were erased, co-opted and corrupted in various ways by the unfolding of colonialism. Similarly, the unfolding of colonialism in particular ways on the continent, and hence the unfolding of decoloniality as an 'existential thought' (Mignolo 2011), can be traced back decades prior to the current euphoria about the decolonial school. As we noted earlier, the project of transforming higher education has had many edifying iterations on the continent since the 1960s – from Dakar to Dar-es-Salaam, from Rabat to Kampala. Some writings that emerged during these times tended to be defensive, and even nativist, in their attempt to recover and reconstruct pure, authentic and independent knowledge. For newly independent nations in Africa, much like the South Asian context, as the political theorist Aditya Nigam (2021) observes, decolonisation of thought has run parallel with nationalist discourses and projects of 'rediscovering the greatness' of the nation.

The 1970s was when the global economic crisis hit Africa and its newly independent nations. The continent saw its fair share of dictatorships and related political crises. In the world of higher education, this shifted conversations away from the politics of transformation and epistemology to the political economy of education and funding issues. The 1990s brought another layer of crises, predominated by the Bretton Woods structural adjustment programmes and World Bank mandates on every aspect of life, including the world of teaching and learning. This set the stage for the corporate university or what Mamdani (2011) labels 'corrosive consultancy culture'. In this neo-liberal paradigm, university researchers and postgraduate students are forced to sustain themselves through paid research. The decades between 1960–1990 unfolded rather differently for South Africa. The 1960s, the golden age of Africanisation of higher education in the rest of the continent, was when South Africa was in the throes of tyrannical oppression – apartheid – and resistance to it.

This continued oppression in the form of apartheid and settler colonialism makes the South African trajectory similar yet different from other colonised spaces that saw the colonising personnel and persons depart at the moment of liberation. It is also different from colonising spaces where the indigenous populations were decimated or coercively assimilated into the colonial project (Pillay 2018, 2021). The so-called native in many parts of Africa was imagined and represented in Western art and science as essentially different from the coloniser – primitive, savage and unchanging. In South Africa, reinforcing the separation of coloniser and colonised, the apartheid regime created tribal homelands (which were reinvented as traditional authorities after 1994). To understand the specific challenges confronting South African universities, it is imperative to pay heed to these racialised and ethnicised histories of the country, and its entangled modernities and traditions. Without perpetuating narratives of national exceptionalism, an understanding of the particular character of South Africa's colonial and liberation journey is needed to develop a full appreciation of what decolonial theory can do in this context.

Building on decades of trial and error in 'thinking independently', and of breaking with 'Euro-normality', contemporary South Africa does not have the excuse of remaining merely defensive or self-referential. Nor can our decolonial present be imagined in simple binaries of 'West versus non-West'. It is time for progressive academics to move beyond polemics and theorising and seize the challenge of the everyday in local contexts, putting theory to work dialogically, in ways that are truly useful for living and working in this place.

PEDAGOGICAL PRACTICES

Articles and books about decolonial theory, which have proliferated in recent years, allow tensions and ambiguities to be held open to a certain degree. In contrast, the constraints of timetables, packed lecture theatres, large and diverse classes, essays, tests and examinations, and the highly pressured, multivalent nature of academic roles in contemporary universities, demand that much is 'fixed', at least within a particular year. Given such challenges, as well as the limited (or nonexistent) pedagogical training that most academics receive, educators in higher education tend to fall back on their own experience of being taught as undergraduate students, thus replicating and perpetuating existing patterns. There is little time within the academic calendar for serious reflection on teaching practice, and it is a truism that teaching is undervalued at universities, despite managerial narratives to the contrary.

These genuine constraints notwithstanding, academics from diverse disciplines, such as the contributors to this volume, *are* creating spaces of change within our universities, and documenting their experiences and ideas. Those represented in this collection are often working against the grain of the academy, to design and teach new content as well as to imagine and enact new modes of engagement in spaces of teaching and learning. This book thus builds on a growing field of published work which we explore briefly here. It also emerges from engagements in multiple material and/or discursive spaces where educators are both challenging the status quo that rests on colonial legacies and practising decolonial pedagogies in ways that make sense for African contexts. Particular attention has been paid in these shifts to spaces of curriculum development and, to a lesser degree, to the material and embodied spaces of teaching and learning.

The first of these, the academic curriculum, has probably been the most visible space of pedagogical decolonisation in recent years (Morreira 2017; Luckett, Morreira and Baijnath 2019). For some, it has been seen as a site through which to achieve a 'quick fix' (Okech 2020) in the wake of protests and resistance. But a deeper look at the calls for curriculum transformation and at experiences of pushing for change, highlights more than issues of representation while also broadening what matters in terms of representation itself. For example, while the UK-based movement 'Why is my curriculum white?' (Peters 2015) asks a seemingly simple question, the response should not be limited to addressing the racial or ethnic identity of the authors whose work appears on course syllabi. As Suren Pillay (2018, 33) observes, 'you could still have an entirely Eurocentric course even if it is filled with African authors'. This does not dismiss the importance of representation but expands the question so that it interrogates assumptions about what is valued as knowledge and academic authority.

Critical questions about representation as well as other systemic issues were certainly asked at UCT in conversations about the transformation and decolonisation of curricula, energised from 2015 onwards through student-led plenaries, public lectures, assemblies, study circles, performances and marches. Thus, while there is no doubt that African authors and texts are represented much more fully now in the curricula of a wide range of disciplines at UCT, the barriers to achieving meaningful curriculum change remain significant. This is not unique to UCT. Scholars across the continent and in other postcolonial contexts remark on similar difficulties. There are numerous reasons for this but here we highlight two that are particularly significant. The first is the power of the canon in diverse disciplines, sometimes because the discipline *as* a discipline took shape around certain writings. Writing that came later than those deemed seminal, or from different sites, is therefore always already relegated to the status of Other.

It is hence important to interrogate who is reflected in the curriculum and where, through the lenses of both race and gender. Awino Okech (2020, 319) raises the question of which authors are listed as 'required' reading, and whose work is recommended or supplementary reading: 'Where material is placed as additional readings, it is de-prioritised by students and not taught in the classroom.' As she rightly argues, there is 'an underlying structural problem in relation to women's publishing', and especially Black womxn's publishing, that is 'reproduced in syllabi that inform teaching' (Okech 2020, 319). It is essential that we recognise that the citation practices of academics, not only in published research but also in curricula, play a major role in reinforcing the existing canon and the principles along which it takes shape.

The second major barrier to the decolonisation of our curricula also raises the question of what is validated as academic knowledge but goes beyond the question of representation. It lies in our cultures of theory and empirical practice (Roy 2016), which very often reproduce Africa as the source of case study material, or the site of 'the manual labour of collecting empirical research' (Mather 2007, 155). Much African scholarship is strongly developmentalist, an orientation that is facilitated and encouraged by funders' imperatives to address material inequalities, as well as by African scholars' own problem- and solution-oriented approaches to all sorts of questions. This 'theory/development dualism' (Robinson 2006) that positions the metropoles of the global North as sites of theory production and normative desires, and the global South as the sites through which Northern theories and norms are applied, not only results in our failure to provincialise Europe (Chakrabarty 2000) but also limits our capacity for research that can make sense of 'what is really going on' (Edjabe and Pieterse 2010) in everyday African lives, or imagine other ways of being on the African continent. Consequently, it fails to constructively critique and reimagine received understandings of democracy, development, freedom or the good life that would be truly just.

The curriculum, being in many ways the core of our teaching practice, must be a central focus in the move to initiate that critique and reimagination. However, the methodologies of teaching which, as Morreira, Taru and Truyts (2020, 138) note, constituted 'the second half of the RMF demand', are 'only just beginning to come under consideration'. Turning our attention to material spaces and interactions demands that we recognise the different forms of work in, and the micropolitics of, teaching and learning. Emotional and administrative forms of labour in teaching are deeply gendered, and seldom recognised as core to the pedagogical project. In addition, the everyday ways in which educators' actions, choices and omissions perpetuate oppression and damaging hierarchies, are difficult to confront in academic contexts that neither value nor make space for such conversations. Yet if careful work does not take place at the scale of the classroom (virtual or physical), and involve actively recognising and resisting the innumerable racist, sexist, ableist and anti-poor microaggressions that many experience in our spaces (Adams-Hutcheson and Johnston 2019), the project for epistemic justice will fail to launch.

Decolonial pedagogies require that educators (and students) work to become aware of our silences, such as who we respond to timeously or at all; whose names we don't remember, can't pronounce, or confuse with others; whose actions and words we fail to criticise, and whose complaints are heard and acted upon (Ahmed 2012; Tolia-Kelly 2017). Generating spaces of epistemic justice demands that we begin actively to 'see' who is interrupted and who is granted deference, who is credited for a good idea, who is called upon in classes and seminars, and who is rewarded for good performance on the basis of which criteria. Teaching, like all academic practice at the scale of the office, the lecture theatre, the laboratory, the corridor and the seminar room, is raced, classed and gendered, and decolonial pedagogies must find ways to bring these dynamics into relief. The aim here should not be to critique for the sake of critique but rather to enact resistance while also fostering the practices of care, collegiality, trust and reciprocity that already exist in teaching practice and mentoring relationships (Johnston-Anumonwo 2018). Love and care, in the academy, are radical acts, and while they seldom enter conversations about teaching, the shift to decolonial thinking provides an opportunity to shift our pedagogical vocabulary as well.

There is naturally a close relationship between the activities of teaching and learning and all the microscale decisions and interactions they involve, and the overarching disciplines, paradigms and theories within which these are carried out. While these may be distinguished as different aspects of the academic project, they are inevitably entangled, and the chapters in this volume demonstrate the impossibility of discussing knowledge as separate from practice, or vice versa. Some authors focus closely on experiments in the classroom and related spaces, while others take a wider view of the discipline that frames their teaching. Collectively, however, the chapters emphasise the importance of attending to the prevailing norms of our disciplines and, simultaneously, to imagining what greater justice might look like 'on the ground' of our teaching and learning spaces.

The contributors to this volume are situated predominantly (though not exclusively) in disciplines within the social sciences and humanities. It is in these spaces of debate that postcolonial and decolonial thinking first gained traction at UCT, as in many other institutions, and it is here that these approaches have effected the most change in curricula and academic practices. The staff and student activism that forced new conversations in 2015 and beyond originated from academic and political work that had been under way in the social sciences and humanities for years prior.

The natural sciences are not exempt from the need to rethink their histories, cultures and paradigms, despite the universality of many of their basic principles. Indeed, there have been important discussions, experiments and initiatives in this regard, in disciplines including mathematics, chemistry, geology, and more. Their relative silence in this volume is not a denial of the work being done in these spaces, but it does reflect the fact that, on balance, the engagement of natural scientists in debates about epistemic justice is less vibrant or at least, perhaps, less documented than that of their colleagues in the so-called softer sciences.

All that said, we are not aiming for comprehensive coverage of all the disciplines represented in, or adjacent to, the faculty of humanities. This collection is inevitably partial and incomplete, and we have no doubt omitted important and influential pedagogical experiments in spaces both in the humanities and beyond. As noted, the book grew out of a workshop series that was first initiated in 2016, and took years to develop into the collection you are now reading. In compiling this volume, we have sought to remain true to both the initial aims of the project for which the seed funding was secured, and to its evolution as some contributors moved on in the course of the workshop series while others came on board through word of mouth and personal, often serendipitous, connections.

It is our hope that the book will bring about many more such 'happy accidents' of connection and expand the spaces within which we converse with each other as scholars, teachers and colleagues. With many of the authors here, we see this book as a call for more inclusive participation in the conversations about justice, transformation and inclusion in the academy but also, and more specifically, for collaborative and interdisciplinary modes of working. The boundaries between faculties at UCT can be rigid, and meaningful cross-faculty engagement is hard to achieve. The creation and nurturing of shared spaces within the institution is sorely needed, not least to enable academics and students to share ideas and techniques for achieving greater justice in our curricula and pedagogical practices.

STRUCTURE AND CONTENT OF THE BOOK

The book is structured in three parts, each exploring particular challenges and experiments in shaping just curricula and institutional spaces at UCT and beyond. Each author works with the idea that a reading of epistemic justice in postcolonial academic spaces must take a multiscalar approach, one that addresses the global geographies of disciplinary and theoretical developments, as well as the institutional and classroom spaces where transformative pedagogies are imagined, designed and practised.

Chapters in part I of the volume, Aesthetics, Politics and Languages, exemplify the inventive crossing of disciplinary, genre, linguistic and national boundaries that is crucial for generating new paradigms for apprehending our realities and remaking them. Chapter 1 opens with Nomusa Makhubu's examination of the Fallist uprising in UCT's creative disciplines between 2015–2016, and her exploration of a number of art collectives, networks and schools on the African continent. Their 'itinerant interventions' compel us to ask what it might mean to reassemble our modes and places of learning, and make them more public, communal and decommodified. Staying with the theme of transcending boundaries, in chapter 2, Rike Sitas renders a provocative exploration of how artful performative practices are offering public pedagogies capable of reconstituting urban studies. Engaging with three interdisciplinary performance art projects, Sitas shows how their historicised, intentionally political and playful form of 'Southerning', trespassing and transgressing of spatial and disciplinary limits can help imagine new futures for our cities. In chapter 3, Shari Daya and Rike Sitas, co-teaching in the inherently interdisciplinary academic space of urban studies, present some of the complexities of working in the interstices of disciplinary norms, and the rich contributions to teaching and learning that can result. They argue for art, film and literature to be taken seriously as texts that are theoretical in their own right, a shift in thinking that can have powerful effects in debates about cities that are persistently developmentalist in nature.

In chapter 4 in this section, Athambile Masola reflects on the political and pedagogical possibilities that open up as historians turn to multilingual and visual archives to recover Black womxn's presence and voices in their curricula and classrooms. Embodied ways of telling and teaching African history that attend to the womxn's words, tones and tilts of their heads have, as Masola suggests, the capacity not only to vivify experiences of conquest and imperial power but also to rethink current nationalist narratives. Drawing on those voices and images, however, calls for another kind of attunement that established methodologies rarely teach. Masola's chapter offers pathways towards crafting such an attuned methodology, recovering but also responding in multiple languages and genres to heretofore silent womxn's voices in the archive.

Part II of the book, Justice, Curriculum and the Classroom, unpacks pedagogical experiments within psychology, history and law. The three chapters in this section take on disciplinary histories, politics and interventions to argue for new ways of seeing established academic norms, and practising both teaching and research. First, in chapter 5, drawing on Hal Cooper's research, Shose Kessi and Cooper historicise the practices and paradigms of contemporary psychology and through a case study of Fela Kuti's music. They argue for a decolonial approach that could tap into 'alternative rationalities' and reframe the discipline in ways relevant to African experiences and locations. Turning to historical studies, in chapter 6, Koni Benson and Kerusha Govender offer a thoughtful reflection on the experiences of designing, teaching and tutoring a course that challenged 'the myths of the "miraculous" 1994' moment in South Africa. The authors map the profound challenges inherent in confronting and subverting power relations in the classroom and beyond. In chapter 7 in this section, Jameelah Omar reflects on her experience of teaching criminal procedure in law, a topic that demands attention to theories of policing. Through a focus on heavy-handed racialised policing, a reality much in evidence in South African society, Omar links societal and legal issues to the Fallist protests of 2015–2017, and the ways in which these opened up her students' appreciation of the interdisciplinary subject of policing.

Part III, Contested Histories and Ethical Spaces, begins with an interview with Lungisile Ntsebeza, one of South Africa's leading scholars on land reform and democracy (chapter 8). As a student, staff member and now professor emeritus at UCT, Ntsebeza, interviewed by Sepideh Azari, offers an insightful first-person institutional history of the Centre for African Studies (CAS), and the people and projects that have passed through it. Azari's interview with Ntsebeza renders African studies and aligned units at UCT as spaces of hurt and hope, anxieties and aspirations to undo the injustices of the past. From the grounds of that fraught history emerged recent student movements and calls for intensive transformation and decolonisation of the university. This interview is followed by chapter 9 on the history and development of the African Gender Institute (AGI) at UCT, by Kealeboga Mase Ramaru. Ramaru, who was actively involved in the RMF movement, brings three generations of feminist perspectives together: Jane Bennett and Yaliwe Clarke as directors, and herself as a student and later as a staff member of the AGI, during the heady and challenging RMF and FMF days. The chapter provides a much-needed historically oriented analysis of AGI's pan-African vision, its relationship to wider university structures and institutional culture, and the role that it played in incubating and fostering the Black feminist orientation of many critical members of the student movements.

The section closes with chapter 10 in which Ari Sitas revisits some of the difficult debates within the student movements about violence and change, aggressive contestations and the possibility of a new ethic of reconciliation. Drawing on first-hand experience of struggles for liberation and social emancipation globally, Sitas cautions against the construction of otherness and recourse to violence as strategies of resistance, arguing instead for an ethic of reciprocity and 'humanitude'. Ari Sitas' purview is the scale of the national and the global; at the same time, his arguments speak to the contexts of academic corridors, meeting rooms and lecture theatres, both physical and virtual. They ground the critical call for an ethical and just postcolonial university, and close off the book with an outline for a new curriculum to help realise that vision.

Collectively, all these chapters make clear that if decolonial theory is to have real purchase, it must be embedded at the human scale of the institution, and in the spaces that we inhabit in our work as educators. The authors bring to life the work of operationalising epistemically just thinking through their accounts and reflections on the many efforts and experiments under way in classrooms and other spaces of teaching and learning. Each of the contributions highlights the many challenges inherent in translating complex and important theories of power and knowledge into the everyday working spaces of curricula and pedagogical practice. In analysing tangible areas of resistance and transformative intervention, they remind readers how, in each material space of teaching and learning, difficult choices have to be made, and complex social contexts confronted. But they offer glimpses, too, of the valuable rewards that this hard work can bring.

NOTES

1   University of Cape Town. n.d. 'History Introduction'. https://www.uct.ac.za/history-introduction.

2   Sepidah Azari's unpublished research on the role of the natural and social sciences in the construction of 'the native' in late colonial South African scholarship throws much-needed light on this topic.

3   For further reading on the debates and responses: https://www.news.uct.ac.za/news/debates/ccwg/.

REFERENCES

Adams-Hutcheson, Gail and Lynda Johnston. 2019. 'Flourishing in Fragile Academic Work Spaces and Learning Environments: Feminist Geographies of Care and Mentoring'. *Gender, Place and Culture* 26 (4): 451–467. https://doi.org/10.1080/096636 9X.2019.1596885.

Ahmed, Sara. 2012. *On Being Included: Racism and Diversity in Institutional Life*. Durham, NC: Duke University Press.

Barnes, Teresa. 2015. 'Beyond Protest: The University of Cape Town and Complicity with Apartheid'. Unpublished manuscript. http://www.historicalstudies.uct.ac.za/hst/news/terri-barnes-institutionalized-complicity-at-UCT.

Barnes, Teresa. 2019. *Uprooting University Apartheid in South Africa: From Liberalism to Decolonization*. Oxford: Routledge.

Bauman, Zygmunt. 2013. *Liquid Modernity*. Oxford: Wiley.

Chakrabarty, Dipesh. 2000. *Provincializing Europe: Postcolonial Thought and Historical Difference*. Princeton, NJ: Princeton University Press.

Clingman, Stephen. 2005. 'On Ethical Grounds'. *Law & Literature* 17 (2): 279–290. https://doi.org/10.1525/lal.2005.17.2.279.

Coetzee, John M. 1974. *Dusklands.* Johannesburg: Ravan Press.

Coetzee, John M. 1982. *Waiting for the Barbarians*. Harmondsworth: Penguin Books.

Collis-Buthelezi, Victoria. 2016. 'The Fire from Below: Towards a New Study of Literatures and Cultures (in English?) A Letter from a Literary Scholar in a South African University'. *Arts and Humanities in Higher Education* 15 (1): 67–78. https://doi.org/10.1177/1474022215613609.

Curriculum Change Working Group. 2018. 'Curriculum Change Framework'. University of Cape Town. https://www.uct.ac.za/main/teaching-and-learning/curriculum-change-working-group.

Edjabe, Ntone and Edgar Pieterse. 2010. 'Preface'. In *The African Cities Reader*, edited by Ntone Edjabe and Edgar Pieterse, 1–5. Cape Town: Chimurenga and African Centre for Cities.

Fricker, Miranda. 2007. *Epistemic Injustice: Power and the Ethics of Knowing*. Oxford: Oxford University Press.

Grosfoguel, Ramón. 2007. 'The Epistemic Decolonial Turn: Beyond Political Economy Paradigms'. *Cultural Studies* 21 (2–3): 211–223. https://doi.org/10.1080/09502380601162514.

Grosfoguel, Ramón. 2008. 'World-System Analysis and Postcolonial Studies: A Call for Dialogue from the Coloniality of Power Approach'. In *The Postcolonial and the Global,* edited by Revathi Krishnaswamy and John C. Hawley, 94–104. Minneapolis: University of Minnesota Press.

Hall, Stuart. 1996. 'When was "the Post-Colonial"? Thinking at the Limit'. In *The Post-Colonial Question: Common Skies, Divided Horizons*, edited by Iain Chambers and Lidia Curti, 242–260. London: Routledge.

Hendricks, Fred. 2008. 'The Mafeje Affair: The University of Cape Town and Apartheid'. *Social Dynamics* 67 (3): 423–451. https://doi.org/10.1080/00020180802505061.

IRTC (Institutional Reconciliation and Transformation Commission). 2019. *Final Report*. University of Cape Town. https://www.news.uct.ac.za/downloads/irtc/IRTC_Final_Report_2019.pdf.

Johnston-Anumonwo, Ibipo. 2018. 'Mentoring across Difference: Success and Struggle in an Academic Geography Career'. *Gender, Place and Culture* 26 (12): 1683–1700. https://doi.org/10.1080/0966369X.2019.1681369.

Kessi, Shose, Zoe Marks and Elelwani Ramugondo. 2020. 'Decolonizing African Studies'. *Critical African Studies* 12 (3): 271–282. https://doi.org/10.1080/21681392.2020.1813413.

Knudsen, Britta Timm and Casper Andersen. 2019. 'Affective Politics and Colonial Heritage, Rhodes Must Fall at UCT and Oxford'. *International Journal of Heritage Studies* 25 (3): 239–258. https://doi.org/10.1080/13527258.2018.1481134.

Luckett, Kathy, Shannon Morreira and Mohini Baijnath. 2019. 'Decolonising the Curriculum'. In *Re-imagining Curriculum: Spaces for Disruption*, edited by Lynn Quinn, 23–44. Stellenbosch: SUN Press.

Mafeje, Archie. 1976. 'The Problem of Anthropology in Historical Perspective: An Inquiry into the Growth of the Social Sciences'. *Canadian Journal of African Studies* 10 (2): 307–333. https://doi.org/10.2307/483835.

Maldonado-Torres, Nelson. 2007. 'On the Coloniality of Being'. *Cultural Studies* 21 (2–3): 240–270. https://doi.org/10.1080/09502380601162548.

Mamdani, Mahmood. 1998. 'Is African Studies to be Turned into a New Home for Bantu Education at UCT?' *Social Dynamics* 24 (2): 63–75. https://doi.org/10.1080/02533959808458649.

Mamdani, Mahmood. 2001. *When Victims Become Killers: Colonialism, Nativism, and the Genocide in Rwanda*. Oxford, UK: James Currey.

Mamdani, Mahmood. 2011. 'The Importance of Research in a University'. Keynote Address delivered at the Makerere University Research and Innovations Dissemination Conference, Makerere, Uganda, 11–12 April. https://www.pambazuka.org/resources/importance-research-university.

Mather, Charles. 2007. 'Between the "Local" and the "Global": South African Geography after Apartheid'. *Journal of Geography in Higher Education* 31 (1): 143–159. https://doi.org/10.1080/03098260601033076.

Mignolo, Walter D. 2011. *The Darker Side of Western Modernity: Global Futures, Decolonial Options.* Durham, NC: Duke University Press.

Morreira, Shannon. 2017. 'Steps Towards Decolonial Higher Education in Southern Africa? Epistemic Disobedience in the Humanities'. *Journal of African and Asian Studies* 52 (3): 287–301. https://doi.org/10.1177/0021909615577499.

Morreira, Shannon, Josiah Taru and Carina Truyts. 2020. 'Place and Pedagogy: Using Space and Materiality in Teaching Social Science in Southern Africa'. *Third World Thematics: A TWQ Journal* 5 (1–2): 137–153. https://doi.org/10.1080/23802014.2020.1747944.

Ndebele, Njabulo S. 1986. *Fools and Other Stories.* London: Reader's International.

Ndebele, Njabulo S. 2007. *Fine Lines from the Box: Further Thoughts about Our Country.* Johannesburg: Umuzi-Random House.

Ndlovu-Gatsheni, Sabelo. 2018. *Epistemic Freedom in Africa: Deprovincialization and Decolonization.* Oxford: Routledge.

Nigam, Aditya. 2021. 'Decolonizing Thought – Beyond Indian/Hindu Exceptionalism'. *Kafila.* https://kafila.online/2021/09/11/decolonizing-thought-beyond-indian-hindu-exceptionalism/.

Nkrumah, Kwame. 1965. *Neo-Colonialism: The Last Stage of Imperialism.* London: Thomas Nelson & Sons.

Ntsebeza, Lungisile. 2012. 'African Studies at UCT: An Overview'. In *African Studies in the Post-Colonial University*, edited by Thandabantu Nhlapo and Harry Garuba, 1–22. Cape Town: University of Cape Town in association with the Centre for African Studies.

Ntsebeza, Lungisile. 2014. 'The Mafeje and the UCT Saga: Unfinished Business?' *Social Dynamics* 40 (2): 274–288. https://doi.org/10.1080/02533952.2014.946254.

Nyamnjoh, Francis B. 2016. *Rhodes Must Fall: Nibbling at Resilient Colonialism in South Africa.* Bamenda: Langaa Research and Publishing Common Initiative Group.

Okech, Awino. 2020. 'African Feminist Epistemic Communities and Decoloniality'. *Critical African Studies* 12 (3): 313–329. https://doi.org/10.1080/21681392.2020.1810086.

Peters, Michael A. 2015. 'Why is My Curriculum White?' *Educational Philosophy and Theory* 47 (7): 641–646. https://doi.org/10.1080/00131857.2015.1037227.

Phillips, Howard. 1993. *The University of Cape Town 1918–1948: The Formative Years.* Cape Town: UCT Press.

Phillips, Howard. 2019. *UCT under Apartheid: From Onset to Sit-in: 1948–1968.* Part 1. Johannesburg: Jacana Media.

Pillay, Suren. 2018. 'Thinking the State from Africa: Political Theory, Eurocentrism and Concrete Politics'. *Politikon: South African Journal of Political Studies* 45 (1): 32–47. https://doi.org/10.1080/02589346.2018.1418203.

Pillay, Suren. 2021. 'The Problem of Colonialism: Assimilation, Difference and Decolonial Theory in Africa'. *Critical Times: Interventions in Global Critical Theory* 4 (3): 389–416. https://doi.org/10.1215/26410478-9355201.

Quijano, Aníbal. 2007. 'Coloniality and Modernity/Rationality'. *Cultural Studies* 21 (2–3): 168–178. https://doi.org/10.1080/09502380601164353.

Ramaru, Kealeboga. 2017. 'Feminist Reflections on the Rhodes Must Fall Movement'. *Feminist Africa* 22: 89–97.

Robinson, Jennifer. 2006. *Ordinary Cities: Between Modernity and Development*. London: Routledge.

Roy, Ananya. 2016. 'Who's Afraid of Postcolonial Theory?' *International Journal of Urban and Regional Research* 40 (1): 200–209. https://doi.org/10.1111/1468-2427.12274.

Sanders, Mark. 2002. *Complicities: The Intellectual and Apartheid*. Durham, NC: Duke University Press.

Shilliam, Robbie. 2016. 'The Aims and Methods of Liberal Education: Notes from a Nineteenth Century Pan-Africanist'. *International Journal of Politics, Culture, and Society* 29: 251–267. https://doi.org/10.1007/s10767-016-9227-5.

Spivak, Gayatri Chakravorty. 1988. 'Can the Subaltern Speak?' In *Marxism and the Interpretation of Culture*, edited by Cary Nelson and Lawrence Grossberg, 271–313. Basingstoke: Macmillan Education.

Thiong'o, Ngũgĩ wa. 1986. *Decolonising the Mind: The Politics of Language in African Literature*. Portsmouth, NH: Heinemann.

Tolia-Kelly, Divya P. 2017. 'A Day in the Life of a Geographer: "Lone", Black, Female'. *Area* 49 (3): 324–328. https://doi.org/10.1111/area.12373.

Twidle, Hedley. 2017. *Firepool: Experiences in an Abnormal World*. Cape Town: Kwela.

PART I
AESTHETICS, POLITICS AND LANGUAGES

1 *UKUHAMBA UKUBONA*/TRAVELLING TO KNOW: MOBILITY AS COUNTER-CURRICULUM ACROSS AFRICA

NOMUSA MAKHUBU

DISLOCATED WORLDS

'The art world is a white world.' Reiterated by the art journalist and critic Lloyd Pollak in a 2003 documentary film, *The Luggage is Still Labelled* (Voyiya and McGee 2003), this statement reflects how the vulgar racialisation of space in the arts has shaped art education and, as a result, art practice. Recorded nine years after the fall of apartheid, the documentary collates interviews with art practitioners and writers, most of whom are Black alumni of the Michaelis School of Fine Art (MSFA) at the University of Cape Town (UCT). They testified to the alienation of being few in a class dominated by white students and teaching staff in the institution, as well as the ghettoisation they experienced as Black artists. It was Gavin Younge, the director of MSFA between 1993 and 1999, who pointed out that the 'issue of institutional racism … has to be confronted' and 'there is no doubt that it does exist' (cited in Voyiya and McGee 2003).

In the documentary, the artist Thembeka Qangule (cited in Voyiya and McGee 2003) shares her experiences at MSFA, stating that she 'felt uncomfortable' and 'felt like too much of an outsider' and that 'most of the time' she 'would just take [her] bag and leave [class]', because Black students were 'not being accommodated'. Likewise, the artist Sipho Hlati (cited in Voyiya and

McGee 2003) attests that Michaelis made him resort to the Bikoist adage: 'Black man, you're on your own.' Moreover, artists such as Lionel Davis pointed out that the predominance of European and American art and theory disadvantages Black artists: 'we know everything about European artists' and 'very little about Africa' (cited in Voyiya and McGee 2003). Thembinkosi Goniwe, curator and art historian, posed the question: 'why was there minimal [contemporary] South African art [included in the curriculum]?' (cited in Voyiya and McGee 2003).

Touted as 'one of South Africa's foremost institutions for the study of fine art and new media at an advanced level', MSFA was founded in 1925 following the 1920 bestowal of a chair of fine art to UCT by the German-born art collector and mining magnate Maximillian Michaelis.[1] It is one of the oldest university art schools in South Africa, although the University of Fort Hare is one of the first to offer art education to Black students. By the time MSFA was established, there were already debates about the shaping of art education in South Africa in a context where 'the influence of British models of art education was strongly felt' (Tietze 2014, 4). The Roeland Street School of Art and Cape Town School of Fine Art (CTSFA), which preceded MSFA, were influenced by the British-inspired South Kensington system. CTSFA art teachers were integrated into MSFA, which, in its initial years, had mostly British teaching staff who were graduates of the Slade School of Fine Art (a university art school founded in 1871 at University College London) (Tietze 2014). Since 'most of the Michaelis staff were British and, led by the amiable but rather upright [John Laviers] Wheatley', Tietze (2014, 15) argues, 'they collectively created an atmosphere of cautious correctness that seemed stifling to some of the new, more radical voices in the Cape Town art world'.

This conservatism continued to pervade MSFA, even under different leadership (Edward Roworth, who was the director between 1938 and 1948). Although Rupert Shepard (director of MSFA from 1948 until 1962) fostered pedagogical experimentation, it was only in the 1970s under Neville Dubow's directorship that questions about artists' social engagement would emerge (Tietze 2014). The 1976 Soweto uprising had inspired political consciousness in art practice, and MSFA hosted 'The State of Art in South Africa' national conference from 16–20 July 1979. This conference sought to 'urge artists to refuse participation in state sponsored exhibitions' until there was inclusion of Black artists (SAHO 2019). Notably, most Black artists boy-cotted the MSFA conference, citing the predominance of white presenters in 'an elitist institution' (SAHO 2019). In 1982, Black artists would instead travel to Gaborone, Botswana, for the 'Culture and Resistance' conference organised by Medu Art Ensemble. Not only did this demonstrate the deep racial fissures reinforced by 'the white art world', even when it sought to be socially engaged, it also showed the implications of the dislocation and transplantation of colonial institutions whose cultural obtrusions have yet to be mapped.

The omission of African art in the MSFA curriculum would later be addressed; but even then, it focused narrowly on so-called ethnic artefacts. The inclusion of contemporary African art (validated in European and American institutions) in the curriculum is recent. From around 2013, MSFA went as far as to include in its prospectus that 'special recognition is given to the school's place in Africa'. By this time, African-born curators such as Okwui Enwezor (1963–2019), Chika Okeke-Agulu, Bisi Silva (1962–2019), Koyo Kouoh, Simon Njami, Salah M. Hassan and others had since the 1990s gained international acclaim, changing the way in which contemporary African art was received in institutions globally. To catch up with a fast-changing artworld, MSFA added the word 'Africa' in its public face, and in course titles and descriptions. Nevertheless, the nascent inclusion of African writers, curators and practitioners in the MSFA curriculum did not necessarily indicate a shift in habitual racism entrenched in institutional culture.

This was made explicit in recent years by *Umhlangano* (gathering), a Fallist movement established in 2016. *Umhlangano* was a convergence of students from creative disciplines (theatre and fine art) located at the FKA (formerly known as) Hiddingh Campus at UCT. During the Fallist uprising in 2015–2016 at South African higher education institutions, *Umhlangano* emerged as part of the broader decolonial movement. As a mode of protest, *Umhlangano* created art interventions across FKA Hiddingh Campus, facilitated a renaming symposium and conceptualised a counter-curriculum. FKA Hiddingh Campus came alive with public art installations and renamed buildings.[2] The transdisciplinary counter-curriculum, which ran parallel to formal lectures and studio practice, was facilitated by students with invited staff. It aimed to challenge alienating institutional cultures and their epistemic violence.

Although *Umhlangano* occupied the FKA Hiddingh Campus, it also moved through the city of Cape Town to initiate creative interventions.

In an interview that I conducted with one of the members of *Umhlangano*, Khanyisile Mbongwa, it was clear that any decolonial programme involves an agonistic struggle over neocolonial and economically controlled space at UCT but also Cape Town's racist class geography as a whole (see also Makhubu and Ruiters 2020). Mbongwa (Makhubu and Mbongwa 2019, 20–21) uses an example of Jacques Coetzer's art installation on Long Street, *Open House*, and states:

> We were looking at hierarchies of mobility because in Cape Town there are borders. When they say *Open House*, to whom is it open? It seems cynical considering the housing crisis in South Africa … If you walk up from downtown Long Street, those areas are seen as the black areas and as you go higher up on Long Street into Kloof, it becomes whiter … It is also about how spaces are occupied at different times … When we move through that space now there is a different memory.

The interventions of *Umhlangano* linked the broader privatisation and racialisation of (pseudo-public) space and socio-economic segregation as entrenched in curricula and institutional cultures that reproduce class inequalities, mirroring the society in which it is located. As a point of departure, this emphasis on mobility is key to understanding itinerancy, which I argue is crucial in realising epistemic justice.

Sbonelo Radebe (2020), a South African student activist, points out that 'the reality of higher education as a commodity produces violence'. 'There is no way,' she asserts, 'we as black poor students can be creative in an uninvited space which at every chance strives by violent means to get rid of us' (Radebe 2020). This characterisation of institutions of higher learning as spaces where most feel uninvited resonates with similar reflections from feminist scholar bell hooks, who described being 'unsettled' in previously white institutions as the feeling of being an 'interloper' (hooks 1994, 182). This sense of alienation arises in response to systemic racism, alienating pedagogical methods as well as limited curricula that reinforce and reproduce uneven development as the 'hallmark of the geography of capitalism' (Smith 1990, 4).

In South Africa, the arts were and mostly remain the prerogative of the privileged, with most prominent art schools located in historically white universities, and with historically Black universities either having no art schools or having under-resourced, precarious art departments. Art schools in historically white universities are generally expensive, culturally exclusive, inclined to global commercial circuits, and are perceived to be static and blind to their sociopolitical environments (Newall 2019). Bisi Silva (2017), curator and founder of the Centre for Contemporary Art (CCA) in Lagos, highlighted this unevenness at a larger scale, arguing that there is 'a critical gap that exists across the continent in which unfortunately the art education system does not include critical theory, art history, research methodologies and conceptual strategies that underpin artistic and curatorial practice today'. Artist centres, organisations and collectives intervene by creating alternative art education and knowledge-sharing platforms. Through funds from private and public donors, they have been crucial in positioning art practice as an integral component of epistemic and social justice. As such, they are often located and integrated in professional or marginalised communities and operate across different spaces, prioritising collaboration. The politics of space – *where* practice and learning happen in relation to race, gender and class and *how* people occupy, navigate and traverse different spatial scales – is crucial.

In contrast to the kind of parochial pretentions of UCT's MSFA, in this chapter I reflect on contemporary art collectives, networks and schools which operate mostly through intra-African trans-border movement and collaboration: the Pan-African Circle of Artists (PACA) initiated by Chuu Krydz Ikwuemesi in 1991, the *Exit Tour* spearheaded by Goddy Leye in 2006, Invisible Borders founded in 2009 and led by Emeka Okereke, and Àsìkò art school launched in 2010 by Bisi Silva, while others include Another Roadmap School. The examples of contemporary itinerant interventions that are most documented are those initiated in West Africa. There are also significant examples of similar initiatives in other parts of the African continent, such as the mobility schemes of Kuona Trust (Kenya) and Art Moves Africa. This focus on one region is not definitive since these interventions reach other regions on the continent and endeavour to go beyond.

In criticising the art education system within immobile slow-to-transform universities, these collectives and schools draw from pan-African ideals to develop modes of generating and disseminating creative knowledge, particularly on the African continent. In most cases, they opt for the road trip as opposed to air travel, placing emphasis on epistemic liberation as the physical

experience and traversal of tangible and abstract borders as porous boundaries, points of encounter, entry and exit, and as contested spaces – a material
reality of imperialism. They adopt socially centred pedagogical methods that
are counterposed to the seemingly fixed, immovable, immutable university
structure and, more significantly, expand an understanding of citizenship and
knowledge.

In contrast to the permanence and hubris displayed in the stultifying architecture of imperial and colonial institutions, knowledge is fluid, social and
relational. Generally, levels of access to knowledge are predetermined by the
place in which one is forced by socio-economic circumstance to live, and the
position that one occupies sociopolitically and economically. Moving beyond
the institutions and borders locates the value of knowledge within relational
social processes. Chandra Talpade Mohanty (2003, 238) raises this point:

> … it is the way we position historical narratives of experience in relation to
> each other, the way we theorize relationality as both historical and simultane-
> ously singular and collective that determines how and what we learn when we
> cross cultural and experiential borders.

Addressing specifically feminist pedagogy, Mohanty (2003, 243) emphasises
that it 'should not simply expose students to a particularised academic scholarship but that it should also envision the possibility of activism and struggle
outside the academy'. As a process of meaningful redistribution of resources
and recognition of rights, social justice must begin with the politics of space
and movement through accounting for dispossession as well as racial and
economic segregation. Epistemic justice involves the recognition of multiple
sites in which knowledge is generated and exchanged. It necessitates moving
between boundaries and reclaiming the collective right to space. It is reminis-
cent of the adage *ukuhamba ukubona, ngesiZulu,* which means 'to learn, one
must make a journey'.

ON THE MOVE: ITINERANCY AND THE ARTS IN AFRICA

Itinerant art interventions on the African continent have older genealogies
that can be linked to certain forms of African artists' workshops. These are
platforms for learning which Till Förster and Sidney Kasfir (2013, 4) char-
acterise as institutions and as 'social space[s]'. Although some workshops are

not necessarily itinerant, the key principles that underpin artists' workshops, such as non-hierarchical pedagogical interaction as well as shared knowledge and resources, are reflected in contemporary itinerant artists' collectives and schools. This link is also made by Namubiru Kirumira and Sidney Kasfir (2013, 111) in their acknowledgement that 'workshops in particular have been significant formative spaces in artists' endeavours to become versatile in a globalizing environment'. Itinerant artists' collectives and schools, however, are often established in response to the uneven distribution of knowledge, and the exclusivity and parochialism in colonial institutions on the continent and abroad.

Silva (2017, xvi) links itinerancy, with particular reference to Àsìkò (the itinerant art platform she founded), to 'the lineage of non-formal art and art education initiatives created across the continent since the beginning of the 20th century'. Silva (2017, xvi) traces the genealogy of colonial art education to Christian missionary organisations that focused on technical training for the production of religious artefacts. These were followed by art schools led by Europeans with the objective to 'nurture' an African aesthetic.[3] Counteracting the biases of colonial art education, were collectives of artists, writers and poets such as the Mbari Mbayo in Ibadan, Nigeria, led by Ulli Beier. Silva (2017, xvi) also mentions the Triangle Artists' Workshop of the 1980s that took place in South Africa, organised by David Koloane and Bill Ainslie and 'developed by New York artists Anthony Caro and art patron Robert Loder'. These examples reflect pan-African ideals, where artists from different parts of the continent and beyond worked collaboratively, as well as articulations of political and cultural identities in relation to modernist frameworks, postcolonial independence and post-Cold War politics in African countries.

The significance of transnational movement and collaboration reaches beyond the arts. In the article 'Remove Borders to Free up Knowledge', Tawana Kupe (2020) advocates for transdisciplinary practices and argues that global technological change operates in 'a world that transcends borders' and that such transnational collaboration for 'universities and knowledge creation institutions' can 'achieve scale'. Kupe (2020) asserts: 'borders and boundaries go against the notion that knowledge and ideas know no borders … knowledge and university communities should be enabled to flow freely across borders and boundaries, unhindered and unfettered'. Although he aptly argues for a 'global academic and student passport or a global visa acceptable to all', he states that border controls 'enable orderly mobility' and 'are legitimate; every nation needs them'. Kupe, however, leaves unquestioned the immobile and hierarchical nature of institutions of higher learning, and in this case, the fixity of the neocolonial nation-state. Still, the argument, at least in its more radical sense, would provoke a harsher critique of borders as imperial constructions. It evokes the plea for a borderless world which is argued almost entirely from an economic perspective: similarly, it does not make a case against physical boundaries but rather promotes the flow of goods, resources and information. The movement of people across geographical, political, economic and socio-cultural boundaries, if envisioned as the collectivisation of knowledge, is crucial for epistemic justice. This would entail *repositioning* institutions of higher learning towards decentralisation, decommodification and a multi-sited approach across geographical scales.

Marxist geographer Neil Smith (1992, 64) considers scale as a 'criterion of difference' and spatial mobility as 'a political strategy of resistance'. Spatialised politics, he argues, 'recovers space' from capitalism's 'annihilation of space by time' (Smith 1992, 62–78). As the world continues to be defined by territories and boundaries, mobility and migration are further politicised and regulated. Intolerant nationalism reinforces boundaries, circumscribing them as absolute markers of identity and access to resources. This positions transnational itinerancy and nomadism by artist collectives as an epistemic modality centrally in understanding the material realities of space as experienced and lived. Shifting across spaces (or what Smith [1992, 66] referred to as 'jumping scales'), stealing the liberties to cross and redefine the meanings of space, is key. 'Any revolutionary project,' argues Henri Lefebvre (1974, 166–167), 'whether utopian or realistic, must, if it is to avoid hopeless banality, make the re-appropriation of the body, in association with the re-appropriation of space, into a non-negotiable part of its agenda.' This is emphasised by Stefano Harney, who opts for a peripatetic approach. When defining speculative practice, Harney states: 'I am speaking about walking through study, and not just studying by walking with others … A speculative practice is study in movement for me, to walk with others and to talk about ideas' (Harney and Moten 2013, 118).

Movement is transformative since it potentiates new encounters and fluidity. Kevin J. Burke and Abraham DeLeon (2015, 4) posit that 'meaning in teaching points toward the nomadic' where learning is becoming. The key point, they argue, 'to a nomadic subjectivity is movement, placing bodies in motion, allowing for transformative experiences to occur through the practices and experiences of perpetual forces and flows' (Burke and DeLeon 2015, 4). Pedagogic nomadism is regarded as a possibility that produces the conditions in which to think about the world differently from 'classical vision of the philosophical subject as the quintessential European citizen' (Braidotti 2010, 409). Movement enables us 'to envision alternative educational relationships and practices because it does not allow for stagnation; movement can allow other possibilities to arise' (Braidotti 2010, 409). The pedagogic nomad sees movement as both physical and as conceptual, transgressing multiple forms of social boundaries, even from the space of the class.

A PAN-AFRICAN SCOPE: THE STUDY TOUR AND ITINERANT LEARNING COMMUNITIES

In the catalogue that accompanied the exhibition *Afrika before Our Very Eyes*, held in May 2016 at the Boribana Museum in Dakar, Senegal, the artist and founding member of the PACA, Chuu Krydz Ikwuemesi, states: 'the collection [of artworks on display] captures our place as captives of history and politics' on 'the crossroads of African history' (Adewunmi and Ugiomoh 2016). Like the metaphors used by hooks (1994) as well as Harney and Moten (2013), the notion of captivity, containment, prison, is once again evoked. Located at what Ikwuemesi sees as a critical juncture, African arts, he argues, is heralding a hopeful direction 'in the journey of a people who should have so much to offer the modern world' (Adewunmi and Ugiomoh 2016). Since its establishment in 1991, PACA has been concerned with the injustices of history and addressing, through a political geography, the shortfalls of institutions. As an artist and academic, Ikwuemesi has worked across cultures, including Africa and Japan. PACA, which includes artists such as Helen Uhunmwagho, Ugochukwu-Smooth Nzewi, Abel Mac Diakparomre, Godwin Ufuah, Ayo Adewunmi, Kent Onah, Clement Emoda, Tony Odeh and other members, embarked on study tours across African countries through an initiative called *Overcoming Maps*.

Overcoming Maps was spearheaded by Ikwuemesi in 2000. Between 2001 and 2010, there were three editions of *Overcoming Maps* through which members ventured on study tours to 11 African countries. PACA was constituted of different artists on each study tour and embarked on exhibitions, roundtable discussions and the PACA biennale. In 2001, PACA travelled from Nigeria to Ghana and Ivory Coast. The following year, in 2002, the study tour took place in Bamako, Mali, to coincide with the Afrika Heritage Biennale. Then, in 2004, the study tour was held in Accra, Ghana. PACA held other exhibitions and round-tables in 2012 and 2016 at Dak'Art in Dakar, Senegal. Earlier experimental exhibitions, such as *Crossing Boundaries and Frontiers* (2002) as part of the Afrika Heritage Biennale, were to ascertain the possibility 'to reinvent Afrika Heritage as a roaming biennial, and, in the process, to begin working on collaborative projects with like-minded independent institutions in Africa' (Nzewi 2015).

In a seminal paper on the PACA, Ugochukwu-Smooth Nzewi (2013) rightly points out that pan-Africanism has become 'a rhetoric-laden' and 'passive concept' that is 'represented in pan-African institutions such as the African Union (AU) and the New Partnership for Africa's Development (NEPAD)'. As such it has had salience among the educated male elite. The lack of material people-centred strategies towards intra-African and African diasporic transnational solidarity is thwarted by the focus on regional eco-nomic trade. Nzewi (2013) suggests that interventions such as PACA present a 'critical pan-Africanism' which 'mobiliz[es] the values of solidarity and cul-tural exchange to effect a situation that has political ramifications'.

To build on this notion of critical pan-Africanism, it may be worth reflect-ing on the dialogical (see Kester 2004) and collaborative methodology of PACA as a mode of navigating different scales of community. They also pro-duced publications including the journal *Letter from Afrika* (Nzewi 2015). The roundtable, *Art as a Tool for Cultural Integration*, which took place in 2001, for example, resulted in the 'Abidjan Declaration', a document that served as a framework for the transnational work of PACA. In all its itera-tions, PACA organised discursive events such as roundtables and workshops, recognising knowledge as a dialogical social process. Dialogical practice, Paolo Freire points out, requires that we 'put aside the simplistic understanding of dialogue as a mere technique' (Freire and Macedo 1995, 379); rather, it is an 'epistemological relationship'. Freire perceives dialogue 'as an indispensable component of the process of both learning and knowing', recognising the 'social and not merely the individualistic character of the process of knowing' (Freire and Macedo 1995, 379).

It is perhaps this dialogical and collaborative approach that links PACA and other similar contemporary movements to pan-African artists' collectives in the early independence decades (1950s–1970s), which similarly sought to facilitate radical political and paradigmatic shifts though navigating different scales of community. These are important in understanding transnational itinerant practice in Africa for a number of reasons.

First, the changing conditions within which senses of community could be created were responding to the geopolitics of colonialism and subsequent national independence. The geographic scale of community could therefore specify immediate, local communities of practice but could also be expanded to refer to, for example, national and global political communities of transatlantic pan-Africanism. Indeed, the global anti-apartheid movement was buoyed by transatlantic pan-African solidarity from the late 1950s, through which South African activists and politicians who were exiled could be supported in various African countries and abroad. 'From the 1950s to the 1980s the anti-apartheid movement performed increasingly well-organized transnational collective action, based on a collective identity, an imagined community of solidarity uniting people across large distances' (Thörn 2006, xiv). Similarly, artist movements established transnational solidarity such as the Mbari Mbayo Club in Nigeria, whose members included South African writer Es'kia Mphahlele, Sudanese artist Ibrahim El-Salahi, and Jamaican writer and photographer Carlton Lindsay Barrett, among others. In this period, artists were creating communities across borders and generating knowledge and anti-colonial political ideas from collaborative, interdisciplinary creative social practices.

Second, the significance of popular agency brought together artists, students and intellectuals who shared ideas in critically analysing their sociopolitical circumstances across social classes and cultures, working towards social justice. This form of pan-Africanism was made more palpable in its community-centred dialogical artist interventions as opposed to the abstract pan-Africanism of the elite. Third, re-articulations of socially immersed art formulated counter-hegemonic approaches to colonial and neocolonial structures and borders. The isolation of the art object to galleries and museums and the isolation of the artist to studios, or what the late artist Thami Mnyele (1948–1985) (2009, 26) refers to as the 'quiet corridors in foreign buildings, far away from home', that was becoming part of the modernist normative had transformed and undermined already existing socially immersed, collaborative practices as well as workshop and apprentice system forms of creative practice. The emergence of the modern African gallery artist who was cosmopolitan and global was significant in the independence decades for establishing equal global participation and for shifting the condescending ethnographic register that African art was entrenched in. However, it signalled a struggle of identity between artist as isolated creator of ocularcentric work and artist as socially immersed, creating a bifurcation between individual global African artists and what came to be taxonomically differentiated as traditional cultural practice.

The abstraction of African art from fine art separated social classes where 'fine art' would be the prerogative of the middle class and the bourgeoisie, the 'white art world'. This has contributed to the unconstructive and short-sighted connotations of the term 'community' as poor communities in need of aid. As Tom Finkelpearl (2013, xi) points out, the term 'community' is used in problematic ways: 'what was meant by "community" in this context was people of color, the new ethnic communities'. It conceals the notion of community as a constantly changing flow of people that is fluid, itinerant, volatile but knowledge-generating – a set of contradictions that is prone to socio-economic imbalances and internal conflicts.

TRANS-AFRICANISM: INVISIBLE BORDERS AND THE ROAD TRIP

It could be argued that critical pan-Africanism as suggested by Nzewi opens pathways for conceptualising trans-Africanism. Invisible Borders, which is led by the Nigerian photographer and writer Emeka Okereke, opts for trans-Africanism. Its founding members include Ray Daniels Okeugo (1980–2013), Uche Okpa Iroha, Amaize Ojeikere, Uche James Iroha, Nike Adesuyi Ojeikere (1968–2016), Lucy Azubuike, Charles Okereke, Chriss Aghana Nwobu and Unoma Giese. Founded in 2009 as an organisation or collective of photographers, its key objective is to exchange knowledge and ideas across cultures and borders. Invisible Borders intentionally chooses road trips rather than air travel for participants to traverse different countries in the context of difficult intra-African transnational movement, hampered by cumbersome visa regulations, extortionate prices and harassment by officials (Madowo 2018). This makes a powerful statement about the collective experience and negotiation of physical borders.

The organisation continues to run a number of projects, namely, the Trans-African Road Trip, *The Trans-African Journal*, iVISIBLE (a flagship project of short stories by authors globally about perceptions about Africa), workshops and exhibitions. The Trans-African Road Trip is referred to as 'learning while the landscape is changing'. Between 2017 and 2018, participants of Invisible Borders embarked on a road trip from Lagos, Nigeria, to Maputo, Mozambique. Participants from different creative fields travelled to Nigeria, Cameroon, Central African Republic, Democratic Republic of Congo, Rwanda, Uganda, Zambia, Zimbabwe and Mozambique in one vehicle, which was considered a 'moving studio'. In his reflections on a road trip from Lagos to Kigali, Emeka Okereke (2021) writes:

> As we looked for ways to traverse from Nigeria into Cameroun through the
> Benue River, … I would think of roots and routes. Their correlation and dissi-
> militude. Roots, as in origin – an identity so to speak. Routes: myriad threads
> of paths intersecting, intertwining. I would think of everything that could fit
> or unfit in between. I would think of the root that does not kill other roots
> around it as it searches for its food and water, or its depths – its foundation
> … I would think of borders and of how – elusive to many – they are outward
> manifestations of doctrines of divisions.

Here, transnational solidarity is less about defining a specific unified identity (as with pan-Africanism) but embracing plurality and constant movement. One of the aims was 'to encounter and engage with actors of internal migration between countries of the region' (Okereke 2021). Invisible Borders also nurtures critical thinking and skills transfer on the road trip and in general. Okereke (2021) states that the project is grounded on 'epistemic affirmations [of knowledge(s)] that have been disavowed' and proposes the concept of kinopolitics as the sociopolitics of movement within countries and across their borders, which he defines as: 'I am where I think.'

Embedded in their manifesto, trans-Africanism is focused on grassroots artistic intervention through an in-transit community. In their manifesto they state that '[t]he African society is in flux. But there has never been a time as now that the countries and communities in the continent have been empowered to come to a better understanding of itself', where the 'strong urge to herald this understanding of the contemporary African experience' is what is meant by effecting change and to transform and transcend 'preconceived notions of what Africa is, what African art is, and how artists can engage their audience' (Invisible Borders 2018). At the core of their practice is collaboration, where the organisation is not just 'the harbinger of a movement' but it is aimed at encouraging 'trans-African interaction between artists and art practitioners in the many countries that make up the continent' (Invisible Borders 2018). The work is also aimed at different audiences, recognising the class stratifications that make art accessible only to the elite. They declare: 'Our goal is to openly share our work, cutting across the demarcating lines of classes and proficiency in literacy, thereby expanding the art public to include more of the local audience and those who have been called "layman"'(Invisible Borders 2018).

Okereke (2012) explains that 'the prefix trans- by definition connotes "going beyond", "transcending", and in some cases implies a thorough change'. It is not just about change (transformation), between (transit) or temporariness (transitory) but also about the necessary political antagonisms that are inevitable in all forms of border crossing. Okereke points out the prefix's connotation of exchange but he shifts beyond the use of the term by the AU in collaboration with the African Development Bank in the building of 'Trans-African Highways' (Okereke 2012). Trans-African, rather than connoting the moving of commodities, refers to space, time and the body, the three main loci of colonial theft. Trans-Africanism can be conceived of as the transcendence of colonialism and its new insidious forms as the theft of bodies (slave trade, massacres and forced labour), theft of space (land dispossession and the Scramble for Africa) and theft of time (the ahistoricisation of African people and their cultural and intellectual gains).

This evokes the concept of never settling/unsettling as discussed by Harney and Moten (2013), which is also captured in Marquis Bey's discussion of transness. Thinking through the unsettling race and gender 'positions', Bey articulates the idea of movement as a mode of becoming. For Bey (2019, 55), Blackness and transness are 'political move[s], strategic or tactical move[s] … movement itself, a displacement between established plateaus … [they] reference movement and cultivate space to live, to become-as-being, in this movement'. Transness as being in-transit, transitoriness, transnational and transgressive, places mobility as a rejection or refusal of static subjectivities. For Okereke (2012), 'trans-Africanism is the ability to transform African-ness into fluid forms that need not be defined'. It is decolonial solidarity from below and is practised by invisible borders as a mode of epistemic justice.

As much as it is about points of departure and arrivals – it is about constant movement as a knowledge-making process.

LEARNING FROM ÀSÌKÒ – THE ITINERANT SCHOOL

Established by Bisi Silva, Àsìkò art school sought to fill 'a gap in the educational system in Nigeria and many African countries, which tend to ignore the critical methodologies and histories that underpin artistic practice' (Silva and Byrd 2017, 245). Translated, the word Àsìkò means 'time' (Silva 2017, xvi). It uses 'the format of part art workshop, part residency and part art academy, over the course of 30 days' (Silva and Byrd 2017, 245). There are facilitators rather than lecturers and teachers overseeing students. This model changes the forms of engagement and the sense of community. Each year, the school takes place in a different African city. This itinerant nature also means that hierarchies and social divisions do not solidify and that the flow of community is constituted by different people and occurs in varying sociopolitical conditions each time.

Àsìkò schools have taken place in Nigeria (2010, 2012), Ghana (2013, 2017), Senegal (2014), Mozambique (2015), Ethiopia (2016), Cape Verde (2018), and often coincided with major events such as Dak'Art in Senegal and others such as the Arts Council of the African Studies Association (ACASA), which took place in Ghana in 2017 and where the book about Àsìkò was launched. This has ensured that participants are exposed to internationally renowned curators, critics and art historians. Thus far Àsìkò has benefited 'over 80 young artists and curators from nearly 20 African countries' (Silva and Kazungu 2017).

Silva, a valued curator and writer, was also the founder of the CAA in Lagos. The CAA has one of the largest independent art libraries in Lagos, as well as exhibition and workshop spaces. Since its inception it has served as an important learning resource for scholars internationally. Àsìkò draws on some of the principles of accessible knowledge resources. As a programme, often referred to as a school, however, it is positioned as an alternative to the university or traditional art school. It has a democratic, horizontal configuration and refuses hierarchical bureaucratic structures. Facilitators are constantly changing and are not positioned as voices of authority. By bringing emerging and experienced curators together, the programme ensures mutual exchange of skills and knowledge. Silva and Kazungu (2017) opine: 'In fact sometimes the most experienced or educated participants realise how narrow their specialization or experience can be.'

Àsìkò has a tripartite structure of informal art academy, residency and laboratory and in Silva's (2017) book (with Stephanie Baptist), *Àsìkò: On the Future of Artistic and Curatorial Pedagogies in Africa,* various participants and practitioners contributed texts and visual diaries reflecting exchanges in different geographical spaces. Silva had envisioned Àsìkò as a platform that would eventually become 'a pan-African curatorial network' (Silva and Kazungu 2017).

Likewise, Gabriela Salgado (2017, 130) states that 'the pan-African education project Àsìkò congregates African artists and curators for a focused period of engaged and experimental exercises in knowledge sharing, learning, and practicing'. Salgado (2017, 130) aligns the work of Àsìkò to the Freirean approach based on the premise 'educate to emancipate', noting that facilitators adopted 'a dialogical, non-curricular structure based on praxis and a commitment to empower each other in order to develop the capacity to transform [each other] and our reality'. Salgado (2017, 131) then offers an interesting metaphor on unsettling by arguing that Àsìkò is about the 'dislocation from comfort zones'. That is, by shifting from known territories, known modes of practice, of doing, thinking and working, the Àsìkò programme enables encounters and growth.

The curator Nontobeko Ntombela (2017, 169) proposes that 'in their teaching Àsìkò employs the concept of "practitioning"' as 'an approach that informs making, studying, teaching and writing around curatorial practices in Africa'. Ntombela points out that its learner-centred teaching models that 'focused on drawing out the relevance to local experiences and contexts' evoke intimate knowledge or what Njabulo Ndebele (cited in Ntombela 2017, 170) refers to as 'domesticated knowledge' and what Molemo Moiloa (cited in Ntombela 2017, 170) terms 'practitioning'. Embedded in this concept is the significance of multilocality in knowledge-making. This is captured by Silva in her reference to Ngũgĩ wa Thiong'o, who suggests that:

> ... knowing oneself and one's environment was the correct basis of absorbing the world; that there could never be only one centre from which to view the world but that different people in the world had their culture and environment as the centre. The relevant question was therefore of how one centre related to other centres (cited in Silva 2017, xiv).

This was also surfaced in Silva's interview with Antawan Byrd, where she mentions that the programme was always 'fluid' and not fixed (Silva and Byrd 2017, 246).

CAPTIVE: LEARNING IN THE CONFINES

I believe in the world and want to be in it. I want to be in it all the way to the end of it because I believe in another world in the world and I want to be in that. And I plan to stay a believer, like Curtis Mayfield. But that's beyond me, and even beyond me and Stefano, and out into the world, the other thing, the other world, the joyful noise of the scattered, scatted eschaton, the undercommon refusal of the academy of misery.

— Fred Moten (cited in Harney and Moten 2013, 118)

Thinking about institutions, I was reminded of a spatial metaphor used by one of my former students, Mawande Ka Zenzile (2017). While studying towards his undergraduate degree at MSFA, the artist Ka Zenzile was given an assessment on landscape genres that tasked learners to look out a window at their home and discuss the notion of the sublime.[4] Questioning its premise, Ka Zenzile pointed out that such a task took for granted what one might see while looking through a window of a house in a township, compared to a house in a suburb with a mountain or sea view. This oversight, he contested, revealed an ideological battle – a clash of incommensurate values. It failed to acknowledge class difference and reflected a pedagogical practice in which learners are imagined as a homogeneous group with similar experiences and values, all located within the same space imagined as neutral. Ka Zenzile argued that the curriculum, reinforcing eighteenth - and nineteenth - century frameworks, imposed ways of thinking and overlooked people's relational, complex and intimate knowledge and understanding of space and place within a history of racism, segregation and dispossession. His response to this task suggested that universities engender a particular kind of blindness in which everyday experiences in rural areas or in urban townships are dislocated; or are to be transcended, denied or forgotten in the 'ivory towers' of education and in the aspiration to become an 'educated' job market product. Context is therefore crucial since 'learning is essentially situated or contextual' (Macleod and Golby 2003, 353; see also Laszlo 1996; Robbins and Aydede 2008).

Ka Zenzile points to situated practice which immerses learners in social situations, transformed from the austere, didactic classroom characterised as '"monastic", from which all other worlds are banished' (Michael Oakeshott, cited in Macleod and Golby 2003, 354).

In the narrative, the window is allegorical. It evokes *umbono womhlaba*, a worldview or Weltanschauung – the beliefs and experiences that shape an individual's perceptions. It is a spatial metaphor, distinguishing the inside from the outside, and locating a viewer who is situated on the inside looking out. It implies a contained, neutral, homogeneous and confining space from which 'the world out there' can be imagined. Although it symbolises a transition between inside and outside, it also circumscribes a boundary, albeit a porous one. This containment characterises universities as places with a 'settled' episteme, a captive audience and a view to the overwhelming outside world but with limited experience of it.

Institutions of learning are structured as the sites where knowledge is produced, kept and sold. Fashioning themselves as originators or repositories of knowledge, they place value on originality, as well as quantified and accumulated production. Given the industrial nature of knowledge, the individualist accumulative meritocratic system tends to limit the extent to which scholars can be immersed in multiple sites of knowledge production. Ka Zenzile's narrative reveals how value is assigned to some forms of knowing and not others. Coming from a country that is still burdened with racial-economic spatial segregation reinforced through systemic racism, Ka Zenzile defined the task as epistemic violence – what Gayatri Chakravorty Spivak (1988, 274) called 'a complete overhaul of the episteme' which others the colonial subject.

This, and the quest for epistemic justice, resonates with the call for decolonised education by Fallist students and academics at institutions of higher learning. The built environment (architecture, learning spaces, monuments) that boasts and celebrates colonial violence; the location of the university within a racially zoned city, marginalising and disadvantaging those from distanced Black townships; and the domineering European epistemes within an African university, underpin the significance of space and the control of movement.

In discussing engaged pedagogy, bell hooks (1994, 4–5) described the university classroom as a space that 'began to feel more like a prison, a place of punishment and confinement rather than a place of promise and possibility', which professors used 'to enact rituals of control that were about domination and the unjust exercise of power'. hooks (1994, 137) questions the reinforcement of bourgeois values in teaching spaces and points out the assumption that students 'coming from a poor or working-class background would willingly surrender all values and habits of being associated with this background'. For hooks (1994, 11), teaching is a 'performative act', and the classroom can be a radical space if one teaches 'in varied communities' and establishes 'communities of learning'.

This is echoed by Stefano Harney and Fred Moten (2013, 26), who argue that 'the only possible relationship to the university today is a criminal one', drawing out the socio-pathological nature of the exploitative and alienating neoliberal university where *fugitivity* becomes a mode of never settling within the strongholds of colonial hegemony. Moten points to the normalisation of self-negation as an 'insidious thing, this naturalisation of misery, the belief that intellectual work requires alienation and *immobility* and that the ensuing pain and nausea is a kind of badge of honor, a kind of stripe you can apply to your academic robe or something' (Harney and Moten 2013, 117).

EXIT: ALTERNATIVES AND GATHERING

How are notions like 'a white art world' to be disintegrated? Whiteness, as Sara Ahmed (2007, 150) argues, 'could be described as an ongoing and unfinished history, which orientates bodies in specific directions, affecting how they "take up" space and what they "can do"'. It is an ensnaring social category, trapping people into suffocating relations. The notion of an 'exit' is not just about leaving confinement but also about regeneration. It is a way to transcend institutional spaces and knowledge to which one assimilates by performing outside of local knowledges, finding oneself simultaneously alienated from Europe-centred knowledge and from the local knowledge that is undermined and eroded in universities.

As Sabelo Ndlovu-Gatsheni (2013, 52) notes, 'knowledge production in Africa is deeply ensnared within the colonial matrix of power and reproduces Western ideational domination on the African continent'. Ndlovu-Gatsheni (2013, 52) cites Paul Zeleza, who posits that 'it is incumbent on African universities and African intellectuals to overcome dependence, to Africanise global scholarship and globalise African scholarship in order to produce knowledge that addresses and explains the problems and possibilities facing the peoples, economies, societies and cultures of Africa'. For this to happen, rebellion is necessary or, as Archie Mafeje (2011) puts it, a combative ontology. Mafeje (2011, 40) argued that Africanity had 'become a pervasive ontology that straddles space and time'. Jack Halberstam (2013, 11) points out that 'fugitivity is not only escape, "exit" as Paolo Virno might put it, or "exodus" in the terms offered by Hardt and Negri, fugitivity is being separate from settling ... it is a *being in motion*'. The need to work beyond the formal institutions and lecture halls and through public-centred initiatives, is hindered by parochial imperialism.

To escape this, one needs to look to examples discussed in this chapter and others such as the Cameroon-based ArtBakery. It was established when 'the Cameroonian scene didn't have any educational opportunities' and was regarded as an 'alternative education' (AMET 2017). Initiated by ArtBakery's founder, Goddy Leye (1965–2011), seven artist-adventurers set off on a two-month trip from Cameroon to Senegal in 2006 known as *Exit Tour*. They included Lucfosther Diop, Alioum Moussa, Dunja Herzog, Ginette Daleu, Justine Gaga, Achilleka and Leye himself. In their discussion of *Exit Tour*, Fiona Siegenthaler and Dunja Herzog (2017) foreground performance and public spaces, arguing that artists engaged in public art in Africa assume multiple publics aimed at audiences/participants across different social classes. Justine Gaga explains that she had asked Leye if they 'couldn't take a trip following the path of the underground railroad' (cited in AMET 2017). 'To exit,' she explains, was 'like a child being born' and the *Exit Tour* 'was a kind of school because what we experienced on the road was honestly so huge it's beyond estimation' (cited in AMET 2017). These examples indicate an inclination towards movement as a crucial aspect of epistemic justice. They articulate changing senses of community at different scales. Moving across spatial scales is crucial in *repositioning* institutions of higher learning as decentralised, decommodified, socially integrated and justice seeking.

NOTES

1   The attribution is made in UCT's online information about MSFA (https://humanities. uct.ac.za/departments/michaelis-school-fine-art#:-:text=The%20University%20of%20 Cape%20Town's,art%20at%20an%20advanced%20level).

2   For example, Michaelis School of Fine Art was referred to as the Helen Sebidi School of Fine Art, named after the esteemed modern South African artist whose work was exhibited in the Michaelis galleries, although the exhibition never opened because of the occupation and protest. The names of buildings have not been formally changed.

3   For example, the Poto Poto School in Congo Brazzaville led by Pierre Lods, who
      believed art could not be taught to Africans as it came naturally to them.

4   This springs from the Romanticist idea, formulated on terror or awe, and defines the
      emotion that one would experience when confronted with something overwhelming –
      in this case, nature.

REFERENCES

Adewunmi, Ayo and Frank Ugiomoh. 2016. 'Afrika before Our Very Eyes ... PACA's Dak'Art
      2016'. *The Guardian*, 26 June 2016. https://guardian.ng/art/afrika-before-our-very-eyes-
      pacas-dakart-2016/.

Ahmed, Sara. 2007. 'A Phenomenology of Whiteness'. *Feminist Theory* 8 (2): 149–168.
      https://doi.org/10.1177/1464700107078139.

AMET. 2017. 'Looking Back on the *Exit Tour* 2006: An Epic Art Journey through West
      Africa'. *ContemporaryAnd*, 27 June 2017. https://contemporaryand.com/magazines/an-
      epic-art-journey-through-west-africa/.

Àsìkò Art School. 2022. https://ccalagos.org/asiko-2022/.

Baptist, Stephanie and Bisi Silva, eds. 2017. *Àsìkò: On the Future of Artistic and Curatorial
      Pedagogy in Africa*. Lagos: Centre for Contemporary Art.

Bey, Marquis. 2019. 'Black Fugitivity Un/Gendered'. *The Black Scholar* 49 (1): 55–62. https://
      doi.org/10.1080/00064246.2019.1548059.

Braidotti, Rosi. 2010. 'Nomadism: Against Methodological Nationalism'. *Policy Futures in
      Education* 8 (3–4): 408–418. https://doi.org/10.2304/pfie.2010.8.3.408.

Burke, Kevin and Abraham DeLeon. 2015. 'Nomadic Teaching, Vagabond Dreaming: An
      Examination of the Spaces that Schools Might Become'. *Review of Education, Pedagogy,
      and Cultural Studies* 37 (1): 4–20. https://doi.org/10.1080/10714413.2015.988489.

Finkelpearl, Tom. 2013. *What We Made: Conversations of Art and Social Cooperation*.
      Durham, NC: Duke University Press.

Förster, Till and Sidney Littlefield Kasfir. 2013. 'Re-thinking the Workshop: Work and Agency
      in African Art'. In *African Art and Agency in the Workshop*, edited by Sidney Littlefield
      Kasfir and Till Förster, 1–23. Bloomington, IN: Indiana University Press.

Freire, Paulo and Donaldo Macedo. 1995. 'A Dialogue: Culture, Language, and
      Race'. *Harvard Educational Review* 65 (3): 377–403. https://doi.org/10.17763/
      haer.65.3.12g1923330p1xhj8.

Halberstam, Jack. 2013. 'The Wild Beyond: With and for the Undercommons'. In *The
      Undercommons: Fugitive Planning and Black Study*, edited by Stefano Harney and Fred
      Moten, 5–15. Wivenhoe, UK: Minor Compositions.

Harney, Stefano and Fred Moten, eds. 2013. *The Undercommons: Fugitive Planning and Black Study*. Wivenhoe, UK: Minor Compositions.

hooks, bell. 1994. *Teaching to Transgress: Education as the Practice of Freedom*. New York, NY: Routledge.

Kasfir, Sidney Littlefield. 1999. *Contemporary African Art*. London: Thames and Hudson.

Ka Zenzile, Mawande. 2017. 'Decolonizing Visualities: Changing Cultural Paradigms, Freeing Ourselves from Western-centric Epistemes'. Master's diss., University of Cape Town.

Kester, Grant. 2004. *Conversation Pieces: Community and Communication in Modern Art*. Berkeley, CA: University of California Press.

Kirumira, Namubiru Rose and Sidney Littlefield Kasfir. 2013. 'An Artist's Notes on the Triangle Workshops, Zambia and South Africa'. In *African Art and Agency in the Workshop*, edited by Sidney Littlefield Kasfir and Till Förster, 111–122. Bloomington, IN: Indiana University Press.

Kupe, Tawana. 2020. 'Remove Borders to Free up Knowledge'. *Mail & Guardian*, 15 January 2020. https://mg.co.za/education/2020-01-15-remove-borders-to-up-free-knowledge/.

Laszlo, Ervin. 1996. *The Systems View of the World*. Cresskill, NJ: Hampton Press.

Lefebvre, Henri. 1974. *The Production of Space*. Translated by D. Nicholson-Smith. Oxford: Blackwell.

Macleod, Flora and Michael Golby. 2003. 'Theories of Learning and Pedagogy: Issues for Teacher Development'. *Teacher Development* 7: 345–361. https://doi.org/10.1080/13664530300200204.

Madowo, Larry. 2018. 'Why Is It so Hard for Africans to Visit Other African Countries?' *BBC Africa*, 7 October 2018. https://www.bbc.com/news/world-africa-45677447.

Mafeje, Archie. 2011. 'Africanity: A Combative Ontology'. In *The Postcolonial Turn: Re-Imagining Anthropology and Africa*, edited by René Devisch and Francis Nyamnjoh, 31–44. Cameroon: Langaa RPCIG African Books Collective.

Makhubu, Nomusa and Khanyisile Mbongwa. 2019. 'Radical Love as Decolonial Philosophy: In Conversation with Khanyisile Mbongwa'. *Journal of Decolonising Disciplines* 1 (1): 11–26. doi: 10.35293/2664-3405/2019/v1n1a2.

Makhubu, Nomusa and Greg Ruiters. 2020. '"This Land Is Not for Sale": Post-1994 Resistance Art and Interventionism in Cape Town's Precarious Publics'. *City, Culture and Society* 23: 1–9. https://doi.org/10.1016/j.ccs.2020.100368.

Mnyele, Thami. 2009. 'Observations on the State of the Contemporary Visual Arts in South Africa'. In *Thami Mnyele + Medu Art Ensemble Retrospective: Johannesburg Art Gallery*, edited by Clive Kellner and Sergio-Albio González, 22–26. Johannesburg: Jacana.

Mohanty, Chandra Talpade. 2003. *Feminism Without Borders: Decolonizing Theory, Practicing Solidarity*. Durham, NC: Duke University Press.

Ndlovu-Gatsheni, Sabelo. 2013. *Coloniality of Power in Postcolonial Africa: Myth of Decolonialism*. Dakar: CODESRIA.

Newall, Michael. 2019. *A Philosophy of the Art School*. New York: Routledge.

Ntombela, Nontobeko. 2017. 'Practitioning: A Few Notes on Curatorial Training in Africa'. In *Àsìkò: On the Future of Artistic and Curatorial Pedagogies in Africa*, edited by Stephanie Baptist and Bisi Silva, 167–180. Lagos: Centre for Contemporary Art.

Nzewi, Ugochukwu-Smooth. 2013. 'Performing Pan-Africanism: The Pan-African Circle of Artists Overcoming Maps, 2001–Present'. Conference paper, African Studies Association, Annual Meeting, Baltimore USA, 22 March 2013.

Nzewi, Ugochukwu-Smooth. 2015. 'A Pan-African Circle of Artists'. *Chimurenga Chronic*, 5 August 2015. http://chimurengachronic.co.za/a-pan-african-circle-of-artists/.

Okereke, Emeka. 2012. 'Transcending "Africa"' (Blog). *Diary of a Border-Being*. 16 May 2012. https://borderbeing.com/2012/05/16/transcending-afr.

Okereke, Emeka. 2021. 'A Volatile Negotiation between the Past and Present: Invisible Borders Trans-African Project'. *Field: A Journal of Socially Engaged Art Criticism* 17. http://field-journal.com/issue-17/a-volatile-negotiation-between-the-past-and-present-invisible-borders-trans-african-project.

Radebe, Sbonelo. 2020. 'Don't Blame Students, Blame the Commodification of Knowledge in South Africa'. *IOL*, 23 February 2020. https://www.iol.co.za/news/opinion/dont-blame-students-blame-the-commodification-of-knowledge-in-south-africa-43305117.

Robbins, Phillip and Murat Aydede, eds. 2008. 'A Short Primer on Situated Cognition'. In *The Cambridge Handbook of Situated Cognition*, edited by Phillip Robbins and Murat Ayede, 3–10. Cambridge, UK: Cambridge University Press.

SAHO (South African History Online). 2019. 'The State of Art in South Africa Conference'. *SAHO*, 7 January 2019. https://www.sahistory.org.za/article/state-art-south-africa-conference#endnote-1.

Salgado, Gabriela. 2017. 'Àsìkò: Radical Education to Quench the Thirst for Knowledge'. In *Àsìkò: On the Future of Artistic and Curatorial Pedagogies in Africa*, edited by Stephanie Baptist and Bisi Silva, 129–132. Lagos: Centre for Contemporary Art.

Siegenthaler, Fiona and Dunja Herzog. 2017. 'Artistic Practice and Art Publics in Africa: Exit Tour'. In *Public Art in Africa: Art and Urban Transformations in Douala*, edited by Iolanda Pensa, Marta Pucciarelli, Fiona Siegenthaler, Marilyn Douala Bell, Kamiel Verschuren, Xandra Nibbeling, Lucas Grandin, Asta Adukaite and Maud de la Chapelle. Geneva: Métis Presses n.p. (e-book).

Silva, Bisi. 2017. 'Creating Space for a Hundred Flowers to Bloom'. In *Àsìkò: On the Future of Artistic and Curatorial Pedagogies in Africa*, edited by Stephanie Baptist and Bisi Silva, xiii–xxiii. Lagos: Centre for Contemporary Art.

Silva, Bisi and Antawan Byrd. 2017. 'A Conversation on the Origins of Àsìkò'. In *Àsìkò: On the Future of Artistic and Curatorial Pedagogies in Africa*, edited by Stephanie Baptist and Bisi Silva, 243–251. Lagos: Centre for Contemporary Art.

Silva, Bisi and Martha Kazungu. 2017. 'Curriculum of Connections: Àsìkò Art School Collaborative Criticism'. Interview by Martha Kazungu, *ContemporaryAnd*, 18 April 2017. https://contemporaryand.com/magazines/collaborative-criticism/.

Smith, Neil. 1990. *Uneven Development: Nature, Capital, and the Production of Space*. Athens, GA and London: University of Georgia Press.

Smith, Neil. 1992. 'Contours of a Spatialized Politics: Homeless Vehicles and the Production of Geographical Scale'. *Social Text* 33: 54–81. https://doi.org/10.2307/466434.

Spivak, Gayatri Chakravorty. 1988. 'Can the Subaltern Speak?' In *Marxism and Interpretations of Culture*, edited by Cary Nelson and Lawrence Grossberg, 271–313. Basingstoke: Macmillan Education.

Thörn, Håkan. 2006. *Anti-Apartheid and Emergence of a Global Civil Society*. Hampshire: Palgrave Macmillan.

Tietze, Anna. 2014. 'The Art of Design: Curriculum Policy and the Fine Art vs. Design Debate at Michaelis School of Fine Art, 1925–1972'. *De Arte* 50 (91): 4–17. https://doi.org/10.1080/00043389.2015.11877211.

Voyiya, Vuyile and Julie McGee, directors. 2003. *The Luggage Is Still Labelled: Blackness in South African Art*. United States and South Africa. Video, 60:00.

PUBLICS, POLITICS, PLACE AND PEDAGOGY IN URBAN STUDIES

RIKE SITAS

THE PLACE IS NOW

We are sitting within a very particular historical, contextual and temporal situation that is difficult to think about and beyond. Ultimately, we are expected to think through the past, present and future in unprecedented ways. Historical, political and propositional positions are almost unthinkable in our unequal contexts – from which no city is exempt. But this is a difficult thing to do in reality – particularly in an academic context. We need to think forwards, backwards and sideways all at once. But ultimately forwards … to a world where we no longer exist in the realm of the tangible. The future is not us …

In our current physical forms, we will no longer be – we will be dead. How do we think in this way within the urgency of the now – especially through the murkiness of the social, cultural, political and economic pressures of the present? The course of a degree is relatively short; as are our twenties when we have energy and are in our risk-taking prime. We want change now, or at least a recognition that changes now mean something for the future when we are worm fodder and all sorts of incarnations of ancestry that are crucial to our imagined beings. As intellectuals, we are not driftwood floating around in the mindfulness of the now, however compelling that may be. We tend to be disciplined even when we traverse into other disciplines. Despite our convictions to question, critique, propose and reimagine the institution, many of us are ultimately invested in the so-called knowledge project for a future that will be unashamedly and excitingly urban, young, Black, and savvy in ways we can only try to imagine if we think of the technological and political leaps that have happened in the last 20 years.

The purpose of this book is to propose ways in which epistemic change can be fostered in the institution. In order to speak to this call for transformation, this chapter is separated into three parts. Firstly, it considers a Southerning in urban studies. There has been a marked shift, a decentring of the primacy of experiences in the global North, yet urban studies is typically developmentalist – focusing on 'wicked problems', forgetting that many of the decisions we humans make on a daily basis are not based on making rational sense. This poses a challenge for research and teaching. Secondly, therefore, the chapter draws on Freirean approaches to public pedagogies that value the kinds of learning for liberation that happen outside of, tangential to and in opposition with formal disciplined scholarly projects. This requires trespassing, transgressing and stepping on toes (hooks 1994). Finally, the chapter reflects on how artful and interdisciplinary practices are doing just this through performing with wombs, playing with food and drawing on walls.

NORMAL – INFORMAL

Pick up any academic or popular publication that deals with urban life in Africa and be prepared to be overrun by caricature, hyperbole, stereotype and moralistic hogwash. Urban Africans are either bravely en route to empowering themselves to attain sustainable livelihoods or the debased perpetrators of the most unimaginable acts of misanthropy ... Amidst these registers it is almost impossible to get any meaningful purchase on what is actually going on in the vibrant markets, streets, pavements, taxi ranks, hotel lobbies, drinking halls, clubs, bedrooms, rooftops, gardens, dump sites, beach fronts, river edges, cemeteries, garages, basements, and other liminal spaces of daily life and the imaginary (Edjabe and Pieterse 2010, 5).

We are faced with an urban reality – particularly on this continent – that is atypical of the Northern canon of theorising, although the swell of Southern theory over the last ten years is trying to take it into account. Despite the recent impulse to brand cities with particular homogenising identities, such as being the 'creative', 'cultural', 'sustainable' or 'financial' capital of a particular region (Landry 2007), cities will always defy simplistic classification because they are continually being made and remade; being pushed and pulled in a complex web of relations between the everywhere and the everyday. Although cities are unequal the world over, the level of inequalities is more visible in the South where the vast difference between being rich and being poor is more apparent.

Southern theorists have been trying to make sense of the chaotic cities of the majority world, questioning the Northern canon's epistemological value. This Southerning emerges explicitly in Raewyn Connell's (2007) *Southern Theory*, as well as in Aihwa Ong's (2006) unravelling of neoliberalism in China, and Ananya Roy's (2014) challenge to homogenising 'planetary urbanism', among many others captured in Susan Parnell and Sophie Oldfield's (2014) *Routledge Handbook on Cities of the Global South*. As Gautam Bhan (2019, 642) claims, 'the South is as much a project as a place, a relational geography that insists on calling out hegemonies of knowledge and dominant forms of practice no matter where they emerge'.

Yet, Edgar Pieterse (2008, 1) has cautioned that Southern scholarship tends to be 'divided between those who take an apocalyptic view and those who display an irrepressible optimism'. For Pieterse (2008, 2010), this dwelling only on the dire is most explicitly seen in Mike Davis' *Planet of Slums* (2007), which locates the future of cities in devastating slums where he describes a miserable set of insurmountable conditions with scant possibility for change. The limitation of such an approach is that it negates alternative kinds of agency and resistance that exist in everyday negotiations of the city. For AbdouMaliq Simone (2010, 333), 'if we pay attention only to the misery and not to the often-complex forms of deliberation, calculation, and engagement through which residents try to do more than simply register the factualness of bare existence, do we not inevitably make these conditions worse?' Equally unhelpful is an economy-driven, Africa-rising trope in which Africa is speculated as a rising global economic star, a brilliant place to invest. This is a convenient narrative to extend neoliberal capitalist ventures.

Although sometimes accurate, extremes and simplistic tropes are unhelpful in understanding the very lived reality of the majority. A lot of attention is paid to extremes: the destitute urban poor on the one hand, and the heinously rich on the other – a divide that in South Africa is also crucially racialised. But the reality is that the majority of the world lives somewhere in between and across those extremes: in between and across economies, communities, legalities and city spaces. We therefore have to challenge what is normal.

When the so-called informal is regarded as normal, it can no longer be seen as deviant (although we must not confuse the ordinary with the desirable as many people live in far less-than-ideal conditions). Although urban scholars have recognised this, how this is studied within the academy is only recently starting to shift, and largely in the urban humanities. Despite an exciting emerging terrain at the intersection of the arts and urban studies, it is still often assumed that the 'right way' of conducting research is to pick research subjects according to algorithmic and rigorous criteria, cross-checking dynamics and applying for ethical clearance and three to six months later when the stamp of approval has been signed by all academic entities, and you enter the proverbial field, everyone is already gone, everything is elsewhere.

The modern rational being does not exist in the way post-Enlightenment thinking asserted. The assumption is that the social and political lives of people are essentially rational, which suggests that citizenship is enacted according to rational criteria. Although the many decisions we make on a daily basis are rational, there are also many that contradict rational decision-making; our dubious consumption patterns attest to this. In addition, many of us fluctuate between the now and the then, the spiritual being and becoming. People know what is 'healthy' to buy and what they can afford, but we have all imbibed or done something we know to be unhealthy in the last 48 hours. Is this wrong? Or tactical? Or just being bloody-minded and human (whatever that means)? The way we respond comes from affective catalysts as much as other impulses and therefore 'affect holds the key to decipher deeply embedded dispositions, desires and concerns that steer us towards a particular kind of response that is most resonant, most appealing and most promising' (Sitas and Pieterse 2013, 330). Not even politics is immune to passion; as Ash Amin and Nigel Thrift (2013, 157) exclaim, politics is 'shot through with emotions from start to finish. Political ideas are frequently born out of passionately held beliefs; many political impulses are contagious precisely because they work on feelings'.

In this context, the reliability of rational research alone is no match for the rapidly shifting dynamics in contemporary cities. And cities are not bounded units devoid of relationship to the rural, or just backdrops or vessels for human interactions. They are constitutive in themselves. The material matters. According to Simone (2010), complex and conflictual human and material entanglements constitute 'cityness', characterised by 'an ongoing negotiation, marked by a hustle for survival on the periphery. It is something messy, though not necessarily disorderly, but something that is constituted on a daily basis. It is located within the ordinary and everyday'. Gautam Bhan et al. (2020) call this 'collective life'. The hustle is therefore not just about livelihoods, but also about the carefully negotiated, cooperative, collaborated and conflicted tactics for living in cities. It is as much about money as it is about childcare, safe passage and sharing a spliff. It is social and material and fundamentally shapes where people feel they do and don't belong.

There have been attempts to understand these entangled strategies of survival, but they still run the risk of swinging on a theoretical pendulum between the singular structural evil of global capital on the one hand, and the amorphously relational on the other, rendering that agency so distributed it is no longer powerful. There are critiques of identity politics and political subjectivities. There are critiques upon critiques. We are good at critique! We need new ways of thinking and acting in this ontological and epistemic terrain that are not going to come from merely inserting ourselves somewhere along theoretical binaries rooted in logics from the global North. We also no longer have the luxury of critique alone.

PUBLICS, PEDAGOGIES

[There are art forms] that are critical and politicized in relation to dominant power relations and their spatial constitution, that are involved in but frequently disrupt everyday urban life, that make use of artistic and creative means to question and explore social problems and conflicts without necessarily prescribing solutions, and that resist the processes through which urban spaces are currently produced in the interests of capital and the state as they seek out and encourage more democratic alternatives (Pinder 2008, 730).

In order to be propositional, we need to consider the politics of learning. The urban poor have research fatigue; many people are tired of exposing their intimate lives for others' higher degrees when little material change is apparent. To generate a more radical approach to knowledge production, we need to think of how research and teaching processes are inherently political and imbued with the same myriad power dynamics that populate broader society; and how they are reproduced in our institutions where incrementally, from school onwards, we are faced with curriculum and classroom pedagogies that are detached from reality and do little to disrupt the status quo. Philosophical and historical canons are endlessly replicated, disabling institutional, onto-logical, epistemological and methodological transformation. There is also a generational rift that is filled with unhelpful hyperbole: naïve youngsters who don't know how to struggle, jaded elders who have forgotten how to struggle, and conflicting notions of what is to be done.

Paulo Freire (1970) taught us about liberatory pedagogies a while ago, yet we are still learning in lecture halls where dialogue too easily equals con-sensual conversations as opposed to critical deliberation in all its conflicted messiness: is there really a homogeneous oppressor or oppressed, especially in essentially conservative societies (all of them everywhere), that would rather maintain the institutionalised racist, sexist and homophobic status quo? We need to explore and experiment with what liberatory learning can be for these tumultuous times. Times may be tumultuous but, realistically, when have times been anything else? Undoubtedly, we are facing numerous crises although the ways in which these are engaged, addressed or represented seem to be faltering.

While there are shifts in the ways that research is being translated into new registers, urban studies scholars often tend to think of visual translation as a creative way to re-present academic research, as opposed to as a mode to do research. This is an important shift but it does not adequately rethink episte-mological or methodological positions or tactics. Urban scholars still separate the knowledge product from knowledge production. And although we still need this, and big data sets that more realistically portray counter-narratives to perspectives of crisis and chaos – and new ways to present these data in more palatable ways – there are other pedagogical practices that can comple-ment and deepen these forms of inquiry.

ARTFUL ACTION, URBAN LEARNING

… in the complex world of cities, everywhere, artists working right now may
be onto more far reaching ways of communicating what contemporary city

life and cities are about. The city is always suspended as a case of 'heres' and 'elsewheres', connected yet – yet … and that is why artists may be doing a better job than southern, or northern, theorists in 'painting', 'composing', 'dancing' and 'writing' cities into being. It remains to scholarship to go further (Mabin 2014, 32).

The cultural turn in planning (Zukin 1995; Peck 2005), the spatial turn in art (Suderburg 2000; Kwon 2004), among many other dizzying turns as disciplines tango together, have led to a simultaneity of creative practice – some more subversive than others. It is unsurprising that the formal art market mimics the formal economy, and therefore a market-driven art economy operates at the same time as radical practices of creative emancipation. Urbanists can romanticise the arts in often apolitical ways, or appropriate art in instrumental ways to soften the blow of development, but there are pedagogical experiments that are stretching forms of urban knowledge production through creative means that have the potential to agitate the status quo.

Using creative practice as a tactic for transformation has a rich history in the arts and humanities – particularly in forms of socially and politically engaged theatre and the performing arts (Davis and Fuchs 1996; Peimer 2018). However, these forms of research praxis do not regularly appear in other disciplines beyond studio-based approaches to solving 'wicked problems' which may rely on collaborative and creative problem-solving but not necessarily artful ways of doing so. Architecture studios may use creative means of addressing design challenges, but largely still within an architectural frame that still foregrounds the centrality of the built environment over the more intangible social and cultural dimensions of urban life.

Although art interventions may unsettle the everyday and may make profound statements against the problematic status quo, they are not necessarily pedagogical in public and politicised ways. This is not to say that all art should follow the same pedagogy but it is helpful to recognise that there is politics at play in any artful act. Public pedagogies in the spirit of Freire (1970) and bell hooks (1994) offer sites of learning and knowledge production that can happen outside of formal institutions, and can have radical intentions at their core. Public pedagogues argue that we learn in cinemas, theatres, museums and nightclubs as much as in schools and lecture halls (Sandlin, Schultz and Burdick 2010). Shari Daya and I argue elsewhere in this book (chapter 3) that academic texts are not the only place where theory lies – novels, films, songs and music videos are critical and theoretical in their own right. This has implications for the kinds of methods and materials needed for liberatory learning. If we learn through sensory engagements with people, places and practices, it is perhaps useful to explore more imaginative ways of learning, particularly in disciplines not accustomed to doing so.

Although artful processes may not in themselves be able to fundamentally reshape systemic and structural inequalities, the one thing art can do, as I argue elsewhere (Sitas 2020a), is transcend the real and the rational. If as beings, most of our time is spent struggling, swimming in and squandering social, political and spatialised lives, maybe we need to rethink how we collectively and collaboratively make new and more appropriate meanings of our predispositions and passions. Art practices are well placed to do this. Art does not require consensus. Gert Biesta (2012), drawing on Jacques Rancière (2013), suggests that recognising difference and dissensus is crucial in these spaces. Although this thinking has found traction in some disciplines, it has yet to be fully immersed in curriculum or teaching at academic institutions, especially outside of the humanities.

To illustrate the intersection of art and urban research, the following three examples may be helpful.

Example 1: Wombs in Labour shows that there are other ways of disseminating knowledge with different audiences through participatory theatre.
Wombs in Labour started as a PhD and turned into a book and a series of participatory theatre performances (Pande 2014). The study was on Indian surrogates as a form of transnational exchange – essentially, affluent couples in the North renting wombs from poor Indian women. But the researcher turned the findings into a performance where the different positions of research subjects were acted out – primarily in the places hiring the wombs, but also workshopped and performed within the research community. The performances involved the researcher enacting the various people involved in the exchanges – the tenants and the landlords. At the end of the performance the audiences were invited to ask questions directly of the characters, and the responses were performed back in character. Although uneasy subject matter, breaking the fourth wall of theatre making (Boal 1979) allowed for productive discussions and revelations to emerge. Although this was not the official PhD defence (imagine if it was?), imagine if the audience was not only a row

of esteemed academics but rather a range of experts – those with both tactical and theoretical knowledge.

It is rare to be able to talk to someone else's research – to interrogate the logics and assumptions made by different perspectives that are usually presented in 2D. It allows different kinds of audiences to make sense of unfamiliar positions: a surrogate in India can question a Scandinavian womb renter; a South African scholar can interview a surrogacy home matron. As is argued elsewhere in this volume (chapter 3 by Shari Daya and Rike Sitas), fiction can sometimes be more truthful than fact. Fictionalising the research and performing it back can surface irreconcilable tensions and the dissensus, can reveal irrational and emotional perspectives, and most importantly, can immerse an audience in a transitional space where changing perspectives becomes possible (Von Kotze 2009).

Example 2: Serious Fun: Food for Thought explored alternative ways of doing research using art and gaming.

This was an experimental project with food security specialists from the African Centre for Cities at UCT and the public art organisation, dala. The purpose of the project was to explore food insecurity in Cape Town through a performative game on the Grand Parade. The performance started with 20 shopping trolleys being pushed through the city, loaned from the nearby Shoprite supermarket. The trolleys were mounted into a sculpture on the side of the road near the market traders. Onto the sculpture were attached a range of everyday food items, the higher up the more expensive. Players were passersby who were given an envelope with money matching different income levels' food budgets for the week. Players were asked to make food-purchasing choices according to their budget. If the products they wanted were higher up, they could hire a ladder. The researcher acted as cashier to gather reflections on food-purchasing choices. Having worked as a food researcher for many years, he was surprised by the choices and rationales. One player with the smallest budget bought only chocolate and wine. When asked, he said he had a new girlfriend and that this week pleasing her would be the priority. If approached with a rational set of research questions, he would have answered very differently. He would have answered the 'right' thing. He would have ticked rational responses counter to his immediate reality. This being a game, he was able to answer more honestly without fear of disdain.

I am not arguing that these kinds of tactics should replace other forms of research but they do offer a lens through which to make sense of the kinds of cognitive dissonance that shape how we interact with and in the world. Games blur the boundary between what is 'serious' and what is 'fun' and, as Jessica Baldwin-Philippi and Eric Gordon (2014, 762) argue, serious urban games 'provide players with opportunities to restructure interactions and relationships of power, providing opportunities that are qualitatively different from life outside the game ... thusly conceived, games are particularly suited to the production of civic learning environments'. In the context of this game, food security is not only about calories and nutrients; food is also about love, desire and human connections.

Example 3: Dlala Indima was a hip-hop-led culture-based regeneration programme.

My final example did not happen in a city per se, but also troubles the urban–rural dichotomy so hot in political priorities these days. This project happened in a small town in the Eastern Cape but township typologies are similar everywhere. And there is not a corner of this earth where hip-hop doesn't prevail in some way. Dlala Indima is a hip-hop and graffiti collective from the neighbourhood which used a R150 000 art grant over the course of three months not only to generate debates about the entanglement of humans and the environment, but also to renovate a neighbourhood through graffiti. In a country where delivering on culture often means building award-winning but entirely unsustainable architecture in the form of community arts centres (Sitas 2015), this crew of graffiti vanguards renovated a building as a cultural space for local youth (90 per cent of whom were unemployed), beautified both private and public amenities, and inspired a waste management overhaul of a neighbourhood. In so doing, they harnessed more than 200 participants (artists, academics and residents) in an essentially hip-hop-inspired public pedagogical project that showed that neighbourhood regeneration need not lead to gentrification. The culmination was not the picture of marginalised urban male gangsterist mayhem. It was an uneasy yet convivial mix of kids, elders and dagga-toting, quart-swilling youngsters (Sitas 2020b).

Even though many theoreticians have argued for the critical – albeit conflictual – nature of hip-hop (Haupt 2001; Caldeira 2004; Pieterse 2010; Williams 2010), this is not culture with a capital 'C' that easily makes it into the arts and culture curriculum in South Africa. Imagine if hip-hop and graffiti were not only seen as the urban pariah of indigent youth, or as a muralled marker of cultural zones pandering to the image of the creative city. Could they form part of an epistemological lexicon for mathematics education, or provide an alternative lens on history?

ARTFUL TRESPASSES AND TRANSGRESSIONS

All these examples demonstrate that we need fundamentally to take tactics of knowledge production, and the trespass of knowledge, cultures and spaces, in order to transgress the current, often stagnant and stultifying status quo. Where formal political processes may falter and lecture halls may lull students to sleep, creative work can create a less threatening inroad to making sense of complex and contested terrains. Reality is messy and decision-making murky. Intellectual projects that use artful tactics enable spaces for active engagement between publics and charged and politicised issues, while also engaging the very human and emotional negotiations people make on a daily basis.

Although artful inquiry may not solve the myriad complexities and crises, they may be an alternative starting point for learning how to do so. Finally, epistemic change requires connecting publics, places and pedagogies in politicised, historicised and propositional ways, and can offer new perspectives on the artful, action-oriented critical and generative inquiry of justice. In addition, it can be fun, and as Benjamin (1970, 9) asserts, 'there is no better starting point for thought than laughter. In particular, thought usually has a better chance when one is shaken by laughter than when one's mind is shaken and upset'.

REFERENCES

Amin, Ash and Nigel Thrift. 2013. *Arts of the Political: New Openings for the Left*. Durham, NC: Duke University Press.

Baldwin-Philippi, Jessica and Eric Gordon. 2014. 'Playful Civic Learning: Enabling Reflection and Lateral Trust in Game-Based Public Participation'. *International Journal of Communication* 8: 759–786. https://ijoc.org/index.php/ijoc/article/view/2195/1100.

Benjamin, Walter. 1970. 'The Author as Producer'. *New Left Review* I (62): 1–9. https://newleftreview.org/issues/i62/articles/walter-benjamin-the-author-as-producer.

Bhan, Gautam. 2019. 'Notes on a Southern Urban Practice'. *Environment and Urbanization* 31 (2) 639–654. https://journals.sagepub.com/doi/full/10.1177/0956247818815792.

Bhan, Gautam, Teresa Caldeira, Kelly Gillespie and AbdouMaliq Simone. 2020. 'The Pandemic, Southern Urbanisms and Collective Life'. *Society+Space* 40 (3). https://www.societyandspace.org/articles/the-pandemic-southern-urbanisms-and-collective-life.

Biesta, Gert. 2012. 'Becoming Public: Public Pedagogy, Citizenship and the Public Sphere'. *Social & Cultural Geography* 13 (7): 683–697. https://doi.org/10.1080/14649365.2012.723736.

Boal, Augusto. 1979. *Theatre of the Oppressed*. London: Pluto Press.

Caldeira, Teresa. 2004. 'Hip-Hop, Periphery, and Spatial Segregation in São Paolo'. In *Urban Traumas: The City and Disasters Conference*, 7–9 July 2004, 7–11. Barcelona: Centre de Cultura Contemporània de Barcelona.

Connell, Raewyn. 2007. *Southern Theory: The Global Dynamics of Knowledge in Social Science*. London: Routledge.

Davis, Geoffrey and Anne Fuchs, eds. 1996. *Theatre and Change in South Africa*. Amsterdam: Overseas Publishers Association.

Davis, Mike. 2007. *Planet of Slums*. London: Verso.

Edjabe, Ntone and Edgar Pieterse, eds. 2010. *African Cities Reader 1: Pan African Practices*. Cape Town: Chimurenga and African Centre for Cities.

Freire, Paulo. 1970. *Pedagogy of the Oppressed*. New York, NY: Continuum.

Haupt, Adam. 2001. 'Black Thing: Hip-Hop Nationalism, "Race" and Gender in Prophets of Da City and Brasse Vannie Kaap'. In *Coloured by History, Shaped by Place: New Perspectives on Coloured Identities in Cape Town*, edited by Zimitri Erasmus, 173–191. Cape Town: Kwela Books.

hooks, bell. 1994. *Teaching to Transgress: Education as the Practice of Freedom*. London: Routledge.

Kwon, Miwon. 2004. *One Place after Another: Site-Specific Art and Locational Identity*. Cambridge, MA: MIT Press.

Landry, Charles. 2007. *The Art of City Making*. London: Earthscan.

Mabin, Alan. 2014. 'Grounding Southern City Theory'. In *The Routledge Handbook on Cities of the Global South*, edited by Susan Parnell and Sophie Oldfield, 21–36. London: Routledge.

Ong, Aihwa. 2006. 'Mutations in Citizenship'. *Theory, Culture & Society* 23 (2–3): 499–505. https://doi.org/10.1177/0263276406064831.

Pande, Amrita. 2014. *Wombs in Labour: Transnational Commercial Surrogacy in India*. New York, NY: Columbia University Press.

Parnell, Susan and Sophie Oldfield, eds. 2014. *The Routledge Handbook on Cities of the Global South*. London: Routledge.

Peck, Jamie. 2005. 'Struggling with the Creative Class'. *International Journal of Urban and Regional Research* 29 (4): 740–770. https://doi.org/10.1111/j.1468-2427.2005.00620.x.

Peimer, David. 2018. 'Contemporary Protest Theatre in South Africa'. In *Scenes from the Revolution: Making Political Theatre (1968–2018),* edited by Kim Wiltshire and Billy Cowan, 40–52. London: Pluto Press.

Pieterse, Edgar. 2008. *City Futures: Confronting the Crisis of Urban Development.* Cape Town: Zed Books.

Pieterse, Edgar. 2010. 'Hip-Hop Cultures and Political Agency in Brazil and South Africa'. *Social Dynamics* 36 (2): 428–447. doi: 10.1080/02533952.2010.487998.

Pinder, David. 2008. 'Urban Interventions: Art, Politics and Pedagogy'. *International Journal of Urban and Regional Research* 32 (3): 730–736. doi: 10.1111/j.1468-2427.2008.00810.x.

Rancière, Jacques. 2013. *The Politics of Aesthetics.* London and New York: Bloomsbury.

Roy, Ananya. 2014. 'Worlding the South: Toward a Postcolonial Urban Theory'. In *Routledge Handbook on Cities of the Global South,* edited by Susan Parnell and Sophie Oldfield, 9–20. London: Routledge.

Sandlin, Jennifer, Brian Schultz and Jake Burdick, eds. 2010. *Handbook of Public Pedagogy: Education and Learning beyond Schooling.* London: Routledge.

Simone, AbdouMaliq. 2010. *City Life from Jakarta to Dakar.* London: Routledge.

Sitas, Rike. 2015. 'Community Centres in Crisis: The Story of the Tsoga Environmental Resource Centre'. In *State/Society Synergy*, edited by Mercy Brown-Luthango, 178–197. Cape Town: African Centre for Cities.

Sitas, Rike. 2020a. 'Becoming Otherwise: Artful Urban Enquiry'. *Urban Forum* 31: 157–175. doi: 10.1007/s12132-020-09387-4.

Sitas, Rike. 2020b. 'Creative Cities, Graffiti and Culture-Led Development in South Africa: Dlala Indima (Play Your Part)'. *International Journal of Urban and Regional Research* 44 (5): 821–840. https://doi.org/10.1111/1468-2427.12894.

Sitas, Rike and Edgar Pieterse. 2013. 'Democratic Renovations and Affective Political Imaginaries'. *Third Text* 27 (3): 327–342. https://doi.org/10.1080/09528822.2013.798183.

Suderburg, Erika, ed. 2000. *Space, Site, Intervention: Situating Installation Art.* Minneapolis, MN: University of Minnesota Press.

Von Kotze, Astrid. 2009. 'Zebra Crossings: Public Participation to Remake the City?' *Rizoma Freireano* 3. http://www.rizoma-freireano.org/n3articulos/zebra-crossings.

Williams, Lance. 2010. 'Hip-Hop as a Site of Public Pedagogy'. *Handbook of Public Pedagogy: Education and Learning beyond Schooling*, edited by Jennifer Sandlin, Brian Schultz and Jake Burdick, 221–232. London: Routledge.

Zukin, Sharon. 1995. *The Cultures of Cities.* Maldon: Wiley.

IMAGINING SOUTHERN CITIES: EXPERIMENTS IN AN INTER-DISCIPLINARY PEDAGOGICAL SPACE

SHARI DAYA AND RIKE SITAS

Just as cities in the global South are burgeoning, so urban studies and urban geography are increasingly lively and growing fields. We write as two cultural scholars who have become geographers, and undertake research and teaching at the University of Cape Town (UCT), in a city that is often popularly criticised as the 'last colonial outpost' of South Africa. At this elite university on the mountainside, an urban research institute, the African Centre for Cities (ACC), was established in 2007. The ACC rapidly became a flagship unit for urban studies on the African continent. In 2020, a Google search using the keywords 'urban studies Africa' brought up the ACC in the first three hits. There is no doubt that this centre plays a leading role in many of the debates about urbanisation in Africa, as well as in the global South more widely. Through a focus on the developmental challenges in African cities, and on systemic solutions to these, the ACC supports a wealth of policy-oriented research into issues as diverse as food provision, violence and conflict, finance and governance, climate change, natural resource management, and more.

Both of us have been part of the ACC almost since its inception – Sitas as an ACC-employed researcher, and Daya as an academic based in geography and affiliated to the centre. We realised early on that we shared interests in art, cultural production and urban life, and that while we were participating in many ACC seminars, workshops and conversations about cities in the global South, there was limited resonance in these spaces with the kinds of questions we wanted to ask. Our questions were fundamentally about representation and imagination, and centred on fiction, speculation and playful learning in and about urban spaces. Against the main institutional agenda of solving structural and material problems, these interests were arguably trivial, and certainly less urgent than some others, yet we felt strongly that they should have a place. Our solution was to carve out a new space, and so we designed a semester-long postgraduate human geography course entitled 'Imagining Southern Cities', which has now run twice (in 2018 and 2019), with two different cohorts of students at the Honours and Master's levels.

We imagined and pitched our course as an experiment, an antidote to (though not a replacement for) the development and policy-centred work that has become the heartbeat of urban studies. At the centre of the course was our conviction that paying attention to fictional cities, and fiction about cities, would deepen our understanding of urban lives and systems, and challenge the dominant paradigms of urban studies in productive ways. The aim, far from diminishing the importance of everyday materialities of economic inequality, violence, struggle and livelihoods, was to ask how these and other experiences come to matter to urban citizens in their fullness as human beings. Fiction and film, as critical texts, blur the boundaries of the academy and everyday life, and may be more approachable and 'relatable', for scholars of all stripes, than many traditional academic texts. The best stories capture the social lives of people, and reading about the familiarity of everyday life can forge solidarities where historically there may have been difference and distrust. Further, we wanted to explore how visual and literary texts might help us approach urban challenges, beyond the framings of planning and policies and in the interest of more just imaginaries. And finally, we aimed to challenge the dominance of an idealised Northern city as 'the city' in the academic imagination of the cultural and geographic disciplines, or at least in the imaginations of our students.

In these aims, we took seriously the notion that 'our theory, with its rationalistic faith, fails … to register the same dimensions and to speak meaningfully about those levels of existence which often engage the imagination of both writer and reader most profoundly' (Watson 1990). The Mexican poet

Octavio Paz could have been writing about contemporary urban studies when he observed that our theory is not in resonance with what many consider to be the full truth about the nature of our life; it leaves out too many dimensions. While it champions the human being, it ignores 'half his [sic] nature, that which is expressed in communion, myths, festivals, dreams, eroticism' (Octavio Paz, cited in Watson 1990). We sought to turn our attention to these 'other' dimensions of human nature. Following David Pinder's (2008, 732) lead, we took as our point of departure the idea that 'attending more closely to existing and potential cross currents and collaborative ventures between urban theory, empirical research and artistic and creative practice [could] deepen and widen the analytical and political edge of these interventions'. More specifically, we saw such ventures as opening up questions about justice, through the idea that more holistic engagement with forms of urban life could help us envision and generate more equitable cities.

Urban studies needs art and it needs cultural criticism. The main reason for this is that cities are generated out of stories. The richest urban archive is not in the texts of developers, theorists or planners but in novels and films. A small sample of cities that cannot be thought without their stories might include Dublin (see James Joyce), London (see Charles Dickens, Charlie Chaplin or Zadie Smith), New York (see Woody Allen), Los Angeles (see Joan Didion, *Blade Runner* [1982], or indeed, any of the countless films that have given that city to the global moviegoing public), Mumbai (see Rohinton Mistry) or Tokyo (see Haruki Murakami). If you want to read the history of a particular city, you would be well advised to turn to fiction, textual and visual. Cities everywhere are always already figural. 'To privilege the metaphorics of the city is not to leave the real city behind. It is … to insist that our real experiences of cities are "caught" in networks of dense metaphorical meanings' (Highmore 2005, 5). Urban experiences are therefore not separate from stories of the city; they are better understood as 'lived figuration' – thick, dense, meaningful life through which metaphor and imagination are constantly being threaded. As William Sharpe and Leonard Wallock (1987, 1) put it, 'our perceptions of the urban landscape are inseparable from the words we use to describe them and from the activities of reading, naming and metaphorizing that make all our formulations possible'.

This is recognised more fully with reference to Northern cities, partly because of city branding and tourism marketing exercises, but also because in the public imagination, Northern cities are where stories live. Southern cities tend to be overdetermined by poverty, and are all too often cast either as elusive and unknowable, or as consisting of the kind of 'on the ground' reality that lends itself only to non-fiction. Part of our aim with this course is to ask: what is the artistic urban archive in the South? What are the metaphors that shape cities in Africa, Asia and Latin America; and can they help us both to see the multidimensional realities of Southern cities and to break down simplistic North–South binaries?

Geography and the ACC might seem like the ideal spaces for such a project. The home of geography at UCT is the Department of Environmental and Geographical Science (EGS), an interdisciplinary department that takes roughly half its students from the humanities faculty and half from the science faculty, and whose staff identify variously as human geographers, physical geographers, environmental scientists and climate scientists. Similarly, the ACC, although formally homed in the School of Architecture, Geomatics and Planning in the Faculty of Engineering and the Built Environment (EBE), is a joint initiative of the EBE, and the science and humanities faculties. Urban studies itself is fundamentally interdisciplinary, as the 'studies' in the name implies (much like gender studies, food studies or cultural studies).

In many senses, as this suggests, we were perfectly located for an interdisciplinary project. However, the challenges of genuinely interdisciplinary work are well documented and the institutions in which we found ourselves were certainly not immune to these. Certain frameworks and paradigms dominated, and while 'other' ideas, questions and initiatives might not have been deliberately marginalised, it often felt to us that there was little oxygen available for them to flourish. Imagining Southern Cities was our attempt to create a space where imaginative yet scholarly work could breathe and be nourished. It was our response to what we saw as an urgent need for genuinely interdisciplinary approaches and new pedagogical methods, in the contexts of postcolonial cities that long ago outgrew the modernist visions that gave birth to them.

The course was a call and an opportunity for more attentive engagement with stories and other imaginative representations of cities as an essential component of theory building from Southern locations. In the course design, we sought to bring in texts and experiences that are seldom considered in urban studies conversations, and to ask what new understandings might emerge from these. Consciously working across the boundaries between urban geography, literary studies, film and media studies, the policy-oriented urban studies, and emergent literatures on Southern theory, we asked our students to engage with films and novels from and about cities in the global South, guided by a pedagogical principle of experimentation and experiential learning.

We knew that what we were doing was unusual. For one thing, the course was not a natural 'fit' in the science faculty where it would have to be accredited. For another, EGS students (whether affiliated to the department or to its associated research units, including the ACC and the African Climate and Development Initiative [ACDI]) would not gravitate in large numbers towards a course that had no obvious environmental or policy focus. Thirdly, the kind of collaborative teaching we were undertaking was highly unusual in our academic spaces, and we had never designed or taught a course on this material, or in this way, before. We were experimenting, and we consistently and explicitly invited students to join us in a journey of experimentation and play, as we tried out ideas in teaching and learning spaces that we had not attempted before. Although we were experimenting *empirically*, one might say, with the actual content and structure of the course, the principle was also (and perhaps more importantly) to encourage in our students and ourselves an *attitude* of experimentation.

Part of this experimentation was the underlying principle of *experiential* learning. Because we were asking students to engage with both written and visual texts as well as with the material city, and indeed to work to see these as intertwined, we included both classroom sessions and field trips in the semester-long course. In the classroom, we invited (in fact, required) students to introduce activities for the group when they led a session, so that we did not simply sit at rectangular tables, talking in the disembodied 'seminar' mode that dominates postgraduate teaching and learning. Several of these activities included hands-on, collaborative tasks that generated movement in the room, and prompted imaginative and open-ended engagements with objects, as well as discussion. We did not do away with formal presentations and discussion but rather mixed these with other ways of thinking and doing. Both these dynamic classroom seminars and the field trips, in their material disruption to the conventional mode of postgraduate teaching and learning, generated thoughts, reflections and conversations that we could not have anticipated, and that demonstrated the value of experimental approaches to learning.

We do not want to overstate the impact of Imagining Southern Cities. The cohorts were small, six students in 2018 and ten in 2019, and the course certainly did not explode the conventional pedagogical models at UCT. In some ways it was necessarily conventional: we met weekly, for two to three hours at a time as the university timetable dictated, and students' work was assessed through written assignments and examinations, with the usual weightings and rubrics. Within these parameters, however, we felt that the principles of experimentation and experiential learning yielded something valuable and helped us journey a little way towards achieving our aims. In this chapter, we draw on student work as well as discussions and activities that emerged during seminar sessions and field trips, to reflect on the value of our pedagogical principles for the interdisciplinary field of urban studies at UCT, and beyond. Moving forward, especially in spaces of learning transformed by Covid-19, we seek to use the course as an opportunity to think about what such work can do to develop spaces of greater justice in teaching and learning, in a context where decolonisation and Africanisation are firmly on the agenda.

EXPERIMENTATION AND EXPERIENTIAL LEARNING

As hinted at the outset, the very initiation of this course was, in the spaces in which we found ourselves, an experiment. There was no guarantee that we would attract students or find resonance or support within our home faculties. In this section we unpack four substantive modes of experimentation undertaken in our course. These include: (a) curriculum experiments, or the choice of primary texts and pedagogical modes of engagement; (b) experimental methodologies of watching and reading; (c) experimental writing; and (d) experiential learning. As these indicate, we were trying out new approaches to postgraduate course design and course content, while asking students to be open to new ways of reading, writing and conversing. We were all, together, going to be trying out practices and ideas that were unfamiliar to us. We wanted simultaneously to engage seriously with urban theory and Southern theory, but importantly, also to play and have fun.

Curriculum Experiments

For us as convenors, our first experiment was in setting the primary texts for the course, which we already knew were going to be stories, told through visual and textual means. In line with our aims, we also knew that we were actively seeking to question the dominant imaginary of the city as one built of concrete, glass and steel, driving modernity forward, the imaginary that invokes Los Angeles, London and Paris. Imaginative accounts of Lagos, Santiago, Chennai and many other cities certainly exist, in English and in other languages, but these stories are seldom regarded as constitutive of these cities in the way of, to take the classic example already referenced earlier, Dickens' London novels. But for cities of the global South, where developmental imperatives are so powerfully felt by almost all stakeholders, the need to diversify the available narratives and thus to mitigate what novelist Chimamanda Ngozi Adichie (2009) terms 'the dangers of a single story' is significant. Without the pressure to solve the 'problems' faced by city policymakers, planners and residents, storytellers are among the few urban rapporteurs with an open brief. The very fact that fiction 'does not bear the responsibility of "truthful" representation' (Sharp 2000, 329) enables experimentation and the exploration of alternatives, perhaps even discursive transformation. As Martha Nussbaum (1990, 290) argues, literary forms, by working through emotion and the moral imagination, 'call forth certain specific sorts of practical activity in the reader that can be evoked in no other way'.

In other words, the 'where' of our primary texts was vitally important. Instead of the typical urban reference points that are so familiar to us 'postcolonials' steeped in Euro-American cultures, and that posit cities of the global North as 'the' city, we looked to stories that were not just about Southern cities but that were in a genuine sense *from* them. Our expectation, informed by our own experience and by postcolonial and Southern theory, was that stories that had grown out of Southern, postcolonial, Black and other marginalised ways of being, would foreground alternative modes of being in and knowing the city.

In addition to geographical concerns of setting and authorship, we opted to focus on public culture, rather than on 'literary' or 'arthouse' products. We sought to include imaginative work that has enjoyed mainstream success and both captured and shaped the popular imagination with regard to cities and urban life. Our set texts therefore included award-winning and bestselling novels, easily accessible documentaries and blockbuster films. While we also incorporated more 'niche' texts and films, the emphasis was on those that were already part of the public imagination. We therefore included writing from the Man Booker prize-winning author Aravind Adiga (2011), high-grossing films such as *Black Panther* (2018) and *District 9* (2009), and popular fiction such as Vikram Chandra's (2006) *Sacred Games*, Chibundu Onuzu's (2012) *The Spider-King's Daughter* and Tendai Huchu's (2010) *The Hairdresser of Harare*.

While not everything needs to be 'relevant', the general appeal of the set texts and films made them relatable to our own lives and experiences, and helped us think through contemporary urban issues. The ease with which they opened up familiar urban worlds, yet rendered them strange, was effective in broadening conversations and sparking fresh thoughts, and this was borne out in discussions and student writings.

Through stories from Mumbai, Nairobi, Johannesburg and even Wakanda, our primary texts demonstrated powerfully that there is no singular city. As one student, Amina, observed in an assignment dealing with two films:

> *Jeppe on a Friday* and *Nairobi Half Life* ... do not attempt to know the entirety of Johannesburg and Nairobi, respectively, but present to us those who know the city through their own intrapersonal realities. At this juncture, as we are drawn into the lives of those in the neighbourhoods of Jeppe and Gaza respectively, we can also begin to know the city through them. From what was previously perceived of the city, we reject the notion of the city as that of extremes ... but instead, allows us to begin to see and know the city as ordinary (Amina, coursework assignment, September 2018).[1]

The particularities of the cities in these stories demonstrate the importance of explicitly *partial* urban understandings, and paying attention to context. They highlighted the ways in which our urban imaginations are dominated by universalist notions that are in fact drawn from Northern cities, and the intellectual and creative work that needs to be done to shift that paradigm. The power relations in city-making (both discursive and performative) are inescapable, and questions of justice emerge here both in terms of understanding relations between city residents of all species, and between different cities in a global context. These questions were engaged both analytically and creatively, and through creative analysis, in our classes. In the following section we unpack some ways in which such texts encourage alternative modes of analysis.

Watching and Reading Experimentally

Rather than teaching traditional literary or visual analysis methods, we sought to encourage students to read imaginative texts and watch films as themselves works of theory – that is, as explanations and interpretations of urban space and urban dynamics (Highmore 2005). In other words, we invited students to join us in exploring these texts less as representations of these cities, and more as explanatory, or indeed theoretical, texts themselves. This is in stark contrast to how imaginative work is typically engaged in the social sciences, including geography and urban studies. When these disciplines turn to novels, poems, films or images, it is often to use them as illustrations of theoretical ideas or arguments, or simply as epigraphs and insertions to add texture and colour to an otherwise conventional academic text. This reduces the work of literature to a blunt instrument for a predetermined agenda, as Joanne Sharp (2000, 329) argues when she says:

> By reducing literature to just another source of 'data' on social or cultural phenomena, geographers miss the significance of literature which is its ability to disrupt or challenge conventional meaning not simply through its coverage of 'geographical' topics but also through the particular conventions of literary writing. Literature is different from geographical writing due to the content of the form of literature, its metaphorical and allegorical nature, the fact that it does not bear the responsibility of 'truthful' representation.

Taking seriously the difference of literature, and reading stories as analytical in their own right, not as the thing to be explained but as a thing that does some explaining (Highmore 2005), is an important shift in mindset. It demands that the voice and the narrative force of the imaginative work be taken seriously as the means by which it analyses the urban.

To try to practice such reading, we watched the documentaries *Urbanized*, *Jeppe on a Friday* and *Not in My Neighbourhood*, as well as Kwesta's music video, *Spirit*, as if they were in conversation with each other. *Urbanized* argues through urban experts; *Jeppe on a Friday*, through the experiences of five residents of a single neighbourhood; *Not in My Neighbourhood*, through residents in three cities across the globe; and *Spirit,* through visual vignettes. Reading and watching are essentially experiential acts, and this includes sensory/emotional experiences: imaginative texts trigger senses and engage readers emotionally. In other words, art forms move us. For example, students had very different emotional responses to feeling 'alienated' from an 'aloof' talking head perspective while watching *Urbanized*; angered in solidarity with activists and residents in *Not in My Neighbourhood*; and 'transported' by *Spirit.* As Rike Sitas and Edgar Pieterse (2013, 330) have argued, we need to 'take cognisance of the insights that emerge when people are not perceived as simply calculative beings who operate primarily on the basis of cognitive modes of consciousness … Affect holds the key to decipher deeply embedded dispositions, desires and concerns that steer us towards a particular kind of response that is most resonant, most appealing and most promising'. Recognising the affective dimensions of everyday life and scholarship can open up different spaces for critical enquiry. This is precisely what one student, Jake, observes in his review of *Not in My Neighbourhood:*

> It feels as though we are involved in the conversation; we are not passive in this process, but rather, invited into the experiences of the local residents. Orderson's [director] approach thereby enables the viewer to feel a sense of solidarity with those affected (Jake, coursework assignment, August 2018).

Feelings of recognition and solidarity are expressed, too, in Amina's reflection on *Jeppe on a Friday*:

> The manner in which the five characters experience space and time – their spatiotemporalities, allows us into the intimate ways of their being and into their personalised experience of the city (Amina, coursework assignment, October 2018).

This affective inroad into the lives of characters – fictional or otherwise – humanises urban enquiry while being no less critical than academic texts. And Jake again:

> Orderson's affective approach may be contrasted to news articles or academic writing – mediums that are often more common within gentrification

discourse – as it is clearly intended to elicit an emotional response, not just a rational one. *Not In My Neighbourhood* then realises a powerful representation of the widespread spatial violence occurring around us, which is usually ignored or overlooked. This is ... a vital project as it subverts dangerous apathy towards such pressing issues by encouraging viewers to engage meaningfully with its scope and urgency; Orderson's film inspires an empathy that, through and throughout it, we see is undeniably lacking [more generally] (Jake, coursework assignment, August 2018).

Humour provided another way of thinking about disrupting conventional modes of thinking the urban. In a class discussion of Aravind Adiga's *Last Man in Tower*, the idea emerged that stories can explain through humour and surprise. That is very seldom the case with theory – formal scholarship is rarely funny – but humour, as Sitas observes in chapter 2 in this volume, can be a powerful tool to shake us out of our passivity in the face of the built environment (Spurr 2012). As Walter Benjamin (1970, 9), speaking of theatre, argues:

> It aims less at filling the public with emotion, even if it is that of revolt, than at making it consider thoughtfully, from a distance and over a period of time, the situations in which it lives. There is no better starting point for thought than laughter. In particular, thought usually has a better chance when one is shaken by laughter than when one's mind is shaken and upset.

Through these modes of watching and reading, students began to see urban challenges in multidimensional ways, and to regard urban residents not only as statistics, or casualties of economic and political processes. People have harrowing *and* hilarious encounters with the city. This nuance and ambiguity fostered a criticality in students, who began to question their own assumptions:

> The fact that I could have been someone in the background of the Woodstock scenes caused a discomfort that was important, perhaps even intended by Orderson, pushing me to actively reexamine the way that I interact with my city (Jake, coursework assignment, August 2018).

And Amina:

> Exploration of these identities, narratives and histories necessitates reflection and challenges the ways in which we make sense of the urban – to grapple with the representation of various urban realities beyond our own (Amina, coursework assignment, September 2018).

Experiments in Writing

Through Imagining Southern Cities, we aimed to tease out how popular, Southern cultural representations might reshape ideas and pedagogies in urban studies, by highlighting the kinds of stories being told, and the possibilities of other kinds of stories. The final experiment, then, was our encouragement to our students not only to think differently about what data and theory might be, but also to *write* differently themselves. By engaging them in narratives and visuals seldom considered in urban studies or urban geography teaching, we invited students to critique but also to create, explicitly giving them freedom to produce work that was both theoretically generative and imaginative. The course was experimental in content and form, and we encouraged students also to experiment in their writing and their class engagements. While some students 'played it safe' in their writing and contributions, others took up the invitation and produced experimental essays, poetry and fiction.

An example from a 2018 student assignment illustrates how a non-conventional narrative opens up engagement with both material space and theoretical writings. Llewellyn's piece, for example, included a dream sequence:

> I dreamed of a place exactly like the neighbourhood, except there was no neighbourhood. The view was the same, the smells and light and wind were the same, and yet everything about it was different. I was in a field but it was as if I wasn't there. There were cattle and herders all around but none seemed to notice me. When I tried to speak no sound came out, and when I tried to walk I silently drifted in the air. The night sky was on fire with stars and the full moon hung beside the mountain (Llewellyn, coursework assignment, August 2018).

This may seem to have nothing to do with cities, but because we asked students explicitly to explain their experimental texts and/or visuals in terms of relevant theory and other texts, the student unpacked the connections:

The city is Cape Town but, like *How to Get Filthy Rich in Rising Asia*, it could be anywhere with a rainy season ... The story beats to the weather because, like the landscape, it has affected everyone in all places forever. It can change over time but it has existed, exists, and will exist. The tenses in [my essay] are deliberately jumbled. Places, people, ideas are shaped in the present by the past, making the future. This is inspired by Berman's dialectics of change in *All That Is Solid Melts into Air* (Llewellyn, coursework assignment, August 2018).

In this assignment, Llewellyn experimented with narrative to produce an academic piece that broke with convention yet demonstrated rigorous engagement with theoretical writings and opened up his own understanding of the urban. In playing with tenses and style, he evoked an urban sensibility that was deliberately ambiguous, and provided a counter-narrative to the rational analysis through which urban understanding is typically developed.

Allowing for ambiguity was a central theme in much of our students' work, reflecting both the freedom of fiction and imaginative work to tell more than one truth at a time, and expressing students' own embodied experiences of cities. Even engaging with a documentary on urban planning in a fairly conventional academic assignment – a review – one student suggested that '*Urbanized* doesn't give any answers but challenges us to think in a different way, including and valuing all efforts to create our future cities' (Amelie, coursework assignment, August 2018).

Experimentation also allowed students to explore the ambiguity of experience and understanding through visual means. Amina, for instance, produced for one assignment a collage that included images, media headlines and other texts of, from and about Kenya, and specifically Nairobi. The resulting visual text resisted normative urban ideas through both self-reflexive and theoretically engaged writing. Amina reflected:

Upon embarking on image collection, I had to think about Nairobi and what the city means to me. To immerse myself into the city and critically analyse my own positionality in how I can create Southern theory through imagery ... From the collage we can appreciate that cities are constantly changing, where new conceptions of society and the city are occurring every day. The artwork of Michael Soi and his two-project collection 'I love NBO' and 'China Loves

Africa' [included in the collage] are exemplary depictions of contemporary Nairobi (Amina, coursework assignment, September 2018).

Having placed her own embodied self firmly in the work, itself a radical act in academic writing, Amina works to draw the connections between this personal reflection and theoretical debates on postcoloniality and Southern theory.

> To ask the question *'Nai Ni Who?',* Who Is Nairobi – is to question who can write, speak and create of the city. It is to rely on post-colonial theory as Roy (2015) reiterates, that engages in a critical process that involves realising new narratives for the global south city. The question may be reproduced in multiple ways; Who Is Lagos? Who Is Mumbai? This allows us to narrate ourselves onto a map that is inclusive of our historical differences and allows for a new intimacy and imagination with urban theory. The messiness of urban identity and space is worth exploring where knowledge-making and individual perspectives can begin to decipher the city and centre ourselves at the heart and within the messiness of urban theory (Amina, coursework assignment, September 2018).

Experiential Learning

It was important to us to give equal weight to imagination, on the one hand, and materiality on the other, and to explore these realms as co-constitutive. As Harriet Hawkins (2010, 324) argues, it is important to consider the 'space[s] to which you take your whole body, bringing … an understanding of the experience of art not as grasped by a "solely intellectual act", but by the complex perception of the body as a whole'. To this end we included travel, movement and hands-on activities as structural elements of the course.

Although seminars happened inside, in fairly typical seminar rooms, wherever possible, we tried to challenge the experience of being in traditional academic spaces – reconfiguring the activities and the room. For the student-led classroom seminars, we asked that an activity be included in every session. This opened the gates for puzzles, games and crafts to be brought into the classroom to help us think through questions of dwelling and building, connecting and excluding. Students rose to this challenge imaginatively. In one seminar, we were asked by the students leading the session to work with different media including paper, plastic bottles, coloured pens and other craft materials, while engaging with a series of questions that emerged out of earlier discussions about the affective dimensions of city-making. This was a tactile strategy that facilitated reflections about how cities are made and remade on a continuous basis. The session was as much about what we made as about how our makeshift designs came in contact with others.

Although a fair amount of time was spent indoors, we ensured that the course also took us out of the seminar room, into the streets beyond the university, to continue our conversations. By thus bringing together techniques of close reading and theoretical critique with walking and sensing in the streets of Cape Town, we sought to destabilise the boundary between the 'real' and the 'imagined' city and explore material and embodied experience as equally essential to reading the city. As Shannon Morreira, Josiah Taru and Carina Truyts (2020, 137) assert, corporeal engagement in learning is a powerful political, decolonial strategy, allowing 'for the creation and maintenance of students as embodied, knowledge-making persons situated within communities, rather than as abstracted individuals to whom academia imparts knowledge created by others'. However, through the course we realised that a second, related yet distinct realm of experience, that of the emotional, was also emerging as important. We discuss each of these realms briefly in this section.

Our main field trip in each iteration of the course was to Wynberg, a suburb roughly midway between Cape Town's CBD and the coastline, along the southern suburbs railway line that hugs the Table Mountain range for about 20 kilometres, between Table Bay and False Bay. Originally established as a military base in the nineteenth century precisely because of its midpoint between the central city and the strategic naval base at Simon's Town, Wynberg is both a major transport hub and one of Cape Town's most starkly divided suburbs along lines of racial and economic privilege.

The morning's walk starts on the pavement at a point across the road from the Magistrate's Court, beside which squats the brutalist concrete block that houses the South African Police Service headquarters, and adjacent to the large, green space of Maynardville Park, the site of a former colonist's villa and garden, and now home to an open-air theatre and a children's play park. From this location we meander through Chelsea Village, an affluent and overwhelmingly white neighbourhood replete with quaint colonial heritage architecture, boutique art galleries and coffee shops. We walk east through Maynardville Park and down the few blocks to Main Road, bustling with commercial activity including street trade, high street retail outlets, and the buzz of taxis and bumper-to-bumper traffic. The demographic is now almost entirely Black and brown.

Running parallel to Main Road is the southern suburbs railway line with lower Wynberg on the other side. Our pedestrian path goes under the railway through a dank subway, and is flanked on the other side by informal trader stalls. The buffer zone between the street and the railway line has been occupied by people who have created an informal settlement with tents and other shelters. This interstitial space feels like a neighbourhood in itself, where the social, the spatial and the economic are not only intimately intertwined, but publicly visible.

Lower Wynberg is an old neighbourhood, classified as 'coloured' under the Group Areas Act of 1950, and still home to many residents who have lived there for generations. Since 1994, the suburb has also come to house many migrants from elsewhere on the continent, for whom the location provides an affordable entry point to the southern suburbs more generally, with their relatively low crime levels, greater job opportunities and relatively well-resourced schools, compared to lower-income areas on the Cape Flats and beyond. Lower Wynberg has a political history, from the Luxurama theatre, one of the few places that could admit racially mixed audiences during the 1960s, to the 'Wynberg 7', teenage activists at Wittebome High School who were arrested and imprisoned by the apartheid police in 1985. Our walk through the area ends at a local Cape Malay diner with salomies, gatsbys and sugar bean curry for lunch.

While field trips are not uncommon in urban studies, they are unusual in literary and film studies, where the text is the site of study, and place is often reduced to 'setting'. In urban studies, by contrast, physical spaces tend to be theorised as sites of 'gritty reality', encapsulated in the normative concept of being 'on the ground'. Our aim was to work between these two tendencies, taking place seriously within texts themselves, and also reading the urban environment as textured places of metaphor and imagination. Walking the city with creative texts and images in mind provided an opportunity for embodied geographical learning. As we walked, we summoned images of informality, movement, contestation and 'rubbing along together' (Watson 2006) from texts including *City of God* (Rio de Janeiro), *Last Man in Tower* (Mumbai) and *The Hairdresser of Harare*, bringing these into conversation with traders, pedestrians, dog walkers, nannies, shoppers and taxi drivers in Cape Town. Walking alongside the evocative images from novels and films allowed for critical reflections that may not ordinarily have arisen. Students brought reflections on the films and texts to bear on what they were seeing on the streets of Wynberg.

There are four ways worth mentioning where students surfaced the potential for embodied and affective theorising from the street, emphasising the importance of walking as a critical act of urban encounter (Lyons, Crosby and Morgan-Harris 2018). First, sensory and sonic landscapes create an awareness of the affective and aesthetic layers to city life. For example, students observed how walking and seeing the city cinematically allows one to recognise that which is 'mundanely beautiful' – light refracting between buildings, bouncing off windows, shadows of trees softening the otherwise hard surfaces, and plants peeking through cracks in pavements.

Second, walking raised the question of how these sensory dimensions are not without their own politics. Something as seemingly 'good' and 'given' as nature in cities, is not benign. Trees, for example, may be seen as innocuous, but they played an important role in colonial planning and the construction of parks such as Maynardville where right of access was reserved. The presence of many exotic trees in the park is the consequence of the Victorian fashion for collecting species, an exercise of power over the colonies as much as of scientific endeavour. Similarly, green spaces such as the corridor alongside the railway line are an enactment of power, creating buffer zones that are used to divide. The fact that these are increasingly encroached upon and transgressed emphasises their boundary-ing intention. Standing under a tree where any chance of sitting down had been thwarted by defensive design, the students remarked that despite the 'greening' ideals of urban planners, there is even a 'politics of shade'.

Third, theory can sometimes rely too heavily on unhelpful binaries – casting city spaces as either affluent and elite on the one hand, or destitute and desperate on the other (Edjabe and Pieterse 2015). Fiction is better able to capture the in between, the irreconcilable and the intersectional. Walking enabled students to see and grapple with the kinds of contradictions active in *Last Man in Tower* and the parallel and interconnected lives in *The Hairdresser of Harare*. The tensions and paradoxes of these narratives were frequently commented on as we observed similar scenes on our walks.

Finally, walking and experiencing the city allowed a space for interrogating the personification of the city and city-fication of people in particular places as well as discussing what this meant for different scales of urban enquiry – how cities are simultaneously real and fictional, local and global, intimate and alienating. We observed how sitting (not always comfortably) in this simultaneity makes for better scholars and scholarship that may be better attuned to imagine spaces of greater urban justice.

POST-CORONIAL PEDAGOGIES?

Films and novels have long provided vital spaces through which cities are represented and made meaningful. Although Hollywood still shapes many of the dominant narratives we see, the comparative success of Bollywood and Nollywood shows how film has permeated every corner of cities everywhere – even when there are no cinemas. The box office success of *Black Panther*, for example, and the popularity of Beyoncé's visual album *Black is King*, demonstrate the reach of global imaginations across national boundaries, creating new spaces for conversations about how cities are represented. Similarly, through e-books and audiobooks, literature is being consumed in new ways, with stories of Southern cities gaining new audiences.

As the world continues rapidly to urbanise, with cities in the global South growing far faster than their Northern counterparts, 'the city' is coming to mean new things to us all. As climate change, too, accelerates, threatening coastal cities around the world with displacement and even disappearance, we urgently need to understand, imagine and enact new urban modes of living. Films and novels have a place in these shifts. As works of art, their main function is to imagine. They do not necessarily bear the burden of rationality, they do not have to be well-meaning. They do not have to concern themselves with acting on issues of justice and inequality and precisely for that reason they might tell us something of those things that we didn't know before.

Art – and particularly film and literature because of their comparatively wide popular appeal and their sustained narratives – can tell truths about what people think and feel in ways that even the best ethnography or participatory research can never do, simply because even the best ethnographer doesn't know what a character/a subject was thinking or feeling. If the subject cannot express it, the researcher cannot document it. But the literary text does know. And just because it isn't 'true' doesn't mean that it is false.

While researchers are bound by rules, traditions and specific forms of ethics, novelists, filmmakers, musicians and artists are more dexterous in their representations of what is happening in the world. For these reasons, they are worth adding to our urban studies canons and curricula.

NOTE

1   All students are referred to by pseudonyms, and excerpts from coursework assignments are cited with permission from the students involved.

REFERENCES

Adichie, Chimamanda Ngozi. 2009. 'The Danger of a Single Story'. Filmed July 2009 at TedGlobal. TED video, 18:21. https://www.ted.com/talks/chimamanda_ngozi_adichie_ the_danger_of_a_single_story?language=n.

Adiga, Aravind. 2011. *Last Man in Tower.* London: Atlantic.

Benjamin, Walter. 1970. 'The Author as Producer'. *New Left Review* 1 (62): 1–9. https:// newleftreview.org/issues/i62/articles/walter-benjamin-the-author-as-producer.

Beyoncé. 2020. *Black is King.* Disney.

Blomkamp, Neill, director. 2009. *District 9.* Tristar Pictures, Block/Hanson. Wingnut Films.

Chandra, Vikram. 2006. *Sacred Games.* New Delhi: Faber and Faber.

Coogler, Ryan, director. 2018. *Black Panther.* Marvel Studios, Disney.

Edjabe, Ntone and Edgar Pieterse. 2015. 'Preface'. In *African Cities Reader III: Land, Property and Value*, edited by Ntone Edjabe and Edgar Pieterse, 1–5. Cape Town: African Centre for Cities and Chimurenga.

Gitonga, David Tosh, director. 2012. *Nairobi Half Life.* One Fine Day Films.

Hawkins, Harriet. 2010. 'The Argument of the Eye? The Cultural Geographies of Installation Art'. *Cultural Geographies* 17 (3): 321–340. https://www.jstor.org/stable/44251352.

Highmore, Ben. 2005. *Cityscapes: Cultural Readings in the Material and Symbolic City.* Houndmills: Palgrave Macmillan.

Huchu, Tendai. 2010. *The Hairdresser of Harare.* Harare: Weaver Press.

Hustwit, Gary, director. 2011. *Urbanized.* Swiss Dots.

Kwesta. 2018. 'Spirit ft. Wale'. YouTube video, 1:16. https://www.youtube.com/watch?v=wFi-BqmTRrw.

Lund, Katia and Fernando Meirelles, directors. 2002. *City of God.* Miramax.

Lyons, Craig, Alexandra Crosby and H. Morgan-Harris. 2018. 'Going on a Field Trip: Critical Geographical Walking Tours and Tactical Media as Urban Praxis in Sydney, Australia'. *Media and Culture Journal* 21 (4). https://doi.org/10.5204/mcj.1446.

Morreira, Shannon, Josiah Taru and Carina Truyts. 2020. 'Place and Pedagogy: Using Space and Materiality in Teaching Social Science in Southern Africa'. *Third World Thematics* 5 (1–2): 137–153. https://doi.org/10.1080/23802014.2020.1747944.

Nussbaum, Martha. 1990. *Love's Knowledge: Essays on Philosophy and Literature*. New York: Oxford University Press.

Onuzu, Chibundu. 2012. *The Spider-King's Daughter.* London: Faber and Faber.

Orderson, Kurt, director. 2017. *Not in My Neighbourhood.* Azania Rising Productions.

Pinder, David. 2008. 'Urban Interventions: Art, Politics and Pedagogy'. *International Journal of Urban and Regional Research* 32 (3): 730–736. https://doi.org/10.1111/j.1468-2427.2008.00810.x.

Roy, Ananya. 2015. 'What Is Urban about Critical Urban Theory?' *Urban Geography* 37 (6): 810–823. doi: 10.1080/02723638.2015.1105485.

Scott, Ridley, director. 1982. *Blade Runner.* The Ladd Company.

Sharp, Joanne P. 2000. 'Towards a Critical Analysis of Fictive Geographies'. *Area* 32 (3): 327–334. https://www.jstor.org/stable/20004085.

Sharpe, William Chapman and Leonard Wallock. 1987. 'From "Great Town" to "Nonplace Urban Realm": Reading the Modern City'. In *Visions of the Modern City: Essays in History, Art, and Literature*, edited by William Chapman Sharpe and Leonard Wallock, 1–4. Baltimore: Johns Hopkins University Press.

Sitas, Rike and Edgar Pieterse. 2013. 'Democratic Renovations and Affective Political Imaginaries'. *Third Text* 27 (3): 327–342. https://doi.org/10.1080/09528822.2013.798183.

Spurr, David. 2012. *Architecture and Modern Literature*. Ann Arbor, MI: University of Michigan Press.

Walsh, Shannon and Arya Lalloo, directors. 2013. *Jeppe on a Friday*. Parabola Films.

Watson, Sophie. 2006. *City Publics: The (Dis)Enchantments of Urban Encounters*. London: Routledge.

Watson, Stephen. 1990. *Selected Essays, 1980–1990*. Cape Town: Carrefour.

INVOKING NAMES: FINDING BLACK WOMEN'S LOST NARRATIVES IN THE CLASSROOM

ATHAMBILE MASOLA

INCOKO: AN ATTEMPT AT CONVERSATION

Makhulu Emma, Makhulu Nonesi, Makhulu Katye; ndiza kuni bantu abadala. Bendithetha ngani eklasini. Ngoku ndibhala ngani ngenxa yokuz-ibuza imibuzo engenampendulo ngendlela enikhunjulwa ngayo. Ndikhule kuthethwa ngeekumkani neekumkanikazi zaseNtshona kodwa nina ndinganazi. Andiyazi nokuba ndithi Makhulu, Khokho, Makhosikazi, Nkosikazi. Xa ben-dithetha ngani, bendisebenzisa iqaqobana lamaphepha asixelela ngobomi benu. Iifoto ezintathu kunye neeleta ezimbalwa. Ezi leta ziqokelelwe encwadini ethetha ngembali yoncwadi yabasetyhini. Kulapho ndaqala ukubona nokufunda ngawe Makhulu Emma. Iifoto zona zibonisa nina Makhulu Nonesi noMakhulu Katye. Nithule kwezi foto. Nihleli, nijongile, nilindile. Ndiye ndazama ukuqwalasela ezi foto. Ndizimamele. Ndiye ndazixhoma e-ofisini yam ukuze ndinisondeze, ndinibone kakuhle. Oko nithe cwaka.

Mhlawumbi ndiyanihlupha nizihlelele. Mhlawumbi bekumele siwayeke amagama enu. Andazi. Isizathu sokuba ndithethe ngani ngumsindo wokubona ukuba indlela endiye ndafundiswa ngayo imbali, yenza ingathi naningekho; iyaninyamalalisa. Ngaphandle kwesizukulwana senu, sibambalwa abayaziyo ukuba naniphila, nanikhona. Ndinento ethi nibukele, nijongile, nimamele, maxa wambi ninikina iintloko xa nibona indlela esithetha ngayo ngembali *yamaAfrika. Emveni kokuba ndithethe ngani eklasini ndiye ndatyelela esiqithini, iRobben Island kunye naseZonnebloem. Bendinethemba lokuba ndiya kuzuza ithuba lokufunda ngani kwiindawo enanikhe nahlala kuzo (nithanda, ningath-andi). Ndibone isimanga esiye sandidanisa: eZonnebloem andilibonanga igama lakho Makhulu Emma. Ngaphandle kwevidiyo enye eveza amagama kunye neefoto zenu Makhulu Katye nawe Makhulu Nonesi, esiqithini kujolwe kum-abali amabanjwa enkululeko ingakumbi. Akukho nenye indawo ebonisa ukuba naniphila njani. Esona simanga – okanye akhonto isisimanga – abona bantu abaye baphakamisa amagama namabali enu kumaziko emfundo nakuncwadi ngabelungukazi. Abantu bayakhalaza, bathi bekungafanelekanga ukuba ibhalwe ngabo imbali yenu. Bekumele ibhalwe ngubani?*[1]

I begin this chapter by addressing Emma, Nonesi and Katye directly. I am not certain yet whether it will be a letter or an attempt at a conversation. Perhaps it is about trying to respond to the gaps in the written archive when it comes to these women whose fragmented stories appear in letters and a few photographs. I write in isiXhosa because that is the language they would have spoken (Emma would have been able to speak English and possibly Dutch as well). These are the royal women I have invoked in my teaching while trying to make sense of the place for stories about Black women in the history cur-riculum, both in higher and basic education.

I address them as '*makhulu*' – grandmother – because they are collective ancestors rather than simply historical figures. I should be using the name '*khokho*' to invoke their position as ancestors but *makhulu* seems more fit-ting as it is more personal. Why would I want to be personal with historical figures? Am I trying to make sense of myself through them? Perhaps I am breaking the boundaries of history which feigns objectivity. Perhaps I am try-ing to imagine them as people whose lives matter enough to be remembered. I am mostly recognising them as *izinyanya* – the living dead; that even while they are historical figures, they are also ancestral spirits who are alive among us, according to an African worldview which deems humans ever-evolving spirits.[2]

I only know these women from what I have read about them. There are no statues, no plaques, few images, no street names to remember them by. Much of what I know about them has been in response to the erasure of women like them who seldom make it into history books; even though they were central to the grand narratives of history, they are overlooked, rendered insignificant.

If they are of any importance at all, it is that they are known in relation to the men who occupy a firm place in the grand narratives: Sandile, Maqoma and Siyolo, all Xhosa chiefs of the nineteenth century whose stories have been revisited over and over again.

Emma, Nonesi and Katye's world in the nineteenth century is characterised by war and displacement. By the 1700s, settler colonial expansion had infiltrated the vast southern area of Africa from west to east that would become the British Cape Colony by the early 1800s. This period was characterised by wars and alliances between the Xhosa and the Khoi, as well as other forms of engagement, since 'the Xhosa saw no reason why Xhosa and European should not merge into a single society rather after the pattern of Xhosa and Khoi … They traded with the Boers as they did other nations' (Peires 1981, 60). However, the wars and resistance to colonial expansion continued, culminating in the cattle killing of 1856/7 which destroyed much of the Xhosa's power (Peires 2013).

The historiography of this period is often dominated by the names of men and their exploits, with little consideration for the ways in which women responded to and negotiated displacement and colonial expansion. Research on Emma Sandile has been more widely available because of her ability to insert herself into the colonial archive through her education at Zonnebloem College in Cape Town.[3] She was born in the 1840s and lived until 1893 (Hodgson 2021). She was the eldest daughter and heir of King Sandile of the Rharhabe and his great wife Noposi (Bhotomane 1967). Princess Emma Sandile arrived in Cape Town in 1858 (in the aftermath of the cattle killing), together with Hester Ngece, Noneko Toney, Nomenteshe (Nomendasha) Maqoma and Nomagatana Toise (Hodgson 2021). The college was a result of a 'collaboration between the British government and the Anglican Church' (Hodgson and Edlmann 2018, 1) and was set up in 1857 'for the education of the sons and daughters of chiefs imprisoned on Robben Island in the aftermath of the … frontier wars' (Hodgson 1975). Much of Emma's life is caught up within this collaboration because of her royal position. Her marriage negotiations were disrupted and eventually she married Stokwe Ndlela (a Mqwathi chief) in a polygamous marriage (Hodgson 2021). She petitioned for land for her co-wives and children, and is known as the first Xhosa woman to own land when she was granted a farm (near Komani in present-day Eastern Cape) by the British government (Hodgson 2021, 155).

There is less information about Katye and Nonesi who appear in the colonial archive only through their husbands, Maqoma and Siyolo, respectively. They both accompanied their husbands into exile in Cape Town in the 1850s (see Stapleton 1994). Stephanie Victor explains 'what little we know about Nonesi and Katye's pre-incarcerated biographies is largely bound up with their husbands' lives' (2014, 154).

WRESTLING WITH MARGINALITY

> Yet how does one recuperate lives entangled with and impossible to differentiate from the terrible utterances that condemned them to death, the account books that identified them as units of value, the invoices that claimed them as property, and the banal chronicles that stripped them of human features? (Hartman 2008, 3).

This is a question Saidiya Hartman poses in her essay 'Venus in Two Acts', which 'examines the ubiquitous presence of Venus in the archive of Atlantic slavery and wrestles with the impossibility of discovering anything about her that hasn't already been stated' (Hartman 2008, 1). This starting point is relevant for this reflection which is about a different kind of wrestling related to invoking the names and voices of Black women in the classroom at the University of Cape Town (UCT). The stories of Emma, Nonesi and Katye are central to their location in Cape Town; however, they appear in 'the scraps of the archive' (Hartman 2008, 4). Unlike the narratives of Jan van Riebeeck, Simon van der Stel and Cecil John Rhodes (to mention a few), whose names are central to how we locate southern African history, the names and stories of Emma, Nonesi and Katye are marginal – as though the scholarship of Janet Hodgson and Stephanie Victor, and oral history, never existed. What does it mean to invoke the names of Emma, Nonesi and Katye in a classroom located at UCT in the twenty-first century, an institution which excluded women and Black people at its inception? Is this a form of justice? When Emma, Nonesi and Katye arrived in Cape Town at different points in the 1850s, the university was in its third decade of existence as a white, male-only institution. Women would only be admitted in 1886. It is impossible to know whether Emma, Nonesi and Katye knew or even cared about UCT; however, knowing what we know about their historical context of war, land dispossession and dislocation, it is possible to assume that their presence at UCT almost 200 years later is a matter of significance.

Penelope Hetherington (1993, 242) offers this:

> In considering the development of women's history generally, most feminist historians would subscribe to three propositions. They would argue that at least until the 1960s, the history of women was neglected in all national historiographies, so that before that time women were almost invisible in the historical record; that the subject matter of history, as written by professional historians (and expressed in the taken-for-granted boundaries between disciplines) has been so narrowly defined that it has excluded many areas that are important for the study of women's past; and that the writing of feminist writing, like all history writing, is a political act. It follows that post-1960 feminist historians were inevitably writing "compensatory" history because there were such gaps in the historical record; that they tended to be interdisciplinary in their approach, with a penchant for asking new questions and for widening the boundaries of history and that they brought a certain passion or commitment to the task of making women visible.

This highlights the political and intellectual context which marginalised Black women in particular in national historiographies. This chapter is not a 'compensatory history' but rather a reflection on the ways in which we engage with the lives of Black women in the context of 'gaps in the historical record'. Beyond the historical record, how do we account for lives that are not memorialised by statues, plaques or extensive scholarship? This results in a fragmented history which ends with an acknowledgement of disappearance rather than a full account of Black women's lives. An attempt at teaching about Black women's lives means thinking through new methodologies to account for these fragments, particularly in a discipline such as history which positions itself as having the ability to provide a narrative about the past.

Over time, these gaps have been addressed and challenged through the works of feminist historians. Helen Bradford highlights that 'female invisibility, it has been argued, is the most dominant trend in African historiography vis-à-vis women' (Bradford 1996, 351). The Women Writing Africa series from The Feminist Press, which features the histories and writings by women from most parts of the continent from as far back as sixth century BCE, has been one of the responses to this invisibility. Even while there has been this attempt at enumerating and anthologising women's narratives and writings, this approach of 'gender-only anthologies can contribute to the tendency to marginalise (ghettoise) women's and gender history' (Erlank and Clowes 2004, 235).

Teaching Black women's narratives in a department which has taken active steps in shedding its imperial origins continues to be a political act. In 2003, the Department of Historical Studies at UCT reflected on the centenary of its existence. While there is a need to reflect again on how this has changed in the past 20 years since this episode of reflection, in 2003 there was an agreement that 'a gender perspective is also often absent from much of the teaching in our courses ... In many universities gender is too often tacked on to courses as one lecture or treated as a theoretical add-on' (Erlank and Clowes 2004, 233). My attempt at teaching about Emma, Nonesi, Katye, Nongqawuse and Nonkosi in a way that does not suggest that they are add-ons to history, is a direct response to this approach which oversimplifies the narratives of women.[4] This chapter is not a speculative history, but rather a reflection on the meaning of teaching in a context of wrestling with knowledge. In 2003, there was also an acknowledgement of two additional challenges to teaching history: who teaches history, and which languages are used? At the colloquium in 2003, Yvette Abrahams pointed out that 'there are only three locally graduated Black female historians in the country, and attempts to recruit a Black female history student to the Sarah Baartmann Biography Project elicited not one suitable female candidate. A similar lack of Black female graduate students is common to history departments around the country' (Erlank and Clowes 2004, 234). It is difficult to see the extent to which these numbers have changed since programmes are still in the process of addressing this history.[5] In short, it matters who is teaching history, and my positionality as a Black woman is an important part of this reflection.

The issue of language is an ongoing challenge which needs a more pointed approach related to who teaches history. At the 2003 colloquium the discussions highlighted:

... the inability of many South African historians (and historians of South Africa) to conduct research in anything other than English and Afrikaans. A South African historical canon presented overwhelmingly in English has several effects. It serves to prioritise exclusionary research agendas, while at the same time provides students with the impression that research undertaken in isiXhosa, Zulu, or Sotho is somehow unacceptable. This is obviously a problem not only for gendered history, and needs to be taken up by academic institutions much more broadly. However, given that much gendered history relies on knowledge of (and acknowledging) the everyday interactions taking place within private and personal spaces, the problem of producing meaningful gendered history, for instance via translation, becomes an issue of representation and power (Erlank and Clowes 2004, 234).

Nomalanga Mkhize's (2018) critique of white academics' dismissal of works in African languages in the case of the Mfecane debate of the 1980s is relevant here.[6] When Richard Tainton Kawa's *Ibali lamaMfengu* was published in 1929, it was 'an expression of Kawa's critique of colonial writing and perspectives on the history of amaMfengu' (Mkhize 2018, 93) and has implications for how the Mfecane debate is understood as a historical event. Mkhize continues to show how Kawa's work was not in isolation but part of a burgeoning culture of historiographers emerging in the early twentieth century among Black intellectuals. These include: 'Walter Rubusana's compendium of African clan histories, *Zemk'inkomo Magwalandini* (1906), and Solomon Plaatje's *Native Life in South Africa* (1916). S. E. K. Mqhayi's canonical novel *Ityala Lamawele* (1914) signalled literary works steeped in historical themes' (Mkhize 2018, 94). Mkhize's discussion of Kawa's work demonstrates the ways in which 'dismissing the likes of Kawa by the academic mainstream can lead to profound epistemic distortions and lacunae within South African historiography' (Mkhize 2018, 105).

The question of language is more complicated, even when sources exist in African languages, because teaching students who are monolingual English speakers creates its own problems. Rather, an approach towards embracing multilingualism and translation, where students learn at least one African language before they reach university, would ensure a different approach to language in the classroom (not only in teaching history, but across the humanities). Part of my attempt in isiXhosa, at beginning this chapter, is to address this language gap and the ways in which the archive is assumed to be accessible only in English. In a sense, I am refiguring and recreating the archive by responding in both isiXhosa and English as a way of experimenting with language.

UKUZILANDA: CALLING OUT NAMES

This pedagogical experiment of listing and evoking names which are not easily searchable on the internet or in many historical documents raises questions about teaching in the humanities more broadly, and in history more specifically. These lists and names are traces and fragments of stories which may never be fully coherent. And even then, this coherence is not possible because 'narratives of survival are lost or could not ever be produced, what is left must be made central to any investigation: autobiographical ephemera, fragments, names, oral stories, songs' (Rak 2018, 546). These lists and names ask the students to witness the nature of erasure as well as think critically about methodologies which respond to erasures and marginality. These methodologies may include creative work as a response to fragments.

I recently joined UCT's Department of Historical Studies and inherited a course titled 'Conflict and Conquest: Southern Africa to 1900', which I taught with Associate Professor Lance van Sittert. The course is framed as follows:

> 'Conflict and Conquest' is aimed at introducing students to historical debates which seek to trouble the often taken-for-granted historical accounts about the making of South Africa as a nation-state leading up to 1900. The course begins with debates related to historiography which attempt to respond to questions of origin. This is related to archival sources and archaeological history and how it accounts for deep history which predates colonialism ... The course will end with a reconsideration of the settler-frontier historical debates with a focus on the South African War and the effects of missionary power. This is the nexus of education, church, colonial governance and colonial capitalism.

In the section related to resistance and frontier narratives, students were prescribed a reading by Jennifer Weir – 'Chiefly Women and Women's Leadership in Pre-colonial Southern Africa' (2006) – which I introduced by asking the students to do a quick Google search of the following names:

Nonesi

Katye

Emma (ka)Sandile

Songiya

Ngqumbazi
Novimbi
Langazane
Mnkabayi kaJama
Nomadada
Nothonto
Nongwane
Thuthula

These are the names of royal women who have always existed in the record but now there is a demand that the names *and* narratives of women be included in historiography. I was deliberate in listing these names in order to show the number of names available, and contrast that with the paucity of information available. Secondly, by listing their names, I invoke the practice of *ukuzilanda*, a concept in isiXhosa which means 'to fetch oneself'. This idea is useful in this context as it is a practice and a methodology which can help us in understanding history. Among amaXhosa, *ukuzilanda* means 'to fetch oneself and connect oneself to the past in the present moment', which is often done through clan names and telling stories (Masola 2018). In history, this means taking seriously the act of listing names which have been ignored, and posing questions about why these names have been ignored, erased, marginalised and otherwise disregarded. *Ukuzilanda* can be seen as a methodology to be read alongside Brittney Cooper's (2017) concept and methodology of listing. Cooper writes about African American women in the nineteenth and twentieth centuries who had to contend with the 'great race men' whose work and narratives often marginalised women's intellectual work. To counter this erasure, these women would create lists in order to account for their public work. Cooper explains:

> I do not merely think of these lists as mere lists. Instead, this intentional calling of names created an intellectual genealogy for race women's work and was a practice of resistance against intellectual erasure … These lists situate Black women within a long lineage of prior women who have done similar kinds of work and naming those women grants intellectual, political, and/or cultural legitimacy to the Black women speaking their names … Black women's long traditions of intellectual production constitute a critical edge, without

which, the broader history of African-American knowledge production would unravel and come apart at the seams (Cooper 2017, 2).

By listing the names of women, mentioned earlier in this chapter, my intention was to highlight the material effects of erasure since many of the students I teach confessed to never having heard of the women on the list. They were also able to see the gaps in knowledge production as there was little to no information on the internet about these women either. The intentional calling of names, that is, *ukuzilanda*, makes us conscious of the nature of knowledge production and the nature of intellectual erasure.

The challenge with this methodology is that it does not fully resolve the question of loss and absence in the archive. Simply being able to list people's names is only half the job. What matters more is the substance of their lives and stories. This remains a gap considering that women did not have the same opportunities as their male counterparts in missionary institutions for participating in the printing presses and publication of their writing. Emma Sandile's peers at Zonnebloem College, as well as similar schools across the region, would have been the likes of Magema Fuze (*c*.1840–1922), Isaac Wauchope (1852–1917), William Wellington Gqoba (1840–1888) and Richard Tainton Kawa (1854–1924), to mention a few. These four men produced writing and publications that have been anthologised and revived in isiXhosa and isiZulu, as well as through English translations. Although the only available writing by Emma comprises her personal letters – available thanks to Janet Hodgson's research on Zonnebloem College – the existence of the letters opens up the possibility that she may have produced other forms of writing.

The poem that follows tries to capture some of these concerns about the nature of erasure; it is titled 'Ukunyamalaliswa' (Masola 2021):[7]

Amagama ethu aphaphatheka nomoya
Amazwi ethu akhaphukhapu njengeli phepha ndibhala kulo
aphela engumgubo
Ubuqu bethu bukhiwa ngetispuni.
Iingcinga zethu zisesithendeni kwezemfundo
Iimbuso zethu zifakwa ezincwadini kodwa kungabikho gama

('For most of history, Anonymous was a woman.')

Abanye bade bazingombe isifuba ngegagu

Besithi zange babhale nto iphucukileyo abantu ababhinqileyo

Xa ndibaphikisa ndivumbulula amagama angenambuso:

Ndiyabazi babephila kodwa andinawo umfanekiso-ngqondweni.

Baluthotho elikhwankqisayo

Ndiyabeva bekhwaza besithi:

Ningavumi!

Ningavumi silityalwe!

Ningarhoxi

Ningatyhafi

Ningarhoxi

Ningatyhafi

Ekhe nabanika ithuba

lokuba bathi sasingekho

niyazi ukuba nani amagama enu azakutshona, kuth'we

anaziwa

anikho

aniyonto

Nani, ninyamalale.[8]

I use isiXhosa in response to this epistemic distortion as a way of responding to the archive (in English), which has sparse evidence of women's voices, not because they were not historically active but because erasure happens when certain voices are dismissed in the archive. In the poem, I show that erasure is systemic rather than haphazard or accidental since people make deliberate choices in causing people to disappear from the archive as well as the cultural imagination. By adding a conversation and poetry to this reflection I am invoking orality, which has the potential to respond to the archive in newly creative and imaginative ways.

TRACING HISTORY THROUGH IMAGES AND VOICES

Emma, Nonesi and Katye show up in the archive in relation to the prominent men who create history. I chose to include these women in the course I taught in order to disrupt the focus on men as the main actors of history.

The context of conflict and conquest is characterised by war, land dispossession, slavery and other forms of sociopolitical interactions dominated by men. When I taught the cattle killing of 1858, I centred the narrative on Nongqawuse, the young female prophet who set rolling the events which led to the destruction of Xhosa people. I introduced students to the debates related to claims about the cattle killing, as well as the glaring questions about a young girl and her own position in the narrative, all of which led to discussions of gender in this context. This was followed by a lecture looking at the aftermath of the cattle killing and the War of Mlanjeni (1850–1853), with a focus on Nonesi and Katye, who had accompanied their husbands to Cape Town when they were incarcerated first in Wynberg Prison and then Robben Island. The next lecture looked at missionary power by focusing on the stories of women such as Jane Waterston (the first principal of the Girls' Institution at the Lovedale Missionary Institute in Victoria West in 1866), Nosutu (mother of the Reverend Tiyo Soga), Paulina Dlamini (a missionary in Natal in the 1880s) and Emma Sandile (daughter of King Sandile and one of the early students at Zonnebloem College in Cape Town in 1858). For the purposes of this chapter, I reflect on Emma, Nonesi and Katye because at least one part of their stories unfolds in Cape Town.

In the course, I used the images Victor writes about to turn the gaze away from the men and zoom in closer on the women alongside them.[9] Since no images of Emma Sandile have survived, I use her letters published in *Women Writing Africa: The Southern Region* (Daymond et al. 2003) in order to bring her voice into the classroom. The photographic images which have survived of Nonesi and Katye allow the opportunity for a different kind of reading of history. In her 2014 article, Victor offers a snapshot as well as a reading of her work, which has since changed during her PhD journey where further information has emerged about the women.[10] Victor's choice of focusing on the images allows for 'looking beyond what we see and attuning our senses to the other affective frequencies through which photographs register. It is a haptic encounter that foregrounds the frequencies of images and how they move, touch, and connect us to the *event* of the photo' (Campt 2017, 9). In the context of fragmented histories, images offer other ways of making meaning of history.

The first illustration used by Victor is by James Glen Wilson, a correspondent for the *Illustrated London News* of February 1853, and marks Nonesi and

Siyolo's arrival in Cape Town and their incarceration at Wynberg Prison with their two attendants, Obeek and Neànte.[11]

Victor focuses on the representation of their dress as 'visually, little remains of their precolonial self' (Victor 2014, 159). However, upon a closer reading, the sketch is also about the representation of captivity. I am struck by the texture of the image: a grainy illustration which almost looks like it was made for a comic book. The four figures are sitting huddled on the floor. Any likeness in the illustration is not the point, which is rather the depiction of what it means to be incarcerated far from home; this would have been a publication for a foreign audience which was 'interested in satisfying its reading public's jingoistic inquisitiveness about an incarcerated Xhosa chief and his entourage' (Victor 2014, 159). The faces of the four figures are not distinct. In fact, they look like a caricature of the same person. This sameness makes it impossible to distinguish who Nonesi is; perhaps the attire is the only clue as one woman has a shawl and the other does not. The size of the headwraps also differs. This lack of distinction demonstrates the ways in which colonial imagination denies the humanity of these subjects in their captivity. The clothing worn by the figures does more than 'represent a transitory period, of a traditional past in a colonially determined present' (Victor 2014, 159) but also highlights the extent of conquest which was not simply about land but also about mundane aspects such as clothing. In a sense, conquest was an all-encompassing experience.

There are two photographic images of Nonesi and Katye with their husbands, from the Grey Collection. The photographer is not recorded, but Victor offers that 'the photographer is unknown but it is probable that the images were taken by Frederick York, an Englishman working in Cape Town at the time, who advertised a selection of portraits of the exiled chiefs on Robben Island in October 1859' (Victor 2014, 165). Much has been said about colonial photography as 'a celebration of the colonial project, serving to camouflage and maintain systems of power and domination inherent in colonial ideology and the colonial effort to categorise, define, and subordinate. Colonial photographs signify a visually documented verification of an alleged innate cultural, economic, political, and intellectual superiority, the raison d'être of European imperial ideology' (Engmann 2012, 53). Furthermore, colonial photography raises questions about gaze – who is being looked at, by whom and why – which further highlights the power dynamics 'in which the

Figure 4.1
'Nkosikazi Nonesi and Nkosi Siyolo, c.1859'. Photographer unknown, possibly Frederick York, an Englishman in Cape Town, who advertised portraits of incarcerated chiefs. Grey Collection. Courtesy of the National Library of South Africa.

omnipotent, colonial, male gaze sees but is never seen' (Engmann 2012, 54). These photographs demonstrate the same power dynamics. I was particularly struck by the posture of the women.

There is a dejectedness in these images. When I zoom in on the women (rather than the men), I am even more curious about their posture. Nonesi's head is slightly cocked to the side – in resignation and exhaustion? She is visibly young but there is a sadness in her youthful face. Katye's posture with her hand on her mouth is more complex to read. There is a defiant look on her face. The position of her hand partly covering her face defies the camera and the male gaze which cannot get full access to her. The posture speaks volumes. In trying to imagine and read closely what the image is saying, the word '*isimanga*' comes to mind.[12] There is a resignation and defiance. There is also a disbelief, *isimanga*: '*Hayi abelungu sisimanga! Abelungu abasiboni!*' (White people never cease to amaze me! White people do not see/respect us.) While photographic images are used to capture a moment which can travel over

Figure 4.2
'Nkosikazi Katye and Nkosi Maqoma c.1859'. Photographer unknown, possibly Frederick York. Grey Collection. Courtesy of the National Library of South Africa.

time and space, if those who are being photographed are subjects, it is possible for the photographer not to see them wholly and therefore only capture a representation that does not recognise their humanity. To not see someone is to render them invisible. To not feel seen or not want to be seen – in the case of Katye's hand position – highlights the complexity behind these images. I am trying to imagine Katye and Nonesi's reaction to the photographer and the idea of having one's image taken: a new technology of subjection in a context of incarceration where there are no choices, no consent and no freedoms. I can also imagine the women being traumatised by the experience; perhaps there was some reluctance in sitting for the photograph? Or perhaps there was excitement as well as anxiety? It is difficult to tell other than trying to read the postures in the photographs. The nature of the clothes becomes a symbol of a change in status: landless royalty who are now dressed in Western clothing to emphasise their capture and subjection.

In 1869, when Katye and Maqoma were released from Robben Island, another picture was taken of them during a visit to Zonnebloem College where they met the warden. Their daughter, Nomendasha Maqoma, was also at Zonnebloem College and returned home with them when they finally left Cape Town. In this later image the postures are quite different. Katye is now standing, looking more confident. She appears much older than the woman who arrived on Robben Island a decade earlier. Maqoma's posture and face are equally defiant, and perhaps more alive at the prospect of finally returning home. Their physical presence in these images seems to be more regal and resonant of their status, even while it is in a context of injustice. Reading this image requires deeper attention as it is taken during an interregnum period of what feels like freedom. The possibility of freedom is not really liberating since they are in fact returning to more conflict and landlessness.

When considering these images and the colonial obsession with portraits, it seems hard to believe that there are no existing images of Emma Sandile while she was a student at Zonnebloem College. I include her in this discussion because her time as a young girl in Cape Town overlaps with Katye and Nonesi's time on Robben Island. In the course I teach, her narrative is included to explore the extent of missionary power and its collusion with colonial governance. In *Women Writing Africa: The Southern Region* (Daymond et al. 2003), six of Emma's written texts appear: a letter to Sir George Grey dated 2 November 1860; two letters to Bishop Gray dated 3 January and 14 January 1864, respectively; a letter to her teacher Miss Matilda Smart dated 26 March 1864; a letter to Charles Levey (magistrate in Southeyville, a Thembu area) dated 27 September 1882; and a submission to the Land Commission dated 10 February 1883. Each of these letters demonstrates the ways in which Emma negotiated power through her ability to use her education as well as her status as a royal woman to advocate for herself and her family. This is in spite of the ways in which the church and colonial government sought to control her life because of her royal status. They curated her education, which was meant to 'civilise' her and the other royal children at the school (Hodgson 2021). They tried to control who she should marry in accordance with the Anglican church; however, this did not succeed and she ended up becoming the great wife of Chief Stokwe of abaThembu. Finally, they sought to control her access to the land.

In the course, students had the opportunity to read Emma Sandile's work closely in order to get a sense of her personhood, her defiance and her voice.

This is particularly apparent in the letter to Charles Levey, which is worth quoting as it appears in the anthology (Daymond et al. 2003, 91–94):

> Sir, I am the eldest daughter of the late Chief Sandile, and the great wife of the late Chief Stockwe. At the present time I am living under your care. Though you have been very kind to me and my children, yet you know that we have no fixed place which we can call our home. Please ask the Government Commission for Thembuland to recommend to the Government that I should get a small farm for my children, and the wives of the late Chief Stockwe. We do not wish to make a native location, but simply want a small place we can call our own. We wish to be always under your care and protection.

This letter is written many years after Emma Sandile experienced the disruption to her life inflicted on her by the colonial government, including the death of her husband in 1880 in battle against the British forces. Emma's admission of living under the 'care and protection' of the British can be read in a myriad of ways, which highlights the complexity of being landless royalty in the context of British occupation. Having 'no fixed place which we can call our home' is a form of truth-telling as well as euphemism given the effects of war and conflict throughout her life. This letter also captures the ways in which women's lives were disrupted by colonial wars and land dispossession, even while the grand narrative of history focuses on men, their negotiations and decisions. Emma's ability to insert herself into the colonial archive meant that her story is present even while it remains marginal. By including her name, writings and narrative in the course, I was able to disrupt this marginality, and in so doing, disrupt the ways in which conquest and conflict are configured. I also place her story in relation to that of Paulina Dlamini, which unfolds in Natal under King Cetshwayo's *isigodlo* (royal homestead) in the 1870s, and ends with her missionary life at the turn of the century. Her story survives through the book written by the German Lutheran missionary, Reverend Heinrich Filter, *Paulina Dlamini: Servant of Two Kings* (published by University of Natal Press and Killie Campbell Africana Library Publications in 1986). By placing these women's stories in conversation with one another, I aim to show the overlaps in their stories which defy exceptionalising them. It is an invitation for more stories of those who were their contemporaries and peers in the nineteenth and twentieth centuries.

AN ONGOING STORY

I began this reflection in an attempt at a conversation with *Makhulu* Emma, *Makhulu* Nonesi and *Makhulu* Katye, tainted by my own ambivalence about their presence and absence in knowledge production. My aim was to show the ways in which bringing these names and narratives into the classroom may be a response to epistemic justice but also an indication that more work is needed to think about the ways in which history as a discipline needs to respond in how it constructs histories. I end with a poem titled 'Imbali' (Masola 2021) as a way of sealing the conversation I began. It is another form of invocation to respond to erasure such as the kind I encountered in the classroom. This reflection is part of an ongoing praxis of thinking through and with erasure – its nature and its implications. The poem speaks to the embodied practice of writing history – the title of the poem means 'history' – which is demonstrated in the analysis of the images and the letters that form part of my discussion here.

'Imbali'

Zibhale kodwa ungabhali esantini
Hleze uhambe namanzi olwandle

Zibhale kodwa ungabhali emthini
Hleze bawugawule okanye bawutshise

Zibhale kodwa ungazibhali ngamafu
Hleze abaleke nomoya okanye abeyimvula

Zibhale kodwa ungabhali ngembola nodaka
Zona zihlambeka lula ngamanzi

Zibhale ngesiqu sakho
Abo banamehlo bakubone

Zibhale ngelizwi lakho
Abo baneendlebe bakuve

Zibhale ngeenyawo zakho
Abo bafunayo bakulandele
Zibhale ngobuqu bakho
Bungaze buvuthuluwe nje ngothuli.[13]

NOTES

1   Grandmother Emma, Grandmother Nonesi, Grandmother Katye: I am coming to you
as elders. I was talking about you in my teaching. And now I am writing about you
because I am asking myself many questions without answers about the ways in which
you are remembered. I grew up hearing stories about kings and queens from the
North, but I did not know about you. I am wondering: how should I address you? As
grandmother, ancestor, queens, queen? When I was talking about you in class I used
a small collection of resources which tell us about your lives. Some images and a few
letters. The letters have been collated into a book which demonstrates women's literary
history. That is where I first read about you, Grandmother Emma. The photographs
show Grandmother Nonesi and Grandmother Katye. You are quiet in these images.
Sitting, looking, waiting. I tried to pay close attention to these images. I tried to listen
to them. I printed them and had them in my office just to make you more familiar and
see you closely. You have been quiet all along.

Perhaps I am bothering you. Perhaps we should leave your names alone. I don't know.
The reason I have spoken about you in my classes is because I am angry about the
ways in which I have been taught history; it is as though you never existed, you have
been made invisible. Other than your own descendants, there are few who know that
you indeed lived; you were here. I have a sense that you are watching, looking and
listening, and at times you shake your heads in dismay when you see the ways in which
we talk about African history. After I spoke about you in class, I visited Robben Island
and Zonnebloem College. I was hoping to learn more about you from the places where
you spent many years (whether you wanted to be there or not is neither here nor
there). I was shocked by what I saw: at Zonnebloem College I did not see your name,
Grandmother Emma. Other than a video that shows your names and photographs,
Grandmother Katye and Grandmother Nonesi, the island focuses on the stories of
freedom fighters. There is no place that shows how you lived while you were on the
island. Another shock – or perhaps there is nothing shocking about this – the people
who have written your stories and elevated your names in research and institutions are
white women. Black people are complaining, saying that it is not their history to tell;
your stories are not for them to tell. Who is meant to write your stories?

2 Their position as royal women warrants more titles: *nkosazana* (princess), *umntwana wegazi* (child of the blood), *nkosikazi* (great wife of a chief/nkosi). For the purposes of the chapter, I will use their first names as these titles are contextual and may cause confusion. I will not use the accepted convention of surnames as using Sandile may add confusion, and Nonesi and Katye lived at a time when surnames were not yet a convention.

3 Emma's family name – Sandile – is used here, as this is how she would have been known at the time of her arrival in Cape Town.

4 For a longer history on their role in the cattle killing, see Peires (2013).

5 At UCT, the History Access Programme, funded by the Andrew W. Mellon Foundation, has focused on 'Everyday Archives' to account for the divide between academic history and public life. 'Vernacular Universals' looks at multilingualism as a tool for using archives which are not available in English, and which are often excluded from the curriculum. The National Institute for the Humanities and Social Sciences has also addressed the question of the number of Black students with PhDs, and has grown the numbers to respond to the critique of their lack of representation at postgraduate level.

6 The debate is too extensive to repeat here; however, much of it can be followed through an experimental digital platform which maps out the debate and the chronology, and includes the resources relevant to the debate, called Emandulo. See http://emandulo.apc.uct.ac.za/. Emandulo is developed by the Five Hundred Year Archive (FHYA) research initiative, a project of Archive and Public Culture (APC), based at the University of Cape Town.

7 Loosely translated, it means 'to be made invisible'. Firstly, I have decided against a line by line translation of the poems used in this chapter. This requires a longer and more painstaking project, which needs a translator who has distance from the poems (I am reluctant to translate my own poems). Secondly, I am currently resisting translation of these poems not because they are untranslatable but rather because the phrasing in English is clumsy, hence the need for more time for revisiting the translation.

8 © Athambile Masola, 2021. Poems first published in *Ilifa* (uHlanga 2021)

9 Stephanie Victor's writing is part of a longer project that culminated in a PhD thesis which was completed in 2022. Much has been unearthed in this project which is yet to be published.

10 Victor's thesis has been embargoed for two years and was not available for quotation at the time of writing this chapter.

11 Obeek and Neànte are unusual names and possibly incorrect spelling.

12 Often translated as shock, awe or wonder, depending on the context.

13 © Athambile Masola, 2021. Poems first published in *Ilifa* (uHlanga 2021)

REFERENCES

Bhotomane, Ndumiso. 1967. 'Imbali'. Interview by Harold Scheud, 10 September 1967. Audio, 10:00. https://search.library.wisc.edu/digital/AIO2B5WLCI3FNE8U.

Bradford, Helen. 1996. 'Women, Gender and Colonialism: Rethinking the History of the British Cape Colony and Its Frontier Zones, c.1806–70'. *Journal of African History* 37 (3): 351–370. https://www.jstor.org/stable/182498.

Campt, Tina M. 2017. *Listening to Images.* Durham, NC: Duke University Press.

Cooper, Brittney C. 2017. *Beyond Respectability: The Intellectual Thought of Race Women.* Urbana: University of Illinois Press.

Daymond, Margaret J., Dorothy Driver, Sheila Meintjes, Leloba Molema, Chiedza Musengezi, Margie Orford and Nobantu Rasebotsa, eds. 2003. *Women Writing Africa: The Southern Region.* New York, NY: The Feminist Press at the City University of New York.

Engmann, Rachel Ama Asaa. 2012. 'Under Imperial Eyes, Black Bodies, Buttocks, and Breasts: British Colonial Photography and Asante "Fetish Girls"'. *African Arts* 45 (2): 46–57. https://doi.org/10.1162/afar.2012.45.2.46.

Erlank, Natasha and Lindsay Clowes. 2004. 'Writing and Teaching Gendered History in Africa in the Twenty-First Century: Centenary of the UCT History Department'. *South African Historical Journal* 50 (1): 231–236. https://hdl.handle.net/10520/EJC93568.

Filter, Heinrich, ed. 1986. *Paulina Dlamini: Servant of Two Kings.* Translated by S. Bourquin. Pietermaritzburg: Killie Campbell Africana Library and University of Natal Press.

Hartman, Saidiya. 2008. 'Venus in Two Acts'. *Small Axe: A Caribbean Journal of Criticism* 12 (2): 1–14. muse.jhu.edu/article/241115.

Hetherington, Penelope. 1993. 'Women in South Africa: The Historiography in English'. *International Journal of African Historical Studies* 26 (2): 241–269. https://doi.org/10.2307/219546.

Hodgson, Janet. 1975. 'A History of Zonnebloem College, 1858–1870: A Study of Church and Society'. MA thesis, University of Cape Town. http://hdl.handle.net/11427/21344.

Hodgson, Janet. 2021. *Black Womanism in South Africa: Princess Emma Sandile.* Cape Town: BestRed.

Hodgson, Janet and Theresa Edlmann. 2018. *Zonnebloem College and the Genesis of an African Intelligentsia, 1857–1933.* Cape Town: African Lives.

Masola, Athambile. 2018. 'Ukuzilanda: Resisting Erasure'. *Ixhanti lam,* 5 December 2018. http://ixhantilam.blogspot.com/2018/12/ukuzilanda-resisting-erasure.html.

Masola, Athambile. 2021. *Ilifa: Imibongo.* Durban: uHlanga Press.

Mkhize, Nomalanga. 2018. 'In Search of Native Dissidence: R. T. Kawa's Mfecane Historiography in *Ibali lamaMfengu* (1929)'. *International Journal of African Renaissance Studies* 13 (2): 92–111. https://doi.org/10.1080/18186874.2018.1533384.

Peires, Jeffrey B. 1981. *The House of Phalo: A History of the Xhosa People in the Days of Their Independence.* Johannesburg: Jonathan Ball Publishers.

Peires, Jeffrey B. 2013 [1989]. *The Dead Will Arise: Nongqawuse and the Great Xhosa Cattle-Killing Movement of 1856–7.* Johannesburg: Jonathan Ball Publishers.

Rak, Julie. 2018. 'Marlene Kadar's Life Writing: Feminist Theory outside the Lines'. *a/b: Auto/Biography Studies* 33 (3): 541–549. https://doi.org/10.1080/08989575.2018.1499486.

Sandile, Emma. 2003. 'Letters and Land Submissions, South Africa 1860–1883'. In *Women Writing Africa: The Southern Region*, edited by Margaret J. Daymond, Dorothy Driver, Sheila Meintjes, Leloba Molema, Chiedza Musengezi, Margie Orford and Nobantu Rasebotsa, 91–95. New York, NY: The Feminist Press at the City University of New York.

Stapleton, Timothy. 1994. *Maqoma: Xhosa Resistance to Colonial Advance.* Johannesburg: Jonathan Ball Publishers.

Victor, Stephanie. 2014. 'Women in Captivity: Nonesi and Katye, the Wives of Xhosa Chiefs'. *Bulletin of the National Library of South Africa* 68 (2): 154–173. https://www.academia.edu/10924147/Women_in_Captivity_Nonesi_and_Katye_the_Wives_of_Xhosa_Chiefs_Published_in_Bulletin_of_the_National_Library_of_South_Africa_68_2_December_2014.

Weir, Jennifer. 2006. 'Chiefly Women and Women's Leadership in Pre-colonial Southern Africa'. In *Women in Southern African History:* Basus'iimbokodo, Bawel'imilambo/*They Remove Boulders and Cross Rivers*, edited by Nomboniso Gasa, 3–20. Cape Town: HRSC Press.

PART II
JUSTICE, CURRICULUM AND THE CLASSROOM

DECOLONISING PSYCHOLOGY IN AFRICA: THE CURRICULUM AS WEAPON

SHOSE KESSI AND HAL COOPER

... every practice produces a theory, and that if it is true that a revolution can fail even though it be based on perfectly conceived theories, nobody has yet made a successful revolution without a revolutionary theory.

— Amílcar Cabral (1966)

Psychology emerged as a discipline in its own right in the late nineteenth century, coinciding with the European imperial conquest of Africa and its partitioning into colonial states. This link is important as it explains the context in which psychologists at the time devoted their attention to scientifically explaining racial differences and became important contributors to 'race science', also referred to as scientific racism (see Howitt and Owusu-Bempah 1994; Richards 1997), which served to scientifically justify the separate and unequal treatment of so-called race groups. Hence, early psychological knowledge written about Africa and Africans was tainted by studies supporting racial oppression. Many South African psychologists during that period used psychometric testing to demonstrate hierarchical differences between racial groups historically defined as 'black', 'coloured' and 'white' to justify oppressive apartheid policies (Foster 1991). Questions about the relevance of psychology only emerged in South African psychology a century later in the 1980s (Macleod 2004) and have been followed by efforts to Africanise and decolonise the discipline (Mkhize 2004; Nwoye 2015; Ratele 2017; Kessi and Boonzaier 2018) and foreground feminist critiques (Shefer, Boonzaier and Kiguwa 2006). These developments have included critiques of global hyper-capitalist and hetero-patriarchal knowledge production (Kessi and Boonzaier 2018), thereby going beyond experimental and individualistic explanations of human thought and behaviour, towards understandings of global forms of power within the discipline and within society. In this chapter, we attempt to demonstrate how psychologists can make psychology relevant to African contexts if sufficient attention is given to unpacking its problematic European roots as well as adopting a decolonial agenda.

CHANGING THE PSYCHOLOGY CURRICULUM

Psychology, as a discipline that focuses on the mind and the role of the mind in social relations, is intrinsically linked to questions of human behaviour and understanding what it means to be human. In mainstream psychology curricula, the mind tends to be theorised as located in the individual and operating outside of the social environment. Indeed, the teaching of psychology largely focuses on the conceptualisation of the human mind as having robotic qualities, responding in particular ways to external stimuli. Even social psychology, as the branch of psychology interested in the individual–social interface, tends to be largely individualistic in approach. Attitudes and attributions theories followed by the widely recognised Solomon Asch (1950s), Stanley Milgram (1960s) and Philip Zimbardo (1970s) laboratory experiments on social norms and conformity (see Hogg and Vaughan [2018] for examples of these theories, or any general social psychology textbook) all attempt to test responses to external stimuli on individuals who are seen to make 'faulty' decisions, which in extreme cases lead to persecution and death. Henri Tajfel's minimum group paradigm and Muzafer Sherif's experiments on intergroup conflict (see Hogg and Vaughan 2018; or for a critical perspective, see Taylor and Moghaddam 1994) explain discrimination as a natural function of group belonging without a broader perspective on cultural and political factors. These studies are rooted in a social cognitive tradition and were designed to understand deviant behaviour as a function of the brain. Prejudice, discrimination or other forms of violence towards others, are theorised as deviations from 'normal' human behaviour, or as so-called biases or errors in cognitive functioning that lead to deviant behaviour. Such approaches to the understanding of human behaviour are problematic and must be challenged on the following premises:

- Unravelling the myth of a single rationality
- Unpacking the political effects of psychology.

THE MYTH OF RATIONALITY

A most critical problem with psychology curricula, which is rarely reflected on, is precisely the focus on cognition to explain prejudice and discrimination (Henwood and Phoenix 1996). Psychological approaches to cognitive theory are based on particular assumptions of human rationality. Human thought and rationality are seen as *fundamentally just* as they present the human as good, and prejudice and discrimination as bad and as errors in cognitive functioning. However, in a neocolonial historical and political context of vast inequalities where violence and conflict are rife as a direct result of colonisation, relying on cognitive approaches and mainstream understandings of rationality would imply that most people living in African contexts could be accused of deficient cognitive functioning or irrationality to explain their subhuman existence. Such theorisations are limited as they deny the existence of alternative rationalities that are guided by a range of historical contexts and political motives. Furthermore, trying to measure and understand the perpetration of violent acts as located in the mind (or as a cognitive function) can have the contradictory effect of exonerating individuals from blame and responsibility (Henriques 1984; Leach 2002). Indeed, if prejudice and discrimination are errors in rationality, then the cause of these errors becomes attributed to those who are discriminated against (Leach 2002). Violent acts are explained away as errors in cognitive functioning and theorised outside of a historical environment, and outside of power relations. A recent study conducted by psychologists in South Africa on the cognitive functioning of 'coloured' women is a case in point. The research findings, based on experiments designed to measure cognitive functioning, reproduced stereotypical images of black women as deficient in cognitive functioning (Boswell et al. 2019) due to explanations such as ethnicity and other socio-demographic factors. Such results are made possible by undermining the social–political context of the population under study, and the reliance on apolitical understandings of cognitive processes. Such work represents contemporary versions of race science (Howitt and Owusu-Bempah 1994; Richards 1997) that are commonplace in psychology (and other disciplines), and often published internationally in what are considered reputable academic journals. Research findings like these have devastating consequences as they impact in very real ways on people's access to resources such as education or employment but also on the resources for identity construction, dignity and psychological well-being. The danger of these studies is that they lead to interpretations about behavioural differences which then become the basis for discrimination in very real ways in everyday life, through institutional policies and cultures, representational projects and interpersonal relations.

THE POLITICAL EFFECTS OF PSYCHOLOGY

Notwithstanding some of the interesting insights into human behaviour derived from experimental studies, it is unclear how findings from laboratory settings can be extrapolated to understanding real-life situations (Taylor and Moghaddam 1994). Critics have suggested that rather than finding solutions to societal conflict and violence, psychological research has in fact served to justify and legitimise genocidal conquests throughout the world. With the Fourth Industrial Revolution upon us, it is of crucial importance to unpack the place of psychology in understanding the human in contemporary contexts. Indeed, the rise of artificial intelligence is predicated on how we theorise human intelligence and rationality in laboratory settings and may thus serve as a basis for re-inscribing inequalities. Much experimental work in psychology on racial difference has been exposed for theorising blackness as inferior (Howitt and Owusu-Bempah 1994; Richards 1997). Gender differences in psychology also have a long history of being theorised in ways that suggest different brain types for men and women (Shefer, Boonzaier and Kiguwa 2006). Psychology as a science is a powerful form of knowledge that, through representational projects, translates into common-sense knowledge and beliefs (Moscovici 1984). Popular representations of the global South in the media or cultural products rely on images of people as poor, inferior, corrupt and lacking in knowledge (Dogra 2012). These representations are also feminised and infantilised with a disproportionate number of images of starving women and children. Anti-immigration policies throughout the world underscore images of migrants (generally black migrants) as criminal, violent, untrustworthy and a drain on national resources. National policies in many post-independent countries are also restrictive and highly punitive in relation to gender and sexual rights. The inferiorisation of blackness consequently intersects with other markers of identity, such as gender, class, nationality and sexuality.

The psychology curriculum and the teaching of psychology therefore have political effects which tend to exonerate those who are dominant in society, and reproduce and legitimise negative conceptions of the marginalised. Alternative approaches are needed that foreground power relations in society, and the experiences and knowledges of those who are oppressed by dominant forms of power. It is for these reasons that foregrounding alternative approaches to psychology is crucial if we are to retain the relevance of psychology (Macleod 2004), and understand human experiences in vastly unequal historical spaces. Psychology curricula need to introduce alternative approaches to rationality based on articulations of cognitive justice (Leibowitz 2017) and the political dimensions of knowledge production. In the sections that follow, we provide an example of what a psychology curriculum could look like by drawing on theoretical frameworks rooted in a decolonial approach to psychology.

A DECOLONIAL FRAMEWORK FOR TEACHING PSYCHOLOGY IN AFRICA

The decolonial approach adopted here draws on Latin American theories of decoloniality in conversation with pan-African concepts of blackness as a tool for identity construction and African-centred practice. Decoloniality refers to the decoloniality of power (Quijano 2000), which is the understanding that global colonial relations of power, be they structural, epistemic, representational or relational (Kessi, Marks and Ramugondo 2020), have persisted despite the formal end of colonial rule. Decoloniality of power has been observed in different forms:

- the decoloniality of knowledge (Mignolo 2012), being the dominance of epistemic constructs that continue to serve white Western interests;
- the decoloniality of being (Maldonado-Torres 2007), referring to the persistent subhuman subjective status of the oppressed; and

- the decoloniality of doing (Ramugondo 2015), which is the ways in which decolonial power is reproduced in everyday occupations.

Of particular interest in the case study that follows (Fela Kuti: Music is the weapon) is how the decoloniality of knowledge, being and doing can intersect in the teaching of psychology. The case study draws on theories of blackness and Black Consciousness to explain racialised difference that disrupts the epistemic violence of early studies on the psychology of 'race'; the case study is about a musical art form that can serve as a political and aesthetic practice to challenge global racism by tapping into alternative (spiritual, sensual, embodied) rationalities and sensitivities; and finally, the case study highlights the ways in which the oppressed sustain colonial relations of power in their everyday practices by trying to emulate a white European identity.

DECOLONIALITY AND THE TEACHING OF PSYCHOLOGY AT UCT

The Department of Psychology at the University of Cape Town (UCT) has a tradition of teaching critical approaches to psychology. The department's curriculum can be seen broadly as comprising three different approaches to psychology: clinical psychology, neuropsychology, and social and critical psychology. The presence of social and critical psychology is reflective of the historical role of South African psychologists in challenging the epistemic violence of psychological knowledge. The field of community psychology in the 1980s until the present has taken a leading role in transforming the psychology curriculum. These 'streams' have in recent years been challenged by students, who have highlighted the contradictory nature of assumptions underlying the conceptualisations of the human mind taught through these different perspectives. The Rhodes Must Fall movement in 2015 gave an additional impetus to these criticisms, which led the department to engage in a curriculum review exercise. While undergraduate students could previously choose a particular stream to focus on, these changes have resulted in a curriculum that provides all undergraduate students with a grounding in all three streams in their first and second years. This has also meant that academics teaching these courses have had to work more closely together to deliver joint courses and craft more comprehensive syllabi. There is still much work to be done in unpacking the contradictions in the teaching of psychology at

UCT and in engaging earnestly with a decolonial approach but these small beginnings are reflective of some of these transformative gains. In 2018, the department also launched the Hub for Decolonial Feminist Psychologies in Africa (known simply as the HUB), funded by the vice-chancellor's office. The HUB is a space for staff and students to engage with the relevance of psychology in African contexts, to explore decolonial, pan-African, feminist and other critical approaches in a transdisciplinary space (see Kessi and Boonzaier 2018). It is within such a context that courses such as the postcolonial psychology Honours course emerged.

The authors of this chapter participated in a semester-long Honours module, 'Postcolonial Psychology', taught in the Department of Psychology. The first author is the lecturer who designed and taught the course and the second author is a former student who chose the course as part of their degree. The module was designed over a 12-week period with each week focusing on a separate theory, ranging from Frantz Fanon and the psychoanalysis of racism, Steve Biko on Black Consciousness, W. E. B. Du Bois on double consciousness, black and African feminist theories, and whiteness studies, to liberation psychology, followed by student presentations. The learning outcomes of the course were to:

- Locate postcolonial theory and psychology within the discipline of psychology;
- Critically assess whether and how to do psychological research in postcolonial settings;
- Discuss the role of psychological research in processes of othering;
- Consider the postcolonial psychological possibilities and conditions for *disrupting* racialising practices and claims to privilege, belonging and knowing.

The curriculum was thus a challenge to the mainstream conceptualisation of prejudice and discrimination in psychology and focused on race, gender and class identities from pan-African and/or Southern perspectives and psychology as a practice of resistance and liberation. Assignments included a presentation on a topic of choice, an analytical book review of an African novel using theories learnt in the course (see Table 5.1), and an essay on transforming or decolonising the discipline of psychology.

Table 5.1: Suggested reading list for book review assignment

Chris Abani	*Graceland* (2004)
Chinua Achebe	*Things Fall Apart* (1958) *A Man of the People* (1966) *No Longer at Ease* (1960) *Arrow of God* (1964)
Chimamanda Ngozi Adichie	*Purple Hibiscus* (2003) *Americanah* (2013) *The Thing Around Your Neck* (2009)
Ama Ata Aidoo	*Our Sister Killjoy* (1977)
Ayi Kwei Armah	*The Beautiful Ones Are Not Yet Born* (1970)
Mariama Ba	*So Long a Letter* (1981)
NoViolet Bulawayo	*We Need New Names* (2013)
Panashe Chigumadzi	*Sweet Medicine* (2015)
Tsitsi Dangarembga	*Nervous Conditions* (1988)
Buchi Emecheta	*Kehinde* (1994) *Second-Class Citizen* (1974) *The Rape of Shavi* (1983) *The New Tribe* (2000)
Bessie Head	*Maru* (1971)
Tendai Huchu	*The Hairdresser of Harare* (2010)
Niq Mhlongo	*After Tears* (2007)
Toni Morrison	*The Bluest Eye* (1970)
Ousmane Sembène	*God's Bits of Wood* (1960)
Ngũgĩ wa Thiong'o	*Petals of Blood* (1977)
Yvonne Vera	*Butterfly Burning: A Novel* (1988)

*The reading list was developed with input from a colleague in the Department of English Literary Studies, pointing to the importance of interdisciplinary collaboration in developing curricula. It was compiled for the second year of the course as it became apparent that students had very little knowledge of African authors, highlighting a critical gap in our undergraduate curriculum.

FELA KUTI: MUSIC IS THE WEAPON

We have chosen to highlight Hal Cooper's class presentation as an example of what an alternative curriculum for psychology can produce. His work illustrates in very poignant, creative and compelling ways how we can engage with the psychology of blackness in order to disrupt the epistemic violence of mainstream psychology, to build consciousness and to contribute ideas towards a decolonised curriculum. His presentation drew on the music of Fela Kuti

(1938–1997), a Nigerian singer and composer, pioneer of Afrobeat, well known for his anti-colonial political activism against corruption and the military state.

Fela Kuti himself said 'music is the weapon', which is also the title of the documentary film produced about his life in 1982. He saw his music as a powerful medium for the education and mobilisation of African people, and thus its content gave expression to his political consciousness, with Black Consciousness and anti-colonialism as significant themes running through much of his work. Thus, during the course of my independent research on Fela Kuti's music, I was able to draw parallels between his work and the subject matter of our postcolonial psychology course. This experience deepened my engagement with and understanding of these theories. Further, the process of pursuing this research in a free and creative way in itself challenged my experience of education, and it will be argued that this has intellectually transformative potential.

Some of the themes running through Fela's music resonated closely with the course content. The central theme of the song 'Black Man's Cry' (1971) challenges the inferiority complex Fela noted in African society. Some notable lyrics are:

> *Who says my black skin is not beautiful?/... Who says your black skin is not beautiful?/... Let the person come out/ There is no better than this your beautiful black skin/ Look at yourselves closely/ There is no better than this my beautiful black skin.*

Thus, through his music, Fela Kuti challenges his listeners to ignore the racist European idea that white skin is beautiful and black skin is not. One can see this as a reaction to what Fanon argued in his book *Black Skin, White Masks* (1986) was an internalisation, or 'epidermalisation', of inferiority. Inferiority was internalised, according to Fanon, by colonised people coming to see themselves through the eyes of their colonial oppressors and taking on racist values to understand themselves. Understanding oneself in the oppressors' terms, as inferior, was profoundly damaging to the psychology of the colonised people. Fela Kuti clearly understood this assault on the dignity and integrity of his people, and his music was an attempt to subvert the cultural dominance of these colonial values and create a counter-discourse – in 'Black Man's Cry' – of affirmation of black skin.

One consequence of the epidermalisation of inferiority was, according to Fanon (1986), a process of 'lactification' – whitening oneself in an attempt to assimilate to the colonial standards of beauty and superiority. This process of lactification did not simply concern pigmentation, but could manifest in an attempt to master the language and culture of the white colonial occupiers, or could be expressed in more explicit physical forms, as explored by Fela Kuti in 'Yellow Fever' (1976). 'Yellow Fever' addresses the practice of skin bleaching which was popular at the time of the song's release in Nigeria. In Nigerian Pidgin, the lyrics polemically attack this practice:

> *You dey bleach, o you dey bleach/ Sissi wey dey go/ Yellow fever/ Stupid thing/ Yeye thing/ Fucking thing/ Ugly thing/ Yellow fever.*

This is a direct attempt by Fela Kuti to challenge the culturally hegemonic discourse of whiteness being something to aspire to, and to encourage a critical state of mind towards this discourse and the practices associated with it. Similar to the themes of inferiority and lactification elaborated by Fanon, Fela Kuti's music resonates closely with the work of Steve Biko. Biko (1978, 29) stated, 'So negative is the image presented to him [the African child] that he tends to find solace only in close identification with the white society.' This analysis resonates with the sentiments expressed by Fela Kuti in 'Black Man's Cry', 'Yellow Fever' and several of his other pieces.

The lyrics to two more of Fela Kuti's songs mirror successfully central themes of the work of Fanon and Biko. The songs 'Gentleman' (1973) and 'Colonial Mentality' (1977) both challenge the assimilation of the historically colonised to the culture and mindset of the colonisers – due to an inferiority complex, and expressed via, for example, forms of lactification. In 'Gentleman', Fela Kuti berates an African man dressing himself in the suit of a European man, attacking this practice by stating,

> *Him be gentleman/ Him go sweat all over/ Him go faint right down/ Him go smell like shit … I no be gentleman at all o!/ I be Africa man, original.*

Thus, Fela Kuti again affirms an authentic African identity, in opposition to the doomed emulation of a white European identity. The song 'Colonial Mentality' critically addresses the persistent colonial mindset of the previously colonised Africans:

> *He be say you be colonial man/ You don be slave man before/ Them don release you now/ But you never release yourself.*

Again, it seems that Fela Kuti's project was one mirrored in the title of Ngũgĩ wa Thiong'o's (1986) seminal book *Decolonising the Mind*. Fela Kuti argued that although Africans had been freed from physical slavery, their assimilation into white European culture meant that their minds had not been freed.

In sum, central themes of Fanon's and Biko's work – the inferiority complex, lactification, cultural assimilation and Black Consciousness – were fundamental to Fela Kuti's music and his ideological and political project. Exploring these themes freely and creatively through this presentation engaged me (as a student and presenter) deeply and enhanced my understanding of these fundamental theories.

CREATIVE LEARNING SPACES FOR ALTERNATIVE RATIONALITIES

Learning in a free and creative way represents a departure from traditional, mainstream educational practice, especially at undergraduate/Honours level. That is, assessment more often consists of essays and exams, the content of which students have no part in determining. Thus, researching a topic of our own choosing and interest for this project on the postcolonial psychology course was in itself a liberating experience, and challenged the compulsoriness of rigid, hierarchical modes of learning in which the teacher and student are distinct categories, with the student lacking in agency.

One can employ Paulo Freire's (1974) (whom we also studied during the course) theoretical framework to analyse the difference in these modes of learning. Mainstream forms of university education, such as written examinations, would align with Freire's 'banking' model of education: the teacher – a distinct entity from the student – deposits information into the student, which the student is then later asked to regurgitate. In this model, the subject matter is often alien to the student, detached from their personal experience, and there is little, if any, space for critical engagement. This is diametrically opposed to the experience of taking the postcolonial psychology course. Indeed, the teacher vs. student dichotomy was subverted. For example, we sat around a table together, in which the 'teacher' was in the same position as the students, and the 'students' were responsible for the majority of the discussion. In the case of the presentations, the students actually became teachers, as they informed the group about a topic they had themselves chosen for special study. Although I chose to do a presentation using PowerPoint slides and music, the project could have been realised in another form, such as a discussion or debate. Thus, in this way, the mode of learning was in line with Freire's conception of a critical pedagogical form of education in which there are student-teachers and teacher-students.

There is enormous emancipatory potential in this mode of learning, especially in the social sciences. Although I chose my research topic based on *interest*, it would have been possible for students to choose their topic based on *experience*. That is, in a critical space in which issues of inequality and oppression are at the centre of discussion, students with experiences of racism, sexism and class inequality could tie the theoretical concepts underlying the course to these experiences. In this way, the content could become more real and relevant to the rest of the class who participate in the learning process. This process of linking theory to reality forms a praxis that should be fundamental to education and mobilisation in an emancipatory movement.

POLITICAL PSYCHOLOGY

Decolonising psychology is a commitment to a continuous process of engagement and reflection with the curriculum and the pedagogies of learning. The Honours course in postcolonial psychology described in this chapter has since evolved into an Honours course called political psychology (see Table 5.2), which has retained some of its previous content but also expanded to include critical approaches to psychology from different parts of the globe, with an emphasis on how the *politics* of knowledge production and how the *political effects* of psychology shape human existence. The idea was to put postcolonial psychology in conversation with contemporary questions of immigration prejudice in Western contexts, political narratives of the Israeli-Palestinian context, diasporan and gendered identities, the impact of social policies such as international aid, and questions of protest and restorative justice from the continent and the diaspora. The reshaping of the course was also prompted by feedback and engagements with students in the classroom, and the need to continuously engage with contemporary social issues in South Africa and their interconnectedness with global movements. A key innovation in this revised syllabus is the introduction of research methodologies in order to provide students with useful tools to conduct their own research projects within a decolonial frame. For each topic of the syllabus, an example of an empirical study was provided to illustrate and critique the approaches to producing psychological knowledge, such as social dominance research, narrative and discourse analyses, and participatory research methods, among others.

Table 5.2: Political psychology seminar overview

1	**Introduction to Political Psychology** This seminar introduces political psychology, interrogates the politics of psychology, covering its history, usual topics of study, as well as the particular theoretical frameworks used in this course. We discuss the differences between formal politics, governance and practices of representation and everyday politics, everyday interactions and relationships, and argue that political psychology plays an important role in showing the connections between these political layers.
2	**Immigration Prejudice and Xenophobia** This seminar introduces students to immigration prejudice and xenophobia in different parts of the world and the role of political psychology in understanding these phenomena.
3	**Political Narratives** This seminar discusses how sociopolitical change is both temporally continuous and dynamic. By exploring the role of narrative research, we can explore how societies adapt and change to dominant political structures where resistance may or may not become a viable strategy.
4	**Whiteness Studies** This seminar explores white identities in political contexts through the lens of whiteness studies. Critical and participatory discussion on whiteness and structures of privilege with emphasis on the post-apartheid context. The discourses and myths underlying white privilege and possibilities for a white anti-racism.
5	**Analysing Political Discourse** This session will introduce discourse analysis as a method for analysing political discourse. Using examples of research on political speeches and televised discussion programmes, students will be encouraged to reflect on the epistemological, methodological and political dimensions of analysis.
6	**Postcolonial Identities, Nationalism and Resistance** This seminar examines the role of racial identities in the construction of the nation with a particular focus on African, black and diasporan identities. The seminar will begin with a discussion on racial privilege and oppression as modes of political organisation. Fanonian concepts of racial alienation and objectification, W. E. B. Du Bois' concept of double consciousness, and Léopold Sédar Senghor on Negritude will be examined as lenses into the role of racism in the construction of nations. Drawing on these forms of African nationalism, we will discuss the possibilities for resistance and decoloniality.
7	**Gender, Citizenship and Nationalism** This seminar examines the role of gendered identities in the political reproduction of the nation. We will examine the significance of gender relations in national projects and problems, such as citizenship and gender-based violence. It will introduce the value of feminism for political psychology, with a particular emphasis on black/African feminisms, the concept of intersectionality, the role of masculinities and sexualities.

8	**Social Policy and Global Governance** This seminar explores the relevance of psychology for understanding how policy acts as a tool for implementing political decisions and strategies with a particular emphasis on aid policies. In order to understand how policy acts as a tool for implementing political ideas, we need to first understand how it is embedded within people's everyday lives. A political psychological approach to policy helps us do this in two key ways: (1) by paying attention to how the surrounding social environment influences the implementation of policy; and (2) by interrogating the psychological factors (including social representations, social identity, agency) that frame how policy impacts on people's lives.
9	**Collective Identities, Social Movements and Liberation** This seminar examines the social and political psychology of collective identities, focusing on the ways in which identities are mobilised in processes of social and political change. It draws together a range of theoretical and empirical approaches to collective identities, examining the ways in which identities are produced in collective protest and action. Studies will highlight the role of social and political ideologies both in provoking and in denigrating political protest and social unrest (such as riots).
10	**Reconciliation and Reparations in Post-Conflict Settings** This seminar examines the psychological conditions for reconciliation and dialogue in post-conflict settings. Examples from diverse settings will be discussed, such as the TRC [Truth and Reconciliation Commission], CARICOM [Caribbean Community], First Nations, Rwanda, and reparations for African Americans who are descendants of enslaved people.

* A number of these seminars have been adapted from Professor Caroline Howarth's political psychology Master's course taught in the Department of Psychology and Behavioural Sciences at the London School of Economics and Political Science (LSE). Shose Kessi taught this course at the LSE in 2017.

These developments in the syllabus are a reflection of how we continue to expand our understanding of the decolonial imperative. The starting point for the development of any curriculum in psychology has to be an acknowledgement of the complicity of the discipline in the colonial project and how this may persist in the afterlives of colonisation. The pursuit of social justice, and the role of psychology as a practice of resistance and liberation, must continuously seek to unravel the often less visible ways in which coloniality and uneven relations of power persist in pathologising the existence of the marginalised and oppressed; it must simultaneously seek to provide the resources for restoring pride and dignity. This seems like an impossible task but so much can be achieved within learning spaces if we trust our students and allow them to be as creative and imaginative as they can be.

It is from them that we learn new, innovative and productive energies for the future.

CRITICAL EDUCATION FOR CONSCIOUSNESS

In many ways, a critical education resembles art, or, as discussed in this chapter, music. Like Fela Kuti's music, the curriculum can be a means of expression, analysing the world that we experience and providing a creative critique of it. The beat, the movement, the voice, the lyrics and sound all weave together in mesmerising ways to reveal the consciousness of a people deeply affected by its colonial history while simultaneously inspiring pride and liberation. Arguably, it is the combination of the affective experience of the music and its theoretical content that has the potential to deepen understandings of human rationality and lived experience, not only for those who experience forms of discrimination but also for those who are privileged in society to begin to develop a sensitivity and awareness of the conditions of the oppressed majority. Fela Kuti's music focuses on his experiences of the problems as he lived them in Nigerian society – often deeply connected to issues fundamental to anti-colonial and Black Consciousness theory – and he expresses these critically and powerfully in an attempt to speak to the experiences of those around him, inviting them to participate in challenging the hegemonic discourses imposed on them by European imperialism. This directly mirrors the experiences of participating in a learning process that analyses issues in contemporary society, continuously linking theory to experience, and subversively inviting students to lead this process. This creative, critical expression resembles a revolutionary art form underpinned by a revolutionary theory. Just as music was the weapon for Fela Kuti, the curriculum too can be a weapon.

In making psychology relevant to a South African context, it makes sense to draw on the pan-African histories of blackness and Africanness on the continent (Kessi, Boonzaier and Gekeler 2021). The philosophy of pan-Africanism placed a strong emphasis on the need for an intellectual and cultural movement. One cannot underestimate the role of a pan-African decolonial aesthetic in building the alternative rationalities necessary for transforming people's understandings of themselves and for developing a psychology of resistance and liberation. Identity and belonging have deeply affective attributes and sensibilities that mainstream psychology fails to address.

The title and theme of this chapter suggest a particular engagement with the pan-Africanism of Amílcar Cabral (1966), whose contribution we believe to be especially significant to psychological research and practice. Unlike many of his contemporaries, Cabral rejected essentialist views of blackness and saw the search for an African identity as a political and cultural revolution, and engagement with the lived experiences of struggle that connect people to the past but also a postcolonial/post-imperial future or a re-Africanisation (Rabaka 2020). This is reflected in the development of the postcolonial psychology module described in this chapter to its reframing as political psychology. This move highlights not only the political dimension and psychological effects of the postcolonial experience but also how these are intrinsically tied to contemporary and continuously shifting global relations of knowledge, power and politics. Cabral understood the inevitability and importance of knowledge production and its effects on society and on people. For Cabral, a revolutionary theory was key to the type of transformative change needed to decolonise African society. Approaching psychology through a political lens is a revolutionary act for a discipline that has historically been complicit in colonial conquest. It is one with the potential to simultaneously critique the discipline and society – including how disciplines and social realities are interlinked – which is at the heart of a decolonial imperative.

REFERENCES

Biko, Steve. 1978. *I Write What I Like*. Johannesburg: Heinemann Publishers.

Boswell, Barbara, Zimitri Erasmus, Shanél Johannes, Shaheed Mahomed and Kopano Ratele. 2019. 'Racist Science: The Burden of Black Bodies and Minds'. *The Thinker: A Pan-African Quarterly for Thought Leaders* 81: 4–8. https://rgsm.fas.harvard.edu/publications/racist-science-burden-black-bodies-and-minds.

Cabral, Amílcar. 1966. 'The Weapon of Theory'. Address delivered to the first Tricontinental Conference of the Peoples of Asia, Africa and Latin America, Havana, Cuba, January 1966. https://www.marxists.org/subject/africa/cabral/1966/weapon-theory.htm.

Dogra, Nandita. 2012. *Representations of Global Poverty: Aid, Development and International NGOs*. London: I. B. Tauris.

Fanon, Frantz. 1986 [1952]. *Black Skin, White Masks*. London: Pluto Press.

Fela Anikulapo Kuti and the Afrika 70, 'Yellow Fever', 1976, A side on Yellow Fever, Afrodisia, 1976, Vinyl LP.

Fela Ransome Kuti and the Africa 70 with Ginger Baker, 'Black Man's Cry', 1971, track 2, A side on Live!, Regal Zonophone, 1971, Vinyl LP.

Fela Ransome Kuti and the Afrika 70, 'Gentleman', 1973, A side on Gentleman, EMI, 1973, Vinyl LP.

Fela Ransome Kuti and the Afrika 70, 'Colonial Mentality', 1977, B side on Sorrow Tears and Blood, Kalakuta Records, 1977, Vinyl LP.

Foster, Don. 1991. '"Race" and Racism in South African Psychology'. *South African Journal of Psychology* 21 (4): 203–210. https://doi.org/10.1177/008124639102100402.

Freire, Paulo. 1974. *Education for Critical Consciousness.* London: Continuum.

Henriques, Julian. 1984. 'Social Psychology and the Politics of Racism'. In *Changing the Subject: Psychology, Social Regulation and Subjectivity*, edited by Julian Henriques, Wendy Holloway, Cathy Urwin, Couze Venn and Valerie Walkerdine, 60–89. London: Methuen.

Henwood, Karen and Ann Phoenix. 1996. '"Race" in Psychology: Teaching the Subject'. *Ethnic and Racial Studies* 19 (4): 841–863. https://doi.org/10.1080/01419870.1996.9993938.

Hogg, Michael A. and Graham Vaughan. 2018. *Social Psychology.* 8th edition. New York, NY: Pearson.

Howitt, Dennis and Kwame Owusu-Bempah. 1994. *The Racism of Psychology: Time for Change.* New York: Harvester Wheatsheaf.

Kessi, Shose and Floretta Boonzaier. 2018. 'Centre/ing Decolonial Feminist Psychology in Africa'. *South African Journal of Psychology* 48 (3): 299–309. https://doi.org/10.1177/0081246318784507.

Kessi, Shose, Floretta Boonzaier and Babette Stephanie Gekeler. 2021. *Pan-Africanism and Psychology in Decolonial Times.* Cham: Palgrave Macmillan.

Kessi, Shose, Zoe Marks and Elelwani Ramugondo. 2020. 'Decolonizing African Studies'. *Critical African Studies* 12 (3): 271–282. https://doi.org/10.1080/21681392.2020.1813413.

Leach, Collin Wayne. 2002. 'The Social Psychology of Racism Reconsidered'. *Feminism & Psychology* 12 (4): 439–444. https://doi.org/10.1177/0959353502012004005.

Leibowitz, Brenda. 2017. 'Cognitive Justice and Higher Education'. *Journal of Education* 68: 93–112. http://www.scielo.org.za/scielo.php?script=sci_arttext&pid=S2520-98682017000100006.

Macleod, Catriona. 2004. 'South African Psychology and "Relevance": Continuing Challenges'. *South African Journal of Psychology* 34: 613–629. https://doi.org/10.1177/008124630403400407.

Maldonado-Torres, Nelson. 2007. 'On the Coloniality of Being'. *Cultural Studies* 21 (2–3):
240–270. https://doi.org/10.1080/09502380601162548.

Mignolo, Walter D. 2012. *Local Histories/Global Designs: Coloniality, Subaltern Knowledges,
and Border Thinking*. Princeton, NJ: Princeton University Press.

Mkhize, Nhlanhla. 2004. 'Psychology: An African Perspective'. In *Self, Psychology and
Community*, edited by Kopano Ratele, Norman Duncan, Derek Hook, Peace Kiguwa,
Nhlanhla Mkhize and Anthony Collins, 24–52. Cape Town: UCT Press.

Moscovici, Serge. 1984. 'The Phenomenon of Social Representations'. In *Social
Representations,* edited by Robert Farr and Serge Moscovici, 3–69. Cambridge:
Cambridge University Press.

Nwoye, Augustine. 2015. 'What is African Psychology the Psychology of?' *Theory &
Psychology* 25: 96–116. https://doi.org/10.1177/0959354314565116.

Quijano, Anibal. 2000. 'Coloniality of Power, Eurocentrism, and Latin America'. *Nepantla:
Views From the South* 1 (3): 533–580. muse.jhu.edu/article/23906.

Rabaka, Reiland. 2020. 'Amílcar Cabral, Cabralism, and Pan-Africanism'. In *Routledge
Handbook of Pan-Africanism*, edited by Reiland Rabaka, 302–316. London: Routledge.

Ramugondo, Elelwani. 2015. 'Occupational Consciousness'. *Journal of Occupational Science*
22 (4): 488–501. doi: 10.1080/14427591.2015.1042516.

Ratele, Kopano. 2017. 'Four (African) Psychologies'. *Theory & Psychology* 27 (3): 313–327.
https://doi.org/10.1177/0959354316684215.

Richards, Graham. 1997. *Race, Racism and Psychology: Towards a Reflexive History*. London:
Routledge.

Shefer, Tamara, Floretta Boonzaier and Peace Kiguwa. 2006. *The Gender of Psychology*.
Cape Town: UCT Press.

Taylor, Donald and Fathali Moghaddam. 1994. *Theories of Intergroup Relations: International
Social Psychological Perspectives*. 2nd edition. London: Sage Publications.

Thiong,o, Ngũgĩ wa. 1986. *Decolonising the Mind: The Politics of Language in African
Literature*. London: James Currey.

THE SHARDS HAVEN'T SETTLED: CONTESTING HIERARCHIES OF (TEACHING) HISTORY

KONI BENSON AND KERUSHA GOVENDER

The course that is at the heart of this chapter was called 'Subjects to Citizens: South Africa since 1900'.[1] Other than the title, taken from Mahmood Mamdani's historical analysis in *Citizen and Subject: Contemporary Africa and the Legacy of Late Colonialism* (1996) which unpacks how colonial systems of indirect rule continue in post-apartheid South Africa, the syllabus was a blank slate. The department offered the course to me, Koni Benson, in 2014 with the invitation to re-politicise the teaching of South African history at the University of Cape Town (UCT) where I was a postdoctoral fellow. I had come to this position after eight years of doing popular political education work with unions and social movements, and was familiar with Mamdani's (1998) critique of the history curriculum at UCT since 1994.[2] I began by speaking to students who had completed degrees in historical studies at UCT, to get a sense of what was and was not covered in their time at the university, and then proceeded to design a course around contemporary histories of some of the most contentious issues in South Africa today. The poster advertising the course read:

What from the past 116 years of history can give us insights into controversies South Africa faces today? South Africa today does not resemble most options of a post-apartheid society imagined during the anti-apartheid struggle. How do we explain this? What happened during the twentieth century in South Africa and how has this informed challenges and debates about the reproduction of power since 1994? The course looks at colonisation and decolonisation through exploring major themes in contemporary South African history, including: land, migration, race, gender, power, resource extraction, labour, urbanisation, resistance, reforms and repression, demobilisation, nationalism, music, identity, and education. It asks students to question the inherited maps and milestones of South African history 1900–2016 and the power dynamics involved in narrating history.

The tutors I was assigned in 2015, and those recruited in 2016, were, each in their own way and from various positionalities, instantly on board and open to the challenge of grappling as much with power dynamics in the present, as with those in the past.[3] Kerusha Govender was the only tutor who was part of both courses. She was assigned to tutor in 2015 while in her Honours year, and chose to be part of this experimental mode of teaching again after she had graduated in 2016.

My goal was to expose struggles in and over history, and share research on the unfolding socio-economic crises, the structures and actions of racism, sexism, xenophobia, landlessness, and forms of challenging power over time. Drawing on this research, the course posits links between narratives of history and material division of wealth and power thereby challenging the myths of the 'miraculous' 1994 period. I was mindful of two sets of urgent issues: the need to question the dangerous mainstreamed and internationally celebrated narrative of the African National Congress (ANC) leading the country to victory against apartheid, which supposedly ended in 1994; and the fact that until this time, courses in the Department of Historical Studies rarely ventured into the 1980s, and almost never dealt with events beyond 1994. My work on ongoing struggles against dispossession and for public services (such as housing, water and education) from the peak of apartheid and into the present was seen, by some, as 'not history'. In 2014, my questions about the politics underpinning the history that we wrote about and that we taught were often met with snickers and comments such as: this is an outdated question, one that 'we' have moved on from since the 1980s.

I was not alone in this dis/orientation and critique. There were many colleagues and students peppered across campus asking similar questions about the overt and covert policing of the politics of the past, in the present. For example, when asked about his experience as a student of history, Asher Gamedze, a tutor on the 2016 course, reflected:

> I studied undergrad history at UCT from 2009–2011. While I enjoyed the content and was a very diligent student, in retrospect I would say one of the most overwhelming critiques I have of the courses, was the sense that the past was finished, something complete to be studied. As a student, even when studying more radical traditions of historiography or radical historical processes, one was never given a sense that studying history was urgent and political. A clear example would be in the course on South African history in the twentieth century. While the course was very interesting and on the whole very good, we were never given the sense that the history was unfinished or that there was any kind of relationship between the political conditions of the present and what we were studying. Studying history seemed to be presented as an apolitical act outside of any social context. There was never any reason presented by lecturers as to why we should study history or what it's for other than an academic exercise (Gamedze 2020).

* * *

As one of the tutors of the course, I (Kerusha Govender) co-produced this piece with Koni Benson. During my time as a student, I rarely encountered lecturers who sought to teach or present material in a novel way. They were usually unable to connect the course materials to students' present-day lives and realities. For the most part, tutors seemed to follow the lecturer's script. Often there was little opportunity for tutors to do more than their marking and tutorials, and it was up to us as students to approach them for help, mostly for support in learning how to write academically. My experience of being an undergraduate student in UCT tutorials included fear of expressing an opinion and sharing alternative views; learning was revision focused and tutors frequently struggled to facilitate dialogue. They struggled to balance skills development and comprehension with the work of facilitating engagement with the material. As a student, if I did not understand, I felt compelled to keep quiet. In tutorials that included more discussion, it would be difficult to participate or keep up with the more articulate students who were confident enough to express strong opinions. However, there were some courses where tutorial questions helped us make relevant connections with our lives – where tutors asked difficult questions that really made you think. It was in those moments where students like myself tentatively attempted to share opinions that I walked away with memorable conversations.

* * *

When the course was being designed in 2014, there was still widespread unchecked denial of the deep and solid connections between 'pre-' and 'post-' 1994. It had been 20 years since the official end of apartheid and now many books were coming out on the history of South Africa since 1994. My (Koni Benson's) question was, what do historians have to offer to these analyses that are circulating and gaining traction? What can historical studies offer to these discussions and understandings of the present? In order to answer these questions, I proposed that we started with new books that focus on histories of South Africa since 1994 and debates on identity, positionality, and the naming and framing of history. We then followed Mamdani's (1996) argument for the need to look back and rethink processes of colonisation, segregation and apartheid, so as to better understand the unfinished tasks of decolonisation in a wider context. This was the method used in the course design to challenge the pre- and post-1994 divide – by studying social histories from the last 115 years to gain insight into contentious issues facing us now. And 'now' at UCT in 2015/2016 looked to many, as the student movement pointed out, much like 1975/1976 (see Rhodes Must Fall 2015; Barnes 2019).

A burning question at the heart of approaching this course was how to teach about power dynamics in the past, without ignoring and reproducing those power dynamics in the present. Studying power to challenge power requires political questions of positionality and pedagogy. Acknowledging, exposing and making space to confront the normalisation of colonial reproduction in the room we occupied was crucial. Everyone has a relationship to the very contentious, painful and unresolved histories we were going to be studying. I therefore began the course with a discussion on the power to name and frame, raising questions of authority and authorship and bringing an awareness of the perspectives from which history books are written, but also initiating a conversation about where these colonial practices land when we now look at neglected, contentious and unresolved histories together in this classroom today. Who is in the room?[4] Why is the lecture hall set up like this – with immovable chairs … and me, a person with white privilege, at a podium? What is the conventional role of education/schooling in society, and disciplining in higher education? What is the banking method (Freire 1970, 53–54), and how can we not only participate differently but account differently, and grapple with our relationships to the history we study, differently?

Guided by a pedagogical approach which draws attention to factors in both the foreground and background of what is being learnt (challenged or reproduced) in the classroom, I lobbied for a room with a flat surface and movable tables. I also sought a double-block time slot. My lectures and assignments, student interactions and, importantly and most often overlooked, engagements with the tutorial space and with the tutors were all driven by this grappling with hierarchies and histories that haunt the worlds in which we live and work.

* * *

Tutors at UCT, and at most universities in South Africa, are postgraduate students hired to work under lecturers by taking on smaller groups of students from large undergraduate classes. In the case of this course, they were mostly students who were doing their Honours (fourth) year, or the first year of their Master's degrees. They were responsible for running eight tutorials during the 14 weeks of lectures, which took place three times a week. In addition to an essay and an exam which the lecturer marks, students are required to do written assignments every other week based on set readings in preparation for the tutorial sessions, which the tutors run and then mark. Lecturers design the written assignments, provide memoranda for marking, and often set the activities for what should happen in the tutorial.

The first iteration of the course in 2015 included films, a field trip and guest lectures to expand the range of modes and tones of learning, and as a way of decentring the lecturer (Koni Benson) as the only figure of authority teaching history, to raise questions of authorship, authority, the production of history and the pedagogies of power. There were weekly check-in meetings with tutors to review the materials and prepare for the running and marking of each tutorial assignment, as well as to gain feedback and enable recalibration in response to where the course was landing for both tutors and students. In the second year, this approach to exposing and understanding course dynamics beyond individualised assignment marks was extended into an experiment involving students as teachers – both in terms of tutors being invited to co-create experimental material, and students working in tutorial groups to research and teach a chosen strand of liberation movement history.[5] The course outline acknowledged its inspiration:

> The course draws on bell hooks (1994), and others to begin to reimagine power and authority in the teaching, creating, and learning of this unresolved (South African) history through discussions, interactive timelines and activities, and student run sessions (Benson 2016).

This methodology was developed in response to important issues about the role of education and the complicit dynamics within educational spaces in reproducing power, raised in the 2015 Rhodes Must Fall (RMF) campus interventions by student activists, who were well represented in the 2015 class. Adding new content was not enough. Critique, without creation, was not enough (Benson, Gamedze and Koranteng 2018). But creating a different space of engagement requires collective effort. Ideas about how to teach and learn differently, and about the prospects of reconstituting how we work – in part – as a 'teaching team', were further developed through ongoing conversations with the interested 2016 tutors (who were also in varying ways involved in RMF). The team was recruited early in the year with a commitment to reviewing the previous syllabus, co-creating more of the 2016 course, and reflecting on the calibrations and recalibrations that played out from the beginning of the semester, through to protest intervention and military securitisation/occupation of campus for the last part of both 2015 and 2016, when our students were scheduled to write exams.

In the rest of this intentional collage-like contribution, we (Koni Benson and Kerusha Govender) share some of the tensions that the curriculum and class discussions sparked. We speak in a single voice at some points and in separate voices at others. We hope that this will convey our various readings of the intentions and intensities at play among students, and between students, tutors and lecturer. Reimagining power in the classroom in this course was done through working with students and collaborating in classroom and curriculum interventions. What we learned, where we learned it, how we learned it, was as much in the content of each piece of reading, in the assignments and in the lecture materials, as it was in pushing ourselves to challenge the spaces of learning, to experiment with vulnerability, with power and with possibility. Relationships as pedagogy enabled us to learn together in our attempts to respond to epistemological violence, and to challenge and expose repressive, authoritative structures and narratives, much of which will require much more than one classroom to subvert. Intention. In tension.

We aim to foreground difficult moments of an attempt to subvert the hierarchies of teaching between lecturers, tutors and students found in colonial education structures but usually relegated to the background/beyond the brief of the classroom space. In order to do so, we juxtapose the curriculum content we were engaging with, with the conversations and dynamics of the pedagogical strategies and challenges. The collage so produced is sculpted out of our archives – out of some of the many notes, correspondence, conversations, evaluations and file folders of articles from this course. Together, they illuminate the politics of decolonial pedagogical practices we were immersed in in 2015 and 2016. These are shards that, like broken glass – a ceiling or shield of power and denial cracked open on the UCT campus – are sharp, reflective, fragmented, unsettled and unsettling.

SUBVERSIONS. SUB-VERSIONS.
Part I: Unpacking the Inherited Maps and Milestones, Names and Frames of SA History 1900–2016. Brick by brick. Tensions in each subversion.
  Week 1 Introduction: Citizens, Subjects, and this History Classroom.

Koni Benson, notes to self, July 2015: And this classroom. Power – ability to control circumstance? Power over. Power with. Power within. How to subvert the multiple sub-versions of colonial dynamics all taking place in this room at the same time? This is not new, there is a local and global history to this challenge. Turn to Neville Alexander's keynote address 'Liberation Pedagogy in the South African Context' at a 1988 experiential learning in formal and non-formal education conference at the University of Natal, Durban (found in a box of rejected Alexander Collection papers at the library). On the question of authority in dialogical classrooms, whether the teacher is equal to the students, he quotes Ira Shor and Paulo Freire (1987, 92–93): 'The dialogical relationship does not have the power to create such an impossible equality. The educator continues to be different from the students … The difference between them, if the teacher is democratic, if his or her political dream is a liberating one, is that he or she cannot permit the necessary difference between the teacher and the student to become "antagonistic". If they become antagonistic, it is because I became authoritarian' (Shor and Freire, cited in Alexander [1990, 58–59]).

'The little-told story of RMF is that our radical point of departure comes by way of realising that existing "progressive" routes are entirely ineffective at changing anything fundamental.'
– Mohammed Jameel Abdulla, 'Letter to the Editor from a "Taliban" at UCT', *Daily Maverick*, 28 April 2016.

Kerusha Govender (2019) reflections on manifesting 2015 RMF calls in our teaching practice: RMF helped me grasp that learning could happen by directly speaking to the experiences students brought with them *into* the university. I took that approach to set the pace of the tutorial by acknowledging who we all were and what we may be grappling with in the university space, in the hope that we could all find a way to get meaningful value from our interactions – be it understanding the material better, sharing different perspectives or learning something new. I thought it was important to bring the tutorial to life by connecting it to the students' experiences and making it a space where the material is relevant to them, too – in the hope that they would be more inclined to engage and understand what they were reading and writing about.

WE ARE NOT FAR AWAY

Week 2 South African History Since 1994. Tutorial 1: Post-Apartheid History? We discussed the inherited milestones of South African history and the relationship between race and racism in pre- and post- 1994 as we read Thiven Reddy (2001) on the politics of naming in the constitution of coloured subjects in South Africa, Naomi Klein (2007) on democracy born in chains, and Mbongiseni Buthelezi and Sithandiwe Yeni (2016) on what is at stake in authorising history of traditional leadership and controversies today. Early in the year, in February 2016, RMF draws attention to the crisis of student housing, erecting 'Shackville' on campus – one of many creative disruptions that raised questions of homelessness at UCT and landlessness more broadly (see Gillespie and Naidoo 2019).

In an article addressing what she calls 'selective white rage' which works to over-shadow histories of racism, a phenomenon common in UCT campus debates on Shackville that took up a lot of space at the beginning of our course, Kelly-Jo Bluen (2016) writes: 'The focus on the paintings as the pinnacle of violence eliminates a consideration of the structural violence that precipitated the burnt paintings, the systemic racism, the exclusion, the police brutality, the everyday oppression of a society premised on white supremacy ... White violence is the extensive and pervasive bedrock of South African society. It is physical, it is economic, it is social, it is psychological, and we consistently refuse to take accountability for it.'

Kaleb Abrahams, student feedback on the Lwandle Migrant Labour Museum field trip, 21 August 2015: I like how this course is not just history.[6]

Tutor feedback, 19 October 2016: Education is usually packaged where you are learning in a way separated from the world. Academic culture discon-nects from society outside. History is emotional. But it's not usually allowed to be. In this course you could not *not* make some connection.[7]

WE ARE NOT A WE

Part II: The Land Question: Settler Colonialism in Rural and Urban South Africa 1900–2016.

Tutorial 3: Migrant Labour. The field trip to the Lwandle Migrant Labour Museum comes after two weeks of lectures on histories of land dispossession, the establishment of the migrant labour system, indirect rule and the creation of ban-tustans, land distribution since 1994, and extractive industries in historical context. The section ends with a lecture on current living and working conditions at the mines in Marikana today, on the anniversary of the Marikana Massacre of 2012, which took place in the same week as a 2015 RMF Marikana solidarity march, and the hoisting of a green blanket on the flagpole above Jammie Hall, renamed Marikana Hall, on the steps of which a thousand students gathered to listen to Joseph Mathunjwa (a speaker from the Association of Mineworkers and Construction Union) pointing out the links between Lonmin and UCT endowments.

Tutor feedback, 14 October 2015: It was so good that we went to Lwandle and did the migrant labour system in this week of the Marikana memorial. I thought I knew about Marikana but then the lectures on the system and dates and laws and turning points woven into real lives and what is going on now just made me get it.

A student, Sino Mzamane, says to the curator, Mani Kunene, at Lwandle Migrant Labour Museum:

> People still get up at 3 am to get to work. It is not over. It's a problem to teach it like it's past. The terminology changed only. RDP [Reconstruction and Development Programme] houses are inhumane. How can the museum present a happy story? What does it mean to have white people come and see the museum and go on being happy as usual?

Mani Kunene replies:

> What changed was that people have schools, have RDP homes in which families can live together. People are free to go to the library. The situation now is better than hostels … this is what people said they wanted. We get involved in the community, we write about living conditions. We use the museum to highlight that, to show people what it was like. What some white people may or may not do with it is not what we do it for. They can run with the stereotypes that white people around here have changed, but it's up to people to decide how to look at things. For example, Black people here faced evictions in 1986 and again in 2014. Are they different?

On the other side of the museum visit a debate between two students escalates:

Sam Kaplan:	My family was from a shtetl in Poland on the one side, and from working class poor England on the other, so I can relate to these living conditions. And I see it as a class issue. But with RMF and its discourse – it is only about race; they [the student movement] are misguided in not seeing class.
Kaleb Abrahams:	This whole museum is about the history of racism, and it is not over – we [Black South Africans] still have family living in these conditions today.
Sam Kaplan:	Well, I am saying that this is about class and anyone who was or is working class can relate to this. RMF makes everything about race yet most of their members are middle/upper class.

Koni Benson:	Is RMF missing class? When we think about racialised capitalism, maybe we need to remind ourselves who makes up the majority of the working class in South Africa? It is not coincidental. Just as women who made it still face sexism – rape, like racism, cuts across class. For so many years, the white left have said it's just about class. Decades of being told race doesn't matter?!
Sam Kaplan:	I am not saying race doesn't matter, you are misunderstanding me and I don't mean to offend you, but I see it as class.
Kaleb Abrahams:	Of course, in your position as a white male you won't see race, but we [Black South Africans] cannot ignore it.

The following week:

Kaleb Abrahams to Koni Benson:	I am not even in RMF, but I just get so angry that white people feel they can tell us it's not about race.
Sam Kaplan to Koni Benson:	I would like to do my essay on the history of liberalism.

CAN WE MAKE SPACE TO FIND AFFINITY?

Tutorial 4 Working Group Session: Preparing to Teach the Class. We discuss which movements of resistance in liberation struggle history groups we want to design classes on and begin thinking about the history and politics of teaching. We read bell hooks (1994) on engaged pedagogy and Henry Giroux (1988) on the dynamics of the hidden curriculum.

Keesha Jones, student, 2015: I like how you changed what a course is supposed to look like.

Koni Benson: It doesn't feel like there is enough space for feedback in class time, but the lectures are so heavy that it feels like violence on violence to ask for people to share their thoughts right after unpacking such difficult histories.

Kerusha Govender, tutor, 2015: Where have you been my whole undergrad? Other classes were on issues that were political but it was as if it was way out there and back then. Distant. And if you said something in class, you were the lone one standing up with feelings about it.

OUR SUCCESS IS DEPENDENT ON STRUCTURAL CHANGE

Week 6 Urbanisation and the Struggle for the City: The Urban Land Question. We discussed the polarised (and arguably purposefully misunderstood) debates about redistribution and decolonisation going on in the campus, putting these struggles in the context of histories of forced removals and the segregation of racialised group areas in the past, and ongoing struggles for housing today, with a guest lecturer from the Cape Town Housing Assembly. We read Yvonne Muthien (1994), Brij Maharaj (1995) and Charles Mather (1987) on histories of segregation; Asanda Benya (2015), Mamphela Ramphele (1993) and Zolani Ngwane (2003) on the gendered dynamics of migration; and we discussed what Fred Hendricks, Lungisile Ntsebeza and Kirk Helliker (2013) call undoing a century of dispossession.

Tutorial discussion prompt: 'Decolonisation is not a metaphor' (Tuck and Yang 2012). Discuss.

A Fallist, Mohammed Jameel Abdulla, responds to a professor's accusations that UCT is 'appeasing a Taliban' which is calling for a 'dumbing down' of the university in a 'fancy new-fangled thing based on a blurry vision of racial quotas and targets' (Hughes 2016). Abdulla's (2016) response: 'We ought to keep in mind that decolonising education cannot be relegated to the realm of "transformation" rhetoric and the empty numbers games of representation. It may perhaps start there but must extend much further and deeper in radically imaginative ways.'

[Koni Benson and Kerusha Govender ask themselves:] What does this mean in a classroom? In a course design? In the relationship between the reading list, the assignments, the discussions, the writing, the thinking, the conversation, the lecturer, the convenor, the tutors, the admin, the department, the university, the student, their friends, their families?

Koni Benson, email to tutors, 16 July 2016: It does not look like we are going to get the classroom for a double period on Thursdays (or any day). So that means that the tuts will be the conventional small group discussions instead of what I had wanted which was to be able to keep everyone together for a two-hour slot so that we could do more interactive activities.

Essay question 1: What was 'influx control' and how has it shifted over time in South Africa? When did it start, how did it change, and can we say that it has ended? Write an essay that critically considers various experiences and perspectives about the programme of 'influx control' in South African history since 1900 and explain why you think this matters today. Please note: The apartheid term 'influx control' is extremely offensive, and in engaging with the readings and in writing your essay, I encourage you to add your thoughts to the much-needed conversation on how we name and speak about this policy today.

WE HAVE A JOB TO DO

Part III: Movements of Resistance. Tutorial groups are assigned to run sessions on histories of Queer Movements; the Pan-Africanist Congress (PAC); the Non-European Unity Movement; and Labour Movement histories.

Leila Khan, tutor, email to students, 8 August 2016: Words and Concepts for Responding to Problematic Terminology and Violent Spaces in Assignments and Tutorials. How do we create safe spaces amidst vocabularies of Taking Up Space in actions and words: Native, Non-White, Tribe, Positionality, Violence, Patronizing, Privilege. Who is an ally?

Kerusha Govender (2019), notes to self on what tutors can, can't, and should be doing: At the end of the day a tutor is also an employee of the university with limited authority – we cannot even, for example, give extensions or permission to miss a tutorial for whatever reasons. A tutor is also often times a student, with their own educational investment, life experiences and political opinions. This has advantages and disadvantages in that it makes them often grasp the students' perspective or be part of student movements. However, a lack of maturity can also mean struggling to strike that balance between activism and fulfilling bureaucratic requirements and protocols. Papers need to be marked and the marks heavily impact the students' future, giving them their academic worth. Ultimately it is what matters to them. So I think whatever good intentions come from creative or different approaches will always be hindered if there is lack of academic skill or knowledge about navigating through academic culture. Many students do not know how to pursue a consistent and successful learning strategy that they truly benefit from. They leave without knowing how to write a powerful paper or get work done on time; they need to be critical and capable.

Hannah Walton (2020), tutor: I agree with Kerusha's comments on the abrupt and sometimes absurd, but pretty much always reductive, bureaucratic needs of the university – grades, deadlines, etc. But this perhaps also gave a useful structure and starting point, or raft to hold onto, in the unsteady terrain we were trying to both navigate and keep unstable.

EXPOSURE

Week 7 Histories of African Nationalism. We traced the shifts within and between the ANC and the PAC, questioned the national borders and watched Cuba, an African Odyssey *(El-Tahri 2007), a documentary about Cuba and the Frontline States. We read about the All Africa Convention of 1935, critiques of nationalism including Frantz Fanon's* 'The Pitfalls of National Consciousness' *(in* The Wretched of the Earth *1961), and Lissoni et al.'s (2012)* One Hundred Years of the ANC: Debating Liberation Histories Today.

Koni Benson, notes to self on day 1, 2015: While I see some white students shifting in their seats when I draw attention to whiteness and the demographics in this history and in this room, an outspoken Rhodes Must Fall student activist (Sino) came to me after the first lecture to challenge the way I referred to people in this history and room as 'white' instead of calling them 'settlers'. He wanted to take me up on the offer to make additions to the reading list and to design his own essay question. Where will the openness to being pushed lead to as the weeks unfold? I see students studying my responses.

'Your inclusion in the anti-racist movement, white ally, cannot and will not happen on your own terms. The sooner you understand that you are not here by choice but by invitation, the sooner you will be allowed space to speak.'
– MrPhamodi, August 2015, 'Face White Supremacy, Good White'.

Student feedback discussion, 13 October 2015: I am more conscious to racist thinking.

Student course evaluation, 30 October 2015: I am a South African student and I have not been involved in the movement but the lectures broadened my mind to what it was really about. That it is about more than Rhodes and decolonization, about Marikana and UCT.

THE WORK IT TAKES

Tutorial 7: Intersections of Gender and Power in South Africa. We discussed the difference between sex and gender, and between various feminisms and women's histories, gender histories and queer histories. We read Nombonisa Gasa (2007) on women's organisation in Bloemfontein in 1913 and Potchefstroom in 1929, and Thuli Gamedze (2015) on 'Azania_House Intersectionality as a Catalyst for Black Imagination' and discussed what an intersectional approach to analysing power in particular moments of South African (gender) history would entail.

Student feedback questionnaire (October 2016):

1. What have you learned/shifted?
2. What has made you angry? Satisfied?
3. What will you take away from this course?
4. What would you suggest/do differently?

Tammy Wilks, tutor feedback, 14 October 2015: It's making all the difference for students to feel they can engage and be spoken to, not lectured at. They can go back to the slides, but the class has space for peoples' opinions and a conversation because of your style. The students also see their tutors there and can say what do you think, etc. and that adds to transforming the space and making students feel part of it. I have never gone to lectures that I tutor for before and I can see that being on this team is changing things in the classroom.

Hannah Walton (2020) tutor reflection: Being responsible for the tutorials and for trying to make sure such a range of students felt able to participate and share, but most especially unlearn and learn, made me aware of how critical the emotional and intimate experience of history and how we learn histories is.

ALIENATION MADE VISIBLE

Week 8 Hearing the 1960s: Music and History. Asher Gamedze (2018) did a series of lectures on his MA research 'Jazz as liberation culture and the so-called "silent" 60s'. We read Julian Jonker (2009) on the historical relationship between jazz and Black Consciousness; Johnny Mbizo Dyani on South Afrikan jazz in exile; and the life history of Sathima Bea Benjamin. We considered the ways in which silence and audibility feature in a piece by Salim Washington and Winston Mankunku Ngozi, and how this relates to historical writing about jazz and (spiritual/social) life then and now.

Kerusha Govender and Koni Benson, emailing reflection notes about epistemological violence, 2016: UCT is a very privileged physical institution removed from the city. It does not like to be reminded of ways in which its institutional culture is part of a bygone era that it continues to create. It is present in the language we read, the language we must use to express ourselves in essays and exams. How do we expose and challenge the violence of ongoing modes of colonial education spaces?

Kerusha to Koni, email, 'Tutorial feedback', 14 August 2015:

> Dear Koni, Today's tutorial was beyond amazing. I am still in shock. In the first tutorial I had not addressed the issue of 'positionality' as I was nervous and uncertain. But after our meeting, I thought that I should give it a shot … As we went around the room I was stunned. People were really honest and open. They displayed such critical thinking about what they learn in such spaces in relation to themselves … I feel like this course is pretty groundbreaking for the history department.

DISCOMFORT

Week 9 Resistance, Repression and Reforms. We read Jabulani Sithole and Sifiso Ndlovu (2011) on the revival of the labour movement in the 1970s, Martin Murray (1994) on destabilisation and counter-revolutionary warfare of the 1980s, and Adam Ashforth (1990) on the history of the reform era. Students used these readings and case studies presented in class on the movements of the liberation struggle to write about the relationship between resistance, repression and reform. From this week forward, in 2016, there were police and private security on campus in attempts to suppress student organising that threatened to disrupt the upcoming exam period.

Student feedback, 13 October 2015: You can't just distance yourself in this classroom/classwork.

Student feedback, 13 October 2015: It is difficult to engage with RMF because I perceive my role as a white person to just listen. I was a bit scared in the tutorial because I am not used to actively debating with people of colour who hold the floor. I was lucky to be there and hear first-hand and be asked to speak. I was not uncomfortable but within myself it was really difficult.

Keesha Jones, conversation walking across campus, 21 August 2015: After the lecture on Marikana on Thursday I looked up and was like, whoah, where am I? It's traumatic. Your class is traumatic – compliment! It's like it put the whole Marikana week in perspective and we came out of that lecture understanding and knowing so much. Like now, after Lwandle, we have to go back to Rondebosch. It's traumatic!

Keesha Jones, Facebook post, 4 October 2019: Five years later in 2019, I am still thinking about our transformative learning experiences.

Koni Benson, email to a friend abroad, 30 October 2015:

Saying the class was intense and catching a hand grenade and managing to acknowledge and deconstruct and find place for it without it going off in what felt like by a hair fracture of possible hit and miss, daily, weekly, does not capture it. But what does? It is I who must do the work of finding a language and words for the past two, ten, months, to be able to answer, how is the class going? Since Oct 6 (shutdown), it has been good to get away from the computer, out of the spotlight of the classroom ... All my phrases feel inadequate to capture what's been going on, all that is or can be said or unsaid because even framing this week as navigating the intensification of protest and the university's militarised responses, falls short of telling you anything. It feels overwhelming to think of trying to consolidate the threads of conversations had in words and in moments of intensity along the way. And at the same time, it is necessary because no general answers feel genuine right now.

INTENSITIES
Part IV, From Subjects to Citizens? Decolonisation and the Search for New Histories.

Kerusha to Koni, email, 'Friday's Tut', 2 August 2015:

... As for the incidents at the tutorial on Friday, Keesha played a central role. It was a charged confrontational moment where Keesha almost shouted and spoke over students. It took away from the things she was saying, because then two girls started talking about how they were feeling attacked and it's not their fault, etc. Pam also lost her temper a little, because she felt that Keesha, as an African American, did not know the struggles of Black South Africans and could not just come and homogenise it all into a lump. She also called Keesha out on the way she was speaking to everyone. Nina then spoke up along with Barry, about understanding the value that Keesha's views and that they were here to learn, and do not proclaim to understand her pain. Barry said something valuable in that often one reads these things but can often distance oneself from the emotions of it … But the two girls Amy and Susan that got offended did not say anything afterwards and I was quite concerned about their reactions. It was very heated and emotional because Keesha was talking about her experiences or things she picked up in Cape Town about queer and women abuse. Strangely, after the tutorial ended, she was back to her usual calmer self. She said that she was a performance artist hence the drama.

Keesha to Kerusha, email, 'Absence from Tut 7 today', 9 October 2015:

Hello Kerusha, I do not feel safe enough to attend today's TUT. I think it is not a conducive learning environment to anyone if I continue to stay in discussion. I ask for your understanding in my decision, after last week's discussion I can no longer manage around the hostility. I have submitted online and will submit a hard copy at the History Department. Best, Keesha

Koni to Keesha, email, 'Tut 7 today', 9 October 2015:

Hello Keesha, Kerusha forwarded me your email about deciding to not go to today's tut. I hear where you are coming from and appreciate what you have said about needing to feel safe, and your concerns about your influence on the learning environment. I would like to think that we can come up with another solution that does not result in you missing tuts.

It is too late to meet in time to discuss this further before today's tutorial, but let's meet on Monday. For attendance and possibly a different space, you are welcome to go to another tutorial group today.

I can meet anytime between 9–5 on Monday so let me know what works. Thanks, Koni

Kerusha Govender to Koni Benson, WhatsApp, 10 August 2015:

Hi Koni, it's Kerusha. Keesha ended up coming to the tutorial. It was really amazing. We talked about whiteness and what it means. It was uncomfortable but fascinating. Will email you.

Koni Benson: Ok wow. That's great.

Kerusha Govender: Chumani came but listened and only spoke at the end. He said he was inspired by them and their level of engagement. It's been a real privilege to tutor for this course. It's making me learn and think about a lot as well.[8]

Koni Benson: Same for me. I'm super inspired by everyone's commitment to diving into the journey with me. The tuts, because of the tutors, have been really central to grappling with the hardest parts of what I've presented in class and via readings – without your willingness to read and probe and feel through the hard probing parts, the course could have remained alienating and distant and left students to struggle through the hardest parts of digesting the past alone!

Student feedback (13 October 2015): My favourite tutorial and best part of my course that will stay with me forever until I am 65 was last Friday. We discussed race and education and got to hear the thoughts and opinion of the founder of the RMF movement and that is huge.

EXPECTATIONS

Essay Question C, Non-Racialism: The dominant anti-apartheid response to disavow apartheid's racial categories was through the ideological concept of 'non-racialism' which is stated as a founding value in the current Constitution. There have been fierce debates about the ideas and political practices of non-racialism both before, during and after the official apartheid period of 1948–1994. What is/was non-racialism and why is its history important for grappling with the past and future of South Africa? Write an essay that critically considers different experiences and perspectives on non-racialism in South African history 1900–2016 and explain why you think this matters today.

Kerusha Govender, email reflection conversation with Koni Benson, 22 July 2019, to prepare to present 'Teaching and Learning of South African History in a Postcolonial Institution', for the Black Academic Caucus Curriculum Collective Workshop, 'Epistemic Violence, the Curriculum and Pedagogy': I think about students who are pressured to make it in life. They come from all spectrums of disadvantage but made it to the classroom and make it diligently but still stare apathetically/blankly when you try to connect them to what they're studying. Some people's degrees mean the world to their families and mean a better future – perhaps these students' primary needs are all they aspire to fulfil. At the same time, in the nature of academia, human experiences are often expected to be dealt with in an objective and serious and academic way.

Student feedback discussion, 13 October 2015: Student A (a white South African student): We haven't really looked into any solutions. We debate important stuff and they lead us to dark and negative conclusions and we haven't had any solutions.

Student B (a Black South African student): It's naïve to ask for solutions to systemic things, to migrant labour, to racism, to forced removals – the answer is, give back the land or the money, but we can't have a course that says that. So we come and have gained an understanding of why the country is in the state it is in.

EXHAUSTION

Week 11 Demobilisation and the Rise of New Social Movements. We explored the differences between democracy and decolonisation, and the history of the negoti-ated settlement of the 'transition' period. We read Neville Alexander (2002) on the historic compromises of the 1990s, and histories by Public Citizen, the Anti-Privatisation Forum and the Coalition Against Water Privatisation (2004) on a community's battle for water rights, and Toussaint Losier (2009) on the struggle for land reform and housing, in conjunction with histories of defining and defying sites of struggle for housing in Crossroads, South Africa, from the 1970s–present (Benson 2015). We had a guest lecture by Faeza Meyer from the Cape Town Housing Assembly. After the lecture, students wrote on some of the controversies between truth and reconciliation raised by Alexander, and gave examples from the articles and lectures on water and housing struggles.

Kerusha Govender, email to Koni Benson, 22 July 2019: History has no answers. This can be exciting, when you engage in themes, draw connec-tions to reality and garner the diverse identities and experiences of students to grapple and discuss and learn, but to what end I sometimes wonder? Does it possibly rattle the psyches of students?

Student feedback, 13 October 2015: It's overwhelming this course.

Ernie Koela, tutor, 27 August 2015: In my tut we divided into two groups and debated what would you do if you had power in 1994? One example used was, would you give back a cellphone that you took, but then upgraded and added airtime, etc.? It lasted two hours but eventually I had to go.

Asher Gamedze, tutor, 19 August 2016: The tut today ... was a bit like pulling teeth. People didn't prepare/read much I don't think.

Student feedback discussion, 13 October 2015: I was raised in small Afrikaaner town. Racist views were drilled into me. Yet we thought we were non-racist and rejected racist ideas. But when I did this course I realised a lot of subconscious biases which the course forced me to confront. Not just how I think of people of colour but an economic understanding of the current situation. Even the questions and answers on the bus to Lwandle about the level of poverty and level of white people's complicity – it helped me get a broader more realistic view of things.

IN TENSION

Week 12 Race, Education, and Decolonisation Today. Koni lectured on the history of the construction of Bantu and White education in South African history, and shared a pre-recorded conversation with Leigh-Ann Naidoo on a history of the South African Students' Organisation (SASO) and the pedagogies used in their Formation Schools. We had guest lectures on the history of RMF by students involved (Brian Kamanzi in 2015, and Thato Pule in 2016). Students read histories of student movements by Shereen Essof (2011), Noor Nieftagodien (2014), Rhodes Must Fall (2015) and Johannesburg Workshop in Theory and Criticism (JWTC) (2015); Robin Kelley (2016) on Black Consciousness, liberalism and racist education; Isaac B. Tabata (1959) on the 1950s; Gail Gerhart (1978) and Leigh-Ann Naidoo (2015) on the 1960s/1970s; and Mahmood Mamdani (1998) and Teresa Barnes (2019) on the 1980s. They about how these readings added to their experiences and thinking on the current debates and issues raised in student protests at UCT.

PrivateSecurityMustFall – UCT petition to the vice-chancellor, registrar and chair of council, organised by students, 18 September 2016:

A new set of private security units have been established on the campus in response to the protest action taking place on site. Some of these members move on the campus in unmarked uniforms and refuse to identify themselves upon engagement. Others garbed in military fatigues carry badges on their lapels named 'Veta Schola' which has been noted as one of the companies used by the university in the past and has been implicated in a number of incidents of assault, intimidation and sexual violence both within the country and beyond ... In reflection of the last engagement on this issue the value of the previous contract, purportedly R2 million per month, was only declared after emails of concern were sent through which also have been neatly erased from the official narrative ... There has been a notable failure on the part of the executive to engage with debates and dialogues on the security issue post-Shackville and the ignoring of critical voices on this issue has arguably facilitated the reckless expenditure manifested in the private security contracts to date (cited in Cairncross 2016; Kamanzi 2016).

Asher Gamedze, email to Koni Benson, reflecting on the context in which we were teaching, 23 August 2020: The liberal political orientation of the department came out very clearly in the 2015/2016 moment when the department was unable to take a stand against the securitisation of campus among other issues.

Kerusha Govender, email correspondence with Koni Benson, 22 July 2019: The past can sometimes be hurtful and feel very negative. To offer empowerment, healing and a solid set of skills in this discipline is a challenge. But then again, when true and deep learning takes place it creates a profound life experience.

'The university is not an engine of social transformation. Activism is.'
– Robin D. G. Kelley, 'Black Study, Black Struggle', *Boston Review*, 1 March 2016.

INCONCLUSIVE CONCLUSIONS

All these snapshots share a selection of an undigested archive of moments from 2015 and 2016. These words expose the explosions and the grunt work, possible foibles and fodder, to re-member the intentions and the tensions that remain. Like the course, this piece account is attempting critical pedagogical shifts by decentring authority and creating different spaces of engagement. Why do we call it an undigested archive? In some ways it is, to us, a valuable resource that can be used to better understand the 2015/2016 (in)tensions over history and occupation of educational experimentations. Such a resource can help us reimagine past and future course work. It is also a record of the ways in which history was being made in 2015 and 2016 while acknowledging that the experiences and confrontations, both personal and interpersonal, are difficult to reflect, conclude and hold on to with clarity and singular meaning. Processing this record demands a much deeper collective process with the rest of the tutor team as well as with students. It is but a sample of the possibilities, complexities and forms of exhaustion that surround teaching and learning in university spaces in the midst of protest, politics and struggles. These struggles bind us within society as a whole, to which each of us belongs and from which each of us comes, from pockets of its spaces with our own identities, biases and insights. The course had all these layers confront one another, and so at times it was uncomfortable, at times messy, at times uncertain. We tried to challenge each other through exposure to difficult questions to be collectively figured out, in the face of the fact that academic structures and protocols can suck the humanity and relevance out of history and the way in which we deal with the past. On this, tutor Hannah Walton commented in an email exchange with Koni Benson in 2020 (19 October 2020):

I feel proud of the way we went about things in 2015 – flawed, necessarily, I'm sure, but I still think we were driven by this sense of responsibility to making it possible for the students – as well as us, the material, the histories, the curriculum, us all – to be able to grow past the confines of the epistemic and experiential horizons we had in varying ways been raised not to look past. I remember this quite direct, strong feeling of being accountable to something that was also unfolding in ways we could only understand by being humble to the process, to peoples' experiences, to the newness of the form and purpose of the course … [which insisted upon] the acknowledgement and structural implementation of the fact that history is visceral and alive … history is emotional, and how critical it is that its emotional reality is part of the teaching and learning of it.

To re-politicise (history) education requires creating transformative, justice-seeking spaces; and spaces of justice are contextual – that is, power is constantly reconfiguring itself. One of the most important contributions historical studies can make to understanding, challenging and shaping the direction of social dynamics and social change is in the tools of understanding context: how have spaces been built, and how can they be deconstructed and reconstructed? Newer ideas such as gender, or now decolonisation, are constantly appropriated and depoliticised into overused catchphrases without any new barometer of assessment, without any political risk, without any real change.

Acknowledging and putting front and centre the politics of pedagogy and power dynamics in the classroom – and between the classroom and the histories we were studying – was what we tried to do in this course. This enabled moments of transformative grappling with the legacies of the historical dynamics (both far and wide) which we were interested in challenging. The teaching team and tutorial space were key to how we modelled and structured pedagogical (as political) intervention. Unsettling the hierarchies that maintain this dynamic resulted in subversion and sub-versions of these moments; questioning of our relationships to the past and the time we are in; exposing the conflicting 'we' and the labour (exploitation) of history/education authorship/authority then and now; opening a space of collective study; welcoming discomfort; experimenting with exposure; drawing lines; facing expectations; and acknowledging alienation and exhaustion.

NOTES

1   We wish to thank the tutors who made up our teaching teams for all that went into the course, and for feedback on previous drafts of this paper. Thanks, too, to Professor Lance van Sittert, head of the Department of Historical Studies at the time, for the space and consistent support for our deliberations and decisions. Many thanks to the organisers of the 2016 workshop on epistemological violence which pushed us to articulate some of the learning and teaching dynamics in this course, and to the editors who created space, again in a moment of campus protest, in 2019, which convinced us to relook at this archive for the sake of collective grappling with and actualising contesting epistemological violence at UCT at this time.

2   The course title had been chosen by Professor Sean Field in Historical Studies at UCT.

3   The tutor team in 2015 included: Tammy Wilks, Kerusha Govender, Hannah Walton, Ernie Koela, Lucy Argent. The tutor team in 2016 included: Asher Gamedze, La'eeqa Mosam, Kerusha Govender, Leila Khan. These were very different years on campus and in this course, but the chapter selects moments most relevant to the theme of this book.

4   In this course, there were about 30 per cent study abroad students (most of whom were white Americans), 30 per cent white South Africans and 30 per cent Black South

Africans. This meant that there were 70 per cent white people in this study space, in a country that has 11 per cent or a city that has 16 per cent white people. Planting these stats as a question for how to bring ourselves into this space, from day one, was an important starting point. Importantly, I did not ask for answers in class, as often this only causes more harm than good. Rather, students were asked to find someone (fellow students, friends, Koni Benson or tutors, as options) or to set up a private journalling practice, to create space to digest what had been unhinged by the course material and course discussions.

5   For example, tutors joined the lecturer in designing and running a history bingo game aimed at interaction and spreading out expertise, as a way of introducing the themes for each section of the course. This required framing the theme being explored, and researching and writing up short questions and summative cue cards, which included: wars of dispossession; 1894 Glen Grey Act/1913 Land Act; mining low grade ore; South African War 1899–1902; Herero and Nama genocide 1904–1908; the settler pact; Bambatha Rebellion, 1906; Clements Kadalie and the Industrial Commercial Union (ICU); 1923 Native (Urban Areas) Act; Hertzog's 'Native Bills' 1926–1936; Greyshirts; Coloured Labour Preference Policy; Sathima Bea Benjamin; Fifth Pan-African Congress, 1945; Cillié Commission into 1976 Soweto uprisings; and grand apartheid.

6   All students' names have been replaced with pseudonyms throughout this chapter. This set of conversations took place at Lwandle Migrant Labour Museum, 21 August 2015.

7   All mention of student or tutor feedback comes from detailed notes that Koni Benson took in regular check-in sessions in class and meetings, as well as from student evaluations submitted anonymously at the end of each course.

8   Chumani Maxwele was the student leader whose direct action on 9 March 2015 of throwing faeces brought from Khayelitsha on the statue of Cecil Rhodes at UCT, with a sign that read 'Exhibit White @ Arrogance UCT', was a significant moment in the lead up to the RMF occupation of the university's administrative building, renamed Azania House, which had begun on 20 March 2015.

REFERENCES

Abdulla, Mohammed Jameel. 2016 'Letter to the Editor from a "Taliban" at UCT'. *Daily Maverick*, 28 April 2016. https://www.dailymaverick.co.za/article/2016-04-28-letter-to-the-editor-from-a-taliban-at-uct/.

Alexander, Neville. 1990. 'Liberation Pedagogy in the South African Context'. In *Education and the Struggle for National Liberation in South Africa: Essays and Speeches by Neville Alexander 1985–1989*, edited by Neville Alexander, 52–70. Johannesburg: Skotaville Publishers.

Alexander, Neville. 2002. *An Ordinary Country: Issues in the Transition from Apartheid to Democracy in South Africa*. Pietermaritzburg: University of Natal Press.

Ashforth, Adam. 1990. *The Politics of Official Discourse in Twentieth-Century South Africa*. Oxford: Clarendon Press.

Barnes, Teresa. 2019. *Uprooting University Apartheid in South Africa: From Liberalism to Decolonization*. London: Routledge.

Benson, Koni. 2015. 'A "Political War of Words and Bullets": Defining and Defying Sites of Struggle for Housing in Crossroads, South Africa'. *Journal of Southern African Studies* 41 (2): 367–387.

Benson, Koni. 2016. 'HST2043S Subjects to Citizens? South Africa Since 1900.' University of Cape Town, undergraduate course syllabus.

Benson, Koni. 'Personal Notes', 21 July 2015.

Benson, Koni. 'Tut 7 Today'. Email, 9 October 2015.

Benson, Koni. 'How Are You Really?' Email, 31 October 2015.

Benson, Koni. 'Email to Tutors'. Email, 26 July 2016.

Benson, Koni, Asher Gamedze and Akosua Koranteng. 2018. 'African History in Context: Toward a Praxis of Radical Education'. In *History's School: Past Struggles and Present Realities*, edited by Aziz Choudry and Salim Vally, 104–117. London: Routledge.

Benya, Asanda. 2015. 'The Invisible Hands: Women in Marikana', *Review of African Political Economy*, 42 (146).

Bluen, Kelly-Jo. 2016. 'Selective White Rage Ignores SA's Racist Truth'. *Business Day*, 25 February 2016. https://www.businesslive.co.za/bd/opinion/columnists/2016-02-25-selective-white-rage-ignores-sas-racist-truth/.

Buthelezi, Mbongiseni and Sithandiwe Yeni. 2016. 'Rural South Africa is on a Precipice'. *GroundUp*, 21 April 2016.

Cairncross, Lydia. 2016. 'UCT Academics Ask Max Price Not to Use Private Security'. *GroundUp*, 2 October 2016. https://www.groundup.org.za/article/uct-academics-ask-vice-chancellor-not-use-private-security/.

El-Tahri, Jihan, director. 2007. *Cuba, An African Odyssey*. Parts I and II. ARTE France 4. YouTube, 190 min (Part 1: 97:00; Part 2: 93:00).

Essof, Shereen. 2011. 'University of Cape Town Workers Support Committee – Committed to Workers' Rights to Decent and Dignified Conditions'. In *My Dream Is to Be Bold: Our Work to End Patriarchy*, edited by Feminist Alternatives, 44–56. London and East Lansing: Pambazuka Press and Michigan State University Press.

Fanon, Frantz. 1961. 'The Pitfalls of National Consciousness'. In *The Wretched of the Earth*, 148–205. New York: Grove Press.

Freire, Paulo. 1970. *Pedagogy of the Oppressed*. New York: Continuum.

Gamedze, Asher. 'Undergrad History at UCT'. Email, 23 August 2020.

Gamedze, Thuli. 2015. 'Azania_House Intersectionality as a Catalyst for Black Imagination'. *The Johannesburg Salon* 9: 122–123. https://studentsnotcustomers.files.wordpress. com/2014/11/vfinal_vol9_book.pdf.

Gasa, Nombonisa, ed. 2007. 'Let Them Build More Gaols'. In *Women in South African History: Basus'iimbokodo, Bawel'imilambo/They Remove Boulders and Cross Rivers*, edited by Nombonisa Gasa, 129–151. Cape Town: HSRC Press.

Gamedze, Simiso Asher. 2018. 'It's in the Out Sides: An Investigation into the Cosmological Contexts of South African Jazz'. MA thesis, University of Cape Town.

Gerhart, Gail M. 1978. *Black Power in South Africa: The Evolution of an Ideology*. Berkeley, CA: University of California Press.

Gillespie, Kelly and Leigh-Ann Naidoo. 2019. 'Between the Cold War and the Fire: The Student Movement, Anti-Assimilation, and the Question of the Future in South Africa'. *South Atlantic Quarterly* 118 (1): 231–233. https://doi.org/10.1215/00382876-7281744.

Giroux, Henry. 1988. *Teachers as Intellectuals: Toward a Critical Pedagogy of Learning*. Granby, MA: Bergin and Garvey Publishers.

Govender, Kerusha. 'Friday's Tut'. Email, 2 August 2015.

Govender, Kerusha. 'WhatsApp to Koni Benson'. WhatsApp, 10 August 2015.

Govender, Kerusha. 'Tutorial Feedback'. Email, 14 August 2015.

Govender, Kerusha. 'My Notes on Tutoring'. Email, 22 July 2019.

Hendricks, Fred, Lungisile Ntsebeza and Kirk Helliker, eds. 2013. *The Promise of Land: Undoing a Century of Dispossession*. Johannesburg: Jacana.

hooks, bell. 1994. *Teaching to Transgress: Education as the Practice of Freedom*. New York: Routledge.

Hughes, Kenneth. 2016. 'Letter to the Editor: Appeasing the UCT Taliban'. *Daily Maverick*, 22 April 2016. https://www.dailymaverick.co.za/article/2016-04-22-letter-to-the-editor-appeasing-the-uct-taliban/.

JWTC (Johannesburg Workshop in Theory and Criticism). 2015. *Salon – Rhodes Must Fall Guest Edition* 9, July 2015. http://jwtc.org.za/the_salon/volume_9.htm.

Jonker, Julian. 2009. 'A Silent Way: Routes of South African Jazz, 1946-1978'. Vlaeberg: Chimurenga Magazine.

Jones, Keesha. 'Absence from Tut 7 Today'. Email, 9 October 2015.

Kamanzi, Brian. 2016. '#PrivateSecurityMustFall'. *Daily Maverick*, 26 September 2016. https://www.dailymaverick.co.za/opinionista/2016-09-26-privatesecuritymustfall/.

Kelley, Robin D. G. 2016. 'Black Study, Black Struggle'. *Boston Review*, 1 March 2016. https://www.bostonreview.net/forum/robin-kelley-black-struggle-campus-protest/.

Khan, Leila. 'Email to Students as Follow Up to Tutorial'. Email, 8 August 2016.

Klein, Naomi. 2007. *The Shock Doctrine: The Rise of Disaster Capitalism.* Canada: Alfred A. Knopf.

Koela, Ernie. 'Tutorial Feedback'. Email, 27 August 2015.

Lissoni, Arianna, Jon Soske, Natasha Erlank, Noor Nieftagodien and Omar Badsha, eds. 2012. *One Hundred Years of the ANC: Debating Liberation Histories Today.* Johannesburg: Wits University Press. https://doi.org/10.18772/22012115737.

Losier, Toussaint. 2009. 'Sekwanele! [Enough is Enough!]: Social Movement Struggles for Land and Housing in Post-Apartheid South Africa'. Left Turn Jan/Feb: 56–61. https://abahlali.org/node/4719/.

Maharaj, Brij. 1995. 'The Local State and Residential Segregation: Durban and the Prelude to the Group Areas Act'. *South African Geographical Journal* 77 (1): 33–41. https://doi.org/10.1080/03736245.1995.9713586.

Mamdani, Mahmood. 1998. 'Is African Studies to Be Turned into a New Home for Bantu Education at UCT?' *Social Dynamics: A Journal of African Studies* 24 (2): 63–78. https://doi.org/10.1080/02533959808458649.

Mamdani, Mahmood. 1996. *Citizen and Subject: Contemporary Africa and the Legacy of Late Colonialism.* London: James Currey.

Mather, Charles. 1987. 'Residential Segregation and Johannesburg's "Locations in the Sky"'. *South African Geographical Journal* 69 (2): 119–128. http://doi.org:10.1080/03736245.1987.10559746.

Murray, Martin. 1994. *Revolution Deferred: The Painful Birth of Post-Apartheid South Africa.* London: Verso.

Muthien, Yvonne. 1994. *Segregation in the Western Cape: State and Resistance in South Africa, 1939–1965.* Aldershot: Avebury.

Naidoo, Leigh-Ann. 2015. 'The Role of Radical Pedagogy in the South African Students Organisation and the Black Consciousness Movement in South Africa, 1968-1973'. *Education as Change* 19 (2): 112-132. doi: 10.1080/16823206.2015.1085614.

Ngwane, Zolani. 2003. '"Christmas Time" and the Struggles for the Household in the Countryside: Rethinking the Cultural Geography of Migrant Labour in South Africa'. *Journal of Southern African Studies* 29 (3) September: 681-699. https://doi.org/10.1080/0305707032000094974.

Nieftagodien, Noor. 2014. *The Soweto Uprising.* Johannesburg: Jacana.

Phamodi, Sekoetlane. 2015. 'Face White Supremacy, Good White'. Blog post, June 2015. http:/mrphamodi.co.za/2015/06/face-white-supremacy-good-white/.

Public Citizen, the Anti-Privatisation Forum and the Coalition Against Water Privatisation. 2004. '"Nothing for Mahala": The Forced Installation of Prepaid Water Meters in Stretford, Extension 4, Orange Farm, Johannesburg, South Africa'. Centre for Civil Society Research Report No. 16. Johannesburg, South Africa.

Ramphele, Mamphela. 1993. *A Bed Called Home: Life in the Migrant Labour Hostels of Cape Town.* Cape Town: David Philip.

Reddy, Thiven. 2001. 'The Politics of Naming: The Constitution of Coloured Subjects in South Africa'. In *Coloured by History, Shaped by Place: New Perspectives on Coloured Identities in Cape Town,* edited by Zimitri Erasmus, 64–79. Colorado Springs, CO: International Academic Publishers.

Rhodes Must Fall. 2015. 'UCT Rhodes Must Fall Mission Statement'. *The Johannesburg Salon* 9: 6–8. https://studentsnotcustomers.files.wordpress.com/2014/11/vfinal_vol9_book.pdf.

Shor, Ira and Paulo Freire. 1987. *A Pedagogy for Liberation: Dialogues on Transforming Education.* Granby, MA: Bergin and Garvey Publishers.

Sithole, Jabulani and Sifiso Ndlovu. 2011. 'The Revival of the Labour Movement, 1970–1980'. In *The Road to Democracy in South Africa* (Volume 2), edited by South African Democracy Education Trust (SADET), 187–241. Pretoria: Unisa Press.

Tabata, Isaac Bangani. 1959. *Education for Barbarism: Bantu (Apartheid) Education in South Africa.* London: Unity Movement of South Africa and Prometheus Publishing.

Tuck, Eve and K. Wayne Yang. 2012. 'Decolonization Is Not a Metaphor'. *Decolonization: Indigeneity, Education & Society* 1 (1): 1–40. https://doi.org/10.25058/20112742.n38.04.

UCT Students. 2016. '"PrivateSecurityMustFall – UCT": Petition to Vice-Chancellor, Registrar and Chair of Council', 18 September 2016. https://docs.google.com/forms/d/e/1FAIpQL ScHXjpAKPltTStUeQ3jYommzkMS8cvb9-oMPW_BKLOSRWQD-Q/viewform.

Walton, Hannah. 'Greetings and Draft Paper on From Subject to Citizen? SA Since 1900'. Email, 19 October 2020.

HEAVY-HANDED POLICING: TEACHING LAW AND PRACTICE TO LLB STUDENTS IN SOUTH AFRICA

JAMEELAH OMAR

DEVELOPING A CRITICAL CURRICULUM FOR CRIMINAL PROCEDURE

Criminal procedure syllabi in law faculties across South African universities are usually focused on the line-by-line study of the Criminal Procedure Act (51 of 1977) (hereafter referred to as 'CPA') and the court rules. At the University of Cape Town (UCT), a more theoretical approach has been taken, focusing less on the individual provisions and more on criminal law's intersections with constitutional law, human rights law or administrative law. Finding the correct balance between theory and a working knowledge of the primary legislation is a difficult task. Future employers, such as the prosecuting authority, Legal Aid or private criminal defence firms, may prefer graduates who enter the profession as already trained criminal lawyers who can 'hit the ground running'. On the other hand, a broader understanding of the context within which the law operates serves to enhance a student's understanding of the rules themselves, but more importantly, to be able to critique them when they do not work.

This tension has been part of my inspiration to work towards a comfortable balance between formal law and the ever-changing social context. In truth, teaching criminal procedure in South Africa requires a blend of law and practice. The kind of practical wisdom needed to bring the subject alive must include both legal practice, such as the ins and outs of court practice, and the context of criminal process in South Africa. As an example, I include in the curriculum topics that demonstrate how social control is embedded in criminal procedure – reflecting on criminal procedure under apartheid offers a useful lens to demonstrate how criminal procedures can be used to control people's ordinary lives, even aspects of their lives that fall outside of the criminal realm. I highlight for my students how the bail procedures in the CPA offer uniform guidelines for the awarding of bail, and yet the implementation of these guidelines often disadvantages economically marginalised groups (Omar 2016).

Since a large part of criminal procedure and the course involves the police at the pre-trial and investigation stages, understanding police powers and the limits thereof is essential. The problem for criminal law lecturers is that the theory of police and policing is situated in the criminology field (which forms a part of the broader sociology discipline). While criminal procedure textbooks may draw on the work of criminologists, police powers in criminal procedure texts are largely restricted to the powers in the Act, and how the rights afforded to arrested, suspected and accused persons in the Constitution, 1996 (section 35) limit these powers. In other words, criminal procedure is confined to the legal and procedural aspects.

I have therefore given a lot of thought to how better to include this theory in a context of limited class time and a large portion of the CPA to cover. Students studying criminal procedure – like all students – are overly focused on what and how they will be assessed. Criminological theory on the reading list is often perceived by them as nothing more than 'background' reading, and therefore not important. Not being a criminologist myself, I can understand the difficulty for law students in knowing how to engage with social science theory. I have found that a focus on heavy-handed policing is a useful topic to highlight the disjuncture between written law and police behaviour in the implementation of policing activities.

My syllabus includes two specific scenarios in which the problem of police heavy-handedness is visible. The first is the use of racial profiling as a policing strategy. This is particularly problematic and nuanced in the South African context where police institutional culture has not overthrown its racial origins but where the majority of police officers are now Black. On the flip side of that, the target of police profiling strategies is also Black men, demonstrating that racial profiling has become woven into the fabric of the South African Police Service (SAPS), and is not simply 'white on Black' racism. This undermines the protective obligation on the police. It also corrupts any notion of effectively upholding the law, when other constitutional rights, namely the rights to equality (section 9 of the Constitution, 1996) and dignity (section 10 of the Constitution, 1996), will be infringed.

The second scenario focuses on the context of protest. I identify lack of training, inconsistent police practice and failure to transform the institution as key causes for the heavy-handed policing visible in many communities. In protest situations, racial profiling is also employed by the police in determining whether a protest is a threat to public order. This poses a risk of infringing the constitutional right to protest (section 17 of the Constitution, 1996), as well as equality before the law and the right to dignity. The term 'protest' used in this chapter is meant as a generic descriptor for group challenges to policy, law or action (state or private). The 'police' or the 'SAPS' may be used interchangeably at times.

During the Fees Must Fall (FMF) student protests, criminal procedure became relevant for many students who experienced or witnessed arrests of their peers, or being tear-gassed, and other public order policing strategies outside Parliament as in 2015. UCT obtained several interdicts against its students, testing the limits of protest and the use of the law to restrict it. This has opened the door for students to understand criminal procedure in a more dynamic way – an opportunity that I have tried to take advantage of, for the purposes of pushing legal education, to adopt a more situated mode.

This chapter is both a reflection of the law on aspects of police powers, and an exploration of what a syllabus might include if policing theory were made a more central part of the reading and discussions of the law. In my opinion, without embedding the law on police powers in this theoretical context, a law student's understanding of the interdisciplinary subject of the police is incomplete. The police, and criminal procedure itself, were tools of injustice used by the apartheid state to oppress and victimise all people that were not classified as 'white' or of European descent (Population Registration Act, 30 of 1950). Parts of the CPA remain identical to that first promulgated under apartheid in 1955. To teach a criminal procedure curriculum as though it is neutral, misses a pedagogical opportunity to develop critical thinking skills in students. Further, there is a moral imperative to attempt to at least unpick the colonial influence on our laws and practices, so that the next generation of lawyers enter the legal profession with an accurate account of the law that they will apply in their work. Through knowledge production and distribution in research and teaching in criminal procedure, I hope to contribute to transformative legal education that will open doors to further epistemic justice in the academy and the legal profession.

GENERAL LEGAL FRAMEWORK FOR POLICING IN SOUTH AFRICA

Being a core course of the LLB, the law on criminal procedure as it stands must be articulated to students to form the foundation of their legal training, from which their knowledge can be built on and scaffolded. I therefore first present the core legal principles that govern police powers linked to racial profiling as a policing strategy and the policing of protests.

The SAPS is the national police service with the constitutional mandate to perform policing functions in South Africa. The South African Police Service Act (68 of 1995) ('SAPS Act') is the primary piece of legislation that governs the police specifically. The SAPS Act creates the South African Police Service. A single police service, namely the SAPS, was created to unify the previous provincial police forces and the police forces operating in the independent 'homelands' (Butler, Rotberg and Adams 1978). It was also a political move to change the leadership of the force. Community Police Forums are also conceived of in the SAPS Act (sections 18–23), allowing for area-specific forums that work alongside community and other actors, including the Department of Social Development. The SAPS Act works in conjunction with the CPA as it deals with obtaining fingerprints and other identifying forensic evidence (sections 36B(1), 36C(1) and 37 of the CPA), while the SAPS Act deals with its storage (section 15A of the SAPS Act).

The process of transformation of a police 'force' to a police 'service' is yet to be fulfilled. The Constitution, 1996, in section 205(3) requires the police service to 'prevent, combat and investigate crime, to maintain public order, to protect and secure the inhabitants of the Republic, and to uphold and enforce the law'. These duties compete or even arguably conflict, pulling the police service in opposite directions – a protective service on the one hand, and a crime control emphasis (heavy-handed policing) on the other. Balancing these competing obligations is a difficult task, and one that without the proper training, resources and relationship building with communities, will continue to fail.

This constitutional provision places immense responsibility on the police, with a number of duties attributed to it. These duties include preventing crime and investigating crimes when they occur. It also includes maintaining public order and enforcing the law. There is a protective duty over all people (and property) in South Africa. This list of duties is a tall order. It is important that law students understand that these duties compete with one another, and can result in a police service that is confused as to its priorities. Students must be prepared for the complexities of policing reform which some of them may be involved in after attaining their qualifications.

The CPA permits the use of force in effecting an arrest, in section 49. This provision, although also applicable to civilians or private security who may be effecting a 'citizen's arrest' (section 42 of the CPA), has relevance to the police more than anyone else. Other portions of the CPA are necessary for the proper functioning of police powers, such as rules regarding search and seizure (chapter 2 of the CPA), arrest (chapter 5 of the CPA), and the trial process more generally in, for instance, the role of the police in ensuring that an accused is brought to court. The police are also governed by regulations and practice directives, which add substance to the legal framework.

The SAPS Act gives power to the minister (of police) to make regulations regarding many different aspects of the day-to-day functioning of the police, including the exercising of police powers; police members' performance of their duties; recruitment and appointment of members and other human resource issues; training of members; and general management and main-tenance (section 24 of the SAPS Act). The national commissioner is given authority to issue orders and instructions that:

> (a) fall within his or her responsibility in terms of the Constitution or this Act; (b) are necessary or expedient to ensure the maintenance of an impar-tial, accountable, transparent and efficient police service; or (c) are necessary or expedient to provide for the establishment and maintenance of uniform standards of policing at all levels required by law (Section 25 of the SAPS Act).

These orders and instructions are often the most important to how the police carry out their functions in practice. For example, Standing Order (General) 262 on Crowd Management During Gatherings and Demonstrations (2004) states in paragraph 11 in respect of the use of force:

> The use of force must be avoided at all costs and members deployed must display the highest degree of tolerance … If the use of force is unavoidable it must meet the following requirements: … the purpose of the offensive actions are to de-escalate the conflict with the minimum force to accomplish the goal … and therefore the success of the actions will be measured by the results of the operation in terms of cost, damage to property, injury and loss of life … and the importance of clear communication and the giving of warnings before the use of force.

The Crowd Regulation and Management During Public Gatherings and Demonstrations National Instruction of 2012 reads very similarly. Both restrict the use of force as measures of last resort that must be executed by those trained in crowd control. Using the Marikana protest situation as a case study in class (see later in this chapter), I discuss how the police engaged with the protesters seemingly in contravention of the above Standing Order. These Orders and Instructions can help students navigate between the written law (largely found in statutes) and the law in its application.

THE CASE FOR TEACHING RACIAL PROFILING IN A LAW CURRICULUM

My students come from many different backgrounds, and it is always interesting to see their different approaches to racial profiling. Some of them, mainly Black students, find parity with their own and others' experiences, and hone in on the 'lived experience' of Black people in South Africa. Some of my white students take a more 'pragmatic' approach, arguing less about whether racial profiling is a 'good' (that is, moral or ethical) policing strategy, and focusing instead on its utility in so far as it gets results. I raise these observations that display views split along racial lines not to be divisive, but to acknowledge that talking about race in a South African university lecture theatre is a difficult and contested terrain, and often *is* divisive.

To illustrate this point, when I provide the following hypothetical example in class, that of a police roadblock set up in an area that would have been designated as 'coloured' under apartheid (the Population Registration Act 30 of 1950 and the Group Areas Act 40 of 1950), I ask the students to reflect on whether it would be reasonable for the police to search for drugs on the person of young men wearing hoodies. This leads to an interesting conversation of policing experiences – that there is a reasonably good chance that searching coloured men will yield the finding of drugs. On the other hand, we can engage with the racial assumptions made and that these assumptions are produced as a result of the consequences of apartheid spatial planning, and the division and destruction of social communities.

Racial profiling is a police strategy used throughout the world in different ways as a means to identify potential criminal threats and act to prevent or apprehend such threats. The American Civil Liberties Union (ACLU) describes racial profiling as 'the discriminatory practice by law enforcement officials of targeting individuals for suspicion of crime based on the individual's race, ethnicity, religion or national origin' (ACLU 2019). Profiling is also referred to as 'identificatory methods' (Adjai and Lazaridi 2013, 199). These methods are evidence of institutional racism and are problematic in the context of police discretion. Certain statutory provisions that authorise search and seizure without a warrant, arrest without a warrant and the use of force, permit the police to act where they have a 'reasonable suspicion' of wrongdoing. This opens the door for police discretion to be corrupted by these methods of profiling. Police heavy-handedness generally is accepted and even advocated for by large parts of the population – almost every radio call-in programme or letter to the editor in community newspapers demonstrates this. There is a misguided conflation of police control measures with safety. This public perception further supported the change from the late 1990s onwards towards harsher police tactics (Gastrow and Shaw 2001, 252).

My students are usually divided on whether the racial history of South Africa remains relevant to evaluating racial profiling as a legitimate policing strategy, particularly in the context of high rates of gangsterism and drugs which the police are tasked with addressing. These conversations are essential to nuanced applications of the legal test for whether there is a 'reasonable suspicion' to arrest or search someone without a warrant.

Following the first days after the FMF protest period at UCT (in 2015), 24-hour security was stationed at certain buildings, including Kramer, the law faculty building. Many students and some staff – all Black – described being stopped and asked to display their staff or student cards before being permitted into the building. It seemed at the time (anecdotally at least) that white staff and students were not being questioned upon entry. Using these experiences of the very students sitting before me enabled a nuanced and layered conversation about the continued profiling of Black bodies at UCT. The threads between what was happening on our own campus and what the textbooks say will be forever drawn in the minds of my students.

Although the police in South Africa may maintain that the law dictates their behaviour, it is more likely that

> ... police behaviour is influenced by situational circumstances and envi-
> ronmental conditions. These include, among others, the nature of police
> organisation, which includes their rules, structures, and culture; the attitudes
> and behaviour of the public; historical relationships between the police and
> the public; levels of crime and disorder, and the power relations that exist with
> the society in which the police operate (Marks 2002, 321).

Moreover, the law permits police discretion, which opens the door for these attitudes, stereotypes and biases to influence the implementation of police duties.

Monique Marks is probably the most prolific scholar on public order policing in South Africa. Being a criminologist, her work is well received by students for being very interesting. However, it is employed only for the purposes of broader discussions, and it is difficult to get students to engage with it in parts of the course that they perceive as 'purely' legal. I use Marks' work to show students how the health of a police force will directly impact on the application of police powers, and therefore the resultant (in)justice that ensues.

Marks provides a case study from New South Wales, Australia, where efforts were made in 1984 to reform dishonourable police conduct (Marks 2002). Notwithstanding, by the 1990s, the New South Wales police were still criticised for the racist and abusive treatment of Indigenous communities. Marks also describes the Los Angeles Police Department in California, USA, and attempts to eradicate discriminatory police conduct (Marks 2002, 321). Focusing on comparable jurisdictions also helps students to move out of the rut of understanding these issues only in terms of the racial history of South Africa. It is a useful study to show that the policing culture of a particular context will not only impact on whether the police use heavy-handed tactics when confronted with a suspect, but may also result in broader criminal activity being perpetrated.

There are three major contributing factors that influence police culture: sociological, psychological and organisational. Sociological refers to the attributes and behaviour of citizens, broader social forces and structures such as crime rates, government priorities and dominant ideologies. Psychological factors include personal attributes such as sex, race, gender, background such as family, education, occupation, as well as attitudes, perceptions, personalities and work styles. This applies both to the personal attributes of the police officers, and also their impressions of the attributes of the persons that they police. Organisational characteristics are policies, structure, leadership and its composition, rules and guidelines, and performance indicators. What seems particularly relevant to the South African context is that the policing environment:

> … provides normative frameworks that are internalised by the police. These are passed from generation to generation and serve both to constrain behaviour as well as shape the police members' world-view and their view of themselves. These norms, in part, constitute and are embedded in the stories and narratives of police. These stories can take the form of memories, often recounted, which serve to commemorate past behaviour and serve as justifications for present behaviour (Marks 2002, 321).

Apartheid provided the kind of normative framework that Marks was referring to, setting the rules for who was policeable and by what means. A key characteristic of policing culture during apartheid was that it was defined by notions of white male supremacy and domination. An essential change to establishing an effective police force was made in the form of diversifying the demographics of SAPS in order to proportionally reflect South Africa's broader population. The transformation of SAPS has been seen as successful in international circles (Newham, Masuku and Dlamini 2006). However, this is an oversimplification because while the SAPS is more racially diverse, it has not separated itself from racial discrimination and apartheid tactics. In fact, I would go so far as to say that it has perpetuated these. Philip Frankel reminds us that the police force under apartheid was not entirely white, and that many Black (including coloured and Indian) persons were recruited into the force (Frankel 1980, 482). He says that:

> ... insofar as rigorous indoctrination and training at institutions such as Hammanskraal, Bishop Lavis, and Wentworth encourages psychologies favorable to the existing order, "non-whites" have become an important, if ambiguous, factor in the white control apparatus (Frankel 1980, 483).

A little-known fact is that the South African Police, the central state's police force, was not the only police force that existed in South Africa pre-1994. There were ten independent police forces in each of the Black African 'homelands' (Gastrow and Shaw 2001, 242). The transference of racist ideologies in the police was thus not only from white apartheid police to a new crop of Black police officers but originated from Black apartheid-era officers too. The addition of non-state actors impacted on the nature of the police, which had until then seen itself as a defensive force not a policing one (Van der Spuy 2019, 247–249). This is often an uncomfortable discussion to have in class, given the already underlying racial tensions in society; however, it is fundamental that an accurate historical picture is understood by law students.

Marks confirms that the police 'are heavily influenced by the images and stereotypes that they hold about members or particular groupings and, consequently, people from stereotyped groupings are responded to in a rehearsed fashion' (Marks 2002, 322). Philip Potgieter reports that discrimination based on racial or cultural group when a crime is reported, was reported by 66.4 per cent of complainants of crime (Potgieter 2014). Because race and class remain intrinsically linked in South Africa (Newham, Masuku and Dlamini 2006), the privileging of white members of the public is analogous to the privileging of persons from certain (wealthier) areas over others. My white male students, for example, report being pulled over at roadblocks late at night and asked whether they have been drinking alcohol. My Black male students report being stopped in various, different places and situations. The main distinguishing feature about the two scenarios of profiling is that it is Black men who are stopped because they are presumed criminals. With an increasing emerging Black middle class, it would be interesting to know whether this link is as strong as it was in the past and for how much longer it will continue, changing instead to an emphasis on class in the future.

A new target of police racism relates to the policing of foreign African nationals in South Africa. The criteria used to identify foreigners include traits such as skin colour, height and vaccination marks (Adjai and Lazaridi 2013, 199). Police officers arrest persons suspected of being in the country illegally, arresting those who are darker than the *average Black South African* (a ridiculous description), or for being present in areas populated by foreign nationals. As a result of the application of this identification feature, it is reported that approximately 30 per cent of those arrested on suspicion of being illegal immigrants turn out to be South African citizens (Adjai and Lazaridi 2013, 199). Language and accent are other markers used extensively. In a UCT LLB class there is a fairly large contingent of foreign nationals from African countries. This discussion raises important related issues of borders, and migration impacts on policing priorities. It also raises the biases and prejudices of everyone, even some who are generally the victims of racial profiling in the country. The layering of policing between and betwixt these social dynamics emerges more clearly for students the deeper the conversation goes.

Another new trend in South Africa is the increased use of private security companies. These companies are contracted to protect a particular workplace, residential or business area. Their modus operandi is to limit access to these spaces, thereby preventing criminal activities. Because of apartheid-era spatial planning, race and class still determine where people live and work – and this determination is demarcated along colour lines. Thus, companies operating in previously white areas will treat Black entrants with suspicion. Where there has been some movement of Black people into these previously white areas, security companies will employ markers such as whether someone is driving or is on foot, or whether they are well-dressed or not. These private security companies fill the vacuum where the state police are not present or active (Carrier 1999, 37). A focus on private security in the curriculum can lead to an important debate about the state monopoly over policing on the one hand, and the lack of regulation of private security on the other.

The use of private security companies during FMF protests was one of the headlining issues. The image of the SAPS being called onto campus was a harsh reminder of South Africa's security-tight days under apartheid.

However, private security, which was initially seen as more palatable, soon drew sharp criticism. One of the key troubling trends was Black women students who reported that they experienced inappropriate sexual comments from security personnel. Thus, a useful angle to the experience of policing is how women are treated. This is an important issue to air since there is otherwise an emphasis placed on the profiling of men, Black men in particular. I might even say overemphasis not because the profiling of Black men is not endemic, but because it is not the only type of abuse of power by the police.

Gareth Newham, Themba Masuku and Jabu Dlamini (2006) conducted an extensive study in 2006, examining racial and gender prejudice among Johannesburg police officers. The following two extracts are worth quoting here. The first is from a white male inspector:

> It is a fact that in the white community there are also criminals but we do not target those as much as we target black people. When it comes to general policing we profile black people more, and as such we stop and search more of them. It is a fact that if you are black driving at night you are more likely to be stopped than if you are white. If you are a man driving at night you are also more likely to be stopped than if you are a woman. It's a fact in South Africa (Newham, Masuku and Dlamini 2006, 40).

Similar sentiments are expressed by a Black male constable:

> Indeed, we target mostly black people in white areas because most of them are involved in criminal activities. Compared with whites involved in crime there are more blacks; as such we target mostly black people. I do not think that is a problem because you cannot target people who are not involved in crime, otherwise we will be wasting resources. Most black people are involved in housebreaking and very few whites are involved (Newham, Masuku and Dlamini 2006, 40).

These quotes and the recent trends of private security and the policing of foreign African nationals show that racial profiling in the SAPS is not restricted to white officers on Black citizens. While Newham, Masuku and Dlamini (2006) point out that those views expressed were by a minority of participants, they do demonstrate that such views exist in the police service and impact on policing strategies. This is to the detriment of effective and fair policing as required by the Constitution.

The purpose of showing this study to law students is this: as much as policing laws are contained in statute and regulations, they are implemented by people. An awareness of the disjuncture between written law and practice can only benefit students who, one way or another, will be engaging with these disputed narratives.

THE PURPOSE OF TEACHING PROTEST LAW TO LAW STUDENTS

Protest law would generally not be included in the core criminal procedure syllabus. The primary textbooks do not include it as a topic either. It makes some sense that it is not included because, while it is a particular form of policing, it is not seen as a part of the criminal process until someone is arrested for committing a crime during a protest. Even then, it is the crime that is alleged to have been committed and not the protest context that is relevant for criminal procedure. I teach protest law because it provides a useful nexus between police powers to maintain security, and the duties to serve and protect. In the grey area where the police are forced into the unenviable position of protecting other citizens from protesters, while still protecting the right to protest, students are able to understand the everlasting conflict that police face. By addressing the issues that protests are challenging, students also grapple with the complexities of policing in an unequal society like South Africa.

The policing of protests is governed by the general policing provisions in the Constitution, the CPA or the SAPS Act, but is also governed by the Regulation of Gatherings Act (205 of 1993). In June 2017, the Social Justice Coalition (SJC), a community organisation based in Khayelitsha, Cape Town, challenged the constitutionality of the Regulation of Gatherings Act ('Gatherings Act') in the Western Cape High Court. This was an appeal from the magistrates court in which 21 members of the SJC were convicted of contravention of section 12(1)*(a)* of the Gatherings Act (*State v Phumeza Mlungwana and 20 others* 2013).

Section 17 of the Constitution, 1996, effectively enshrines the right to protest, and reads: '[e]veryone has the right, peacefully and unarmed, to assemble, to demonstrate, to picket and to present petitions'. The construction of the right therefore includes internal qualifiers to the right to protest.

The implementation of section 17 is also qualified externally through the Gatherings Act. The preamble emulates some of the language of section 17, stating that:

> every person has the right to assemble with other persons and to express his views on any matter freely in public and to enjoy the protection of the State while doing so; and the exercise of such right shall take place peacefully and with due regard to the rights of others.

The Gatherings Act therefore protects not only the right to protest but also the right to state intervention that facilitates the right to protest (Omar 2017, 25).

However, the Gatherings Act falls short of this protection in a number of ways. Firstly, it could be argued that the Act, which was created between the period 1990–1993, was an agreed compromise by the outgoing apartheid government and is therefore tainted by the moment in time (Omar 2018, 45). Secondly, the legal terms used in the Gatherings Act differ from section 17 of the Constitution, by referring to 'assemble' and 'gathering' (defined in section 1 of the Gatherings Act as referring to any 'assembly, concourse or procession of more than 15 persons' in a public place). The reach of the Gatherings Act therefore extends further than the constitutional right, as the Act intends to include in its ambit all gatherings that may interfere with public areas. Linked to this, the third issue with the Gatherings Act relates to the notice procedure required by section 3. The rationale for notice to the local authority is to allow for proper logistical planning, including route planning, road closures or detours, and availability of medical personnel and water stations (Omar 2017, 27). The problems that emerge from these shortcomings relate to the power given to a local authority to use the notice period to prevent a gathering from taking place.

With reference to protests, Marks says that policing strategy requires a determination of which protesters are good or bad – generally making use of stereotypically 'dangerous populations' as the markers of risk in protest situations. These populations are groups that 'police indiscriminately identify as "typical criminal groupings" and they are often policed with more brutality than other groupings' (Marks 2002, 323).

Innocent Madawo confirms that the SAPS operational ethos has not changed much from the time when a white-dominated police force used heavy-handed tactics to quell protests by the Black majority (Madawo 2011, 32). The current police force has a large contingent of former apartheid officers, both white and Black, working alongside former anti-apartheid activists, some of whom were involved with the armed wing (uMkhonto we Sizwe) of organisations like the African National Congress. This has emphasised the combatant culture of the SAPS. The introduction in 2010 of military-style ranks has not helped this ethos to change.

Potgieter (2014) argues in the context of protest that the maintenance of 'social order' is a priority for the SAPS, which results in heavy-handed policing tactics during protests. In my view, these policing tactics are attempts to maintain order, which is not the same as maintaining social order. The police also consistently report violence against their members as the cause for police use of force. While this may be true in some instances, and it cannot be denied that the SAPS in South Africa operate under very difficult and under-resourced circumstances, 'the police have proved to be far from impartial in responding to these protests' (Duncan 2016, 131).

The resource constraints that the police face must be emphasised to students – not to excuse police conduct but to get them to think about how different parts of the criminal justice system are interlinked; when one part is faulty it creates a flawed system overall. The policing resources case brought by the SJC in 2018 highlights the interface between national and provincial planning and budgeting, and the impact on the efficacy of policing in less resourced areas (*Social Justice Coalition and Others v Minister of Police and Others* 2018). This in turn impacts the dissatisfaction of the inhabitants of these areas, as well as the likelihood of more heavy-handed policing as officers will always have to be brought in from elsewhere, since the local branch will not have sufficient personnel to build strong relationships with residents. As Andrew Brown says, in these situations, 'policing turned from neglect to riot control, from indifference to conquest' (Brown 2016, 42).

Protest is a tool of communication for those who lack access to alternative avenues to communicate their dissatisfaction. The important role that protest has played in South Africa's history to a constitutional democracy must continue to be celebrated. The Constitutional Court has noted as follows:

So the lessons of our history which inform the right to peaceful assembly and demonstration in the Constitution, are at least twofold. First, they remind us that ours is a 'never again' Constitution: never again will we allow the right of ordinary people to freedom in all its forms to be taken away. Second, they tell us something about the inherent power and value of freedom of assembly and demonstration, as a tool of democracy often used by people who do not necessarily have other means of making their democratic rights count. Both these historical considerations emphasise the importance of the right (*SATAWU and Another v Garvas and Others* 2013, para. 63).

The heavy-handedness of the police in acting as an agent of the state denies this history.

While the Gatherings Act makes it more difficult to comply with the law and protest lawfully (Omar 2017, 28), police presence at protests can also exacerbate rather than prevent lawlessness. This is in part because of the conflicted history of policing in South Africa, particularly at protests, and the continued mistrust of the police (Brooks 2019, 24–25). Municipal IQ comments that the 'policing of protests appears to add another layer of violence, further destabilising the already vulnerable relationship between communities and authority figures' (Municipal IQ 2017).

Section 9 of the Gatherings Act, which details the powers of the police during a gathering, is especially problematic. While the police would ordinarily have jurisdiction to monitor an event that involves a large group of people in a public space, section 9 gives explicit and specific authority to the police to intervene in various stages of the protest. For example, the police may prevent or move participants to a different place (section 9(1)(b)), may order the participants of a protest to disperse (section 9(2)), or use force in the case of serious damage to persons or property (section 9(2)(d) and (e)).

The court in the well-publicised SJC10 case ('10' referring to the original arrests made), *Phumeza Mlungwana and 20 Others v State and Others* A431/15, reiterated that section 9 demonstrably gives the police powers to manage a gathering reasonably (para. 33). This would seem superfluous in light of the police's general duties and powers in section 205(3) of the Constitution. The need for specific police powers in the Gatherings Act is perhaps a relic of its time and context, where the role of the police in protests was at the forefront of the minds of the legislative drafters and Parliament.

In 2006, the Public Order Policing (POP) units within the SAPS were significantly restructured, reducing their capacity. This was in part to redeploy resources to other units such as the Organised Crime unit, with the increased focus on gangsterism. Prior to the restructuring process, there were 7 227 POP members (Burger and Omar 2009, 10). This was reduced during the restructuring to 2 595 POP members. The wave of xenophobic attacks throughout South Africa in 2008 resulted in a slight increase to the number of POP units; however, capacity was still approximately half of what it had been prior to 2006 (Burger and Omar 2009, 10).

This reduced capacity was a significant factor in the Marikana massacre that unfolded on 16 August 2012 in North West province. On 12 August 2012, a large group of protesters, mainly striking mineworkers, marched to the offices of the primary union, the National Union of Mineworkers (NUM), at Lonmin. Two security guards were killed during this time. Some of the protesters had also attacked employees who had chosen to work, and two were killed. The SAPS established a Joint Operations Centre at the mine. After a week of similar incidents, protesting mineworkers, particularly members of a union more recently operating in the mine, the Association of Mineworkers and Construction Union (AMCU), faced the police in a standoff in which the police shot and killed 34 people. The shootings occurred at two different scenes, 1 and 2. At scene 1, the police formed a line to block protesters from going further towards Lonmin's offices. According to reports, one officer opened fire with live ammunition, which set off a barrage of bullets from the other officers. After this, the protesters retreated to the hill (known as the 'koppie') where officers appear to have shot protesters in the back, or while they were hiding behind rocks (this later interaction on the koppie is referred to as scene 2).

The police in this standoff with the protesters were a mixture of Tactical Response Team members and POP members. The use of the Tactical Response Team – a paramilitary unit in the SAPS – harks back to policing protests under apartheid and is unlikely to facilitate constructive negotiations between the SAPS and protesters (Roberts et al. 2017, 65).

Gary White, an expert in crowd control working in Northern Ireland, provided expert testimony to the Marikana Commission of Inquiry (2015). White was asked by the South African Human Rights Commission to analyse the police strategies employed on 16 August, and the use of force. White provided extensive analysis and only a few points will be emphasised here. Firstly, White criticised the failure to gather intelligence, arguing that information gathering is vital for effective negotiation with a crowd. Should negotiation fail, information is also necessary to develop the best policing strategy to de-escalate the situation (White, in Marikana Commission of Inquiry 2015, paras. 2.3.1–2.3.4). White also compares South Africa to the United Kingdom (UK), arguing that South Africa's permission of tear gas and rubber bullets, neither of which is used in the UK, is not conducive to effective crowd control and risks doing a lot of indiscriminate damage (White, in Marikana Commission of Inquiry 2015, paras. 2.3.5–2.3.7).

The Marikana Commission of Inquiry recommended that police officers should be better trained for crowd management and that experts should be used to redraft or clarify police guidelines for practice. It was also recommended that paramilitary parts of the SAPS, such as the Tactical Response Team, should only be used subject to specific guidelines (Marikana Commission of Inquiry 2015, 549). In 2016, the training for new cadets on public order policing was increased from two weeks to three weeks (Lamb 2018, 14). Having worked for a short while with a team of lawyers at the Centre for Applied Legal Studies (CALS) who were representing the South African Human Rights Commission at the Marikana Commission of Inquiry, I am able to bring personal insights into the classroom about the Commission and the facts of the massacre.

Unless law students understand the full picture – the weakening of POPs, the myriad of social issues, the politics of the unions, the lack of policing strategy and intelligence – they are likely to have a blinkered view of the events, what Nigerian writer Chimamanda Ngozi Adichie (2009) refers to as 'the danger of a single story'. In my experience, this will either be an overemphasis on the politics, or a sole critique of the police. For future legislators, advocates, policy drafters or activists, as I hope all my students will become, the legal, criminological, social and economic issues are relevant.

TEACHING LAW IN A SOCIAL CONTEXT

My colleague and co-teacher of criminal procedure for a time, Professor Dee Smythe, says that the teaching of criminal procedure should have changed fundamentally after Marikana. It is no longer possible (if it ever were) to ignore the social context within which the law is sought to be applied. Similarly, the protests and looting in KwaZulu-Natal and parts of Gauteng in July 2021 raise further controversy around the role of policing in highly charged, politicised contexts. If we do not have these nuanced conversations with law students, we are not fully developing their critical thinking skills. We are also perpetuating the misconception that law is theoretical and is abstracted from reality.

The increase in the number of protests has been accompanied by a clear increase in the number of people arrested or where force is used at protests (Bond 2010). This is a continuation of the apartheid trend of state resistance to dissent. In a context where protest has become the only means for certain groups to communicate their marginalisation, strong-arm tactics by the SAPS are likely to further reduce trust in the police (Tait and Marks 2011, 20).

The problem of racial profiling in protest, but also for all police matters, is a further alienating factor that undermines the possibility of cooperation between the police and communities. Law students need to understand the powers of the police not only through the written law, but through live interactions. Students in fact do understand this, but they are schooled to believe that these 'lived experiences' have to be left at the door to law school. Yet, these perspectives are vital to developing well-rounded lawyers.

Post-apartheid South Africa has a new legal framework but a very similar police service to that which was inherited. There remains an overemphasis on the use of force and racial profiling as a police strategy. These stand in stark contrast to the Bill of Rights and constitutional principles that created a single police service.

Both heavy-handed policing of protests and racial profiling push communities further away from cooperating with the police. The police should be implementing their powers in ways that increase their legitimacy. I argue that unless these fundamental cultural issues are addressed, there will continue to be an emphasis on crime control – resulting in further alienation of the public. Unless these issues are raised and engaged with critically in law courses, the next generation of lawyers will continue the path of increased security without understanding or grappling with the complex social issues. Teaching police powers from a multidisciplinary perspective is one part of the project for epistemic justice.

The complexities of race, class, gender and nationality that are embedded in the way policing is conducted in South Africa must be brought to the front of every law student's consciousness. To teach criminal procedure as a set of laws that are merely rules to be followed, is to take for granted, even ignore, the inequalities and injustices on which South Africa's criminal justice system is built. Whether a law student engages with the police post-LLB or never practises criminal law again, a more interdisciplinary and nuanced approach to police and policing will benefit their legal knowledge and expand their critical thinking skills.

REFERENCES

ACLU (American Civil Liberties Union). 2019. 'Racial Profiling: Definition'. https://www.aclu. org/other/racial-profiling-definition2019.

Adichie, Chimamanda Ngozi. 2009. 'The Danger of a Single Story'. Filmed July 2009 at TedGlobal. TED video, 18:21. https://www.ted.com/talks/chimamanda_ngozi_adichie_ the_danger_of_a_single_story?language=n.

Adjai, Carol and Gabriella Lazaridi. 2013. 'Migration, Xenophobia and New Racism in Post-Apartheid South Africa'. *International Journal of Social Science Studies* 1 (1): 192–205. https://doi.org/10.11114/ijsss.v1i1.102.

Bond, Patrick. 2010. 'South Africa's Bubble Meets Boiling Urban Social Protest'. *Monthly Review* 62 (2). https://monthlyreview.org/2010/06/01/south-africas-bubble-meets-boiling-urban-social-protest/.

Brooks, Heidi. 2019. 'Democracy and Its Discontents: Protest from a Police Perspective'. *South African Crime Quarterly (SACQ)* 67: 1–29. http://doi.org/10.17159/2413-3108/2019/ v0n67a5711.

Brown, Andrew. 2016. *Good Cop, Bad Cop: Confessions of a Reluctant Policeman*. Cape Town: Zebra Press.

Burger, Johan and Bilkis Omar. 2009. 'Can Practice Make Perfect? Security and the 2010 FIFA World Cup'. *SACQ* 29: 9–16. https://doi.org/10.17159/2413-3108/2009/i29a899.

Butler, Jeffrey, Robert Rotberg and John Adams. 1978. *The Black Homelands of South Africa: The Political and Economic Development of Bophuthatswana and KwaZulu*. Berkeley, CA: University of California Press.

Carrier, Ryan. 1999. 'Dissolving Boundaries: Private Security and Policing in South Africa'. *African Security Studies* 8 (6): 37–43. https://doi.org/10.1080/10246029.1999.9628158.

Constitution of the Republic of South Africa, 1996.

Duncan, Jane. 2016. *Protest Nation: The Right to Protest in South Africa.* Pietermaritzburg: University of KwaZulu-Natal Press.

Frankel, Philip H. 1980. 'South Africa: The Politics of Police Control'. *Comparative Politics* 12 (4): 481–499. https://doi.org/10.2307/421837.

Gastrow, Peter and Mark Shaw. 2001. 'In Search of Safety: Police Transformation and Public Responses in South Africa'. *Daedalus* 130 (1): 235–258. https://www.jstor.org/stable/20027687.

Lamb, Guy. 2018. 'Mass Killings and Calculated Measures: The Impact of Police Massacres on Police Reform in South Africa'. *South African Crime Quarterly* 63: 5–16. http://dx.doi.org/10.17159/2413-3108/2018/v0n63a3028.

Madawo, Innocent. 2011. 'The Dilemma of the SA Police'. *New African* 508: 32–33.

Marikana Commission of Inquiry. 2015. *Report on Matters of Public, National and International Concern Arising out of the Tragic Incidents at the Lonmin Mine in Marikana, North West Province.* https://www.gov.za/documents/report-judicial-commission-inquiry-events-imarikana-mine-rustenburg-25-jun-2015-0000.

Marks, Monique. 2002. 'New Methods, New Motives? Appraising Police Behavioural Change in a Post-Apartheid Police Unit'. *Journal of Asian and African Studies* 37 (3): 318–352. http://dx.doi.org/10.17159/2413-3108/2018/v0n63a3028.

Ministry of Police. 2004. SAPS Standing Order No. 262 on Crowd Management.

Ministry of Police. 2012. National Instruction # of 2012: Public Order Police: Crowd Regulation and Management during Public Gatherings and Demonstrations.

Municipal IQ. 2017. '2017 Service Delivery Protests in a High Range, but Downward Trend from May Peak'. Municipal IQ press release, 24 October 2017. https://www.municipaliq.co.za/publications/press/201710241012397864.pdf.

Newham, Gareth, Themba Masuku and Jabu Dlamini. 2006. *Diversity and Transformation in SAPS.* Braamfontein: Centre for the Study of Violence and Reconciliation. https://csvr.org.za/docs/policing/diversity.pdf.

Omar, Jameelah. 2016. 'Penalised for Poverty: The Unfair Assessment of "Flight Risk" in Bail Hearings'. *South African Crime Quarterly* 57: 27–34. http://dx.doi.org/10.17159/2413-3108/2016/v0n57a1273.

Omar, Jameelah. 2017. 'A legal Analysis in Context: The Regulation of Gatherings Act – a Hindrance to the Right to Protest?' *South African Crime Quarterly* 62: 21–31. https://doi.org/10.17159/2413-3108/2017/i62a3044.

Omar, Jameelah. 2018. 'Testing the Judiciary's Appetite to Reimagine Protest Law: A Case Note on the SJC10 Case'. *South African Crime Quarterly* 63: 43–51. http://dx.doi.org/10.17159/2413-3108/2018/v0n63a4509.

Phumeza Mlungwana and 20 Others v State and Others A431/15.

Potgieter, Philip J. 2014. 'Operational Characteristics of Police Officers'. *Acta Criminologica* 27 (1): 90–113. https://hdl.handle.net/10520/EJC162004.

Republic of South Africa. 1977. Criminal Procedure Act (No. 51 of 1977). Pretoria.

Republic of South Africa. 1992. Drugs and Drug Trafficking Act (No. 140 of 1992). Pretoria.

Republic of South Africa. 1950. Group Areas Act (No. 40 of 1950). Pretoria.

Republic of South Africa. 1950. Population Registration Act (No. 30 of 1950). Pretoria.

Republic of South Africa. 1993. Regulation of Gatherings Act (No. 205 of 1993). Pretoria.

Republic of South Africa. 1995. South African Police Service Act (No. 68 of 1995). Pretoria.

Roberts, Benjamin James, Narnia Bohler-Muller, Jare Struwig, Steven Lawrence Gordon, Ngqapheli Mchunu, Samela Mtyingizane and Carin Runciman. 2017. 'Protest Blues: Public Opinion on the Policing of Protest in South Africa'. *South African Crime Quarterly* 62: 63–80. http://dx.doi.org/10.17159/2413-3108/2017/v0n62a3040.

SATAWU and Another v Garvas and Others 2013 (1) SA 83 (CC).

Social Justice Coalition and Others v Minister of Police and Others (EC03/2016) [2018] ZAWCHC 181; 2019 (4) SA 82 (WCC) (14 December 2018).

State v Phumeza Mlungwana and 20 others (case number 14/985/2013).

Tait, Sean and Monique Marks. 2011. 'You Strike a Gathering You Strike a Rock: Current Debates in the Policing of Public Order in South Africa'. *South African Crime Quarterly* 38: 15–22. https://doi.org/10.17159/2413-3108/2011/i38a853.

Van der Spuy, Elrena. 2019. 'The Integration of ANC and PAC Cadres (Non-Statutory Forces) into the South African Police Service, 1994–1996: Facets and Fault Lines'. In *A Reasonable Man: Essays in Honour of Jonathan Burchell*, edited by P. J. Schwikkard and Shannon Hoctor, 246–269. Cape Town: Juta and Company.

PART III
CONTESTED HISTORIES AND ETHICAL SPACES

AFRICAN STUDIES AT UCT: AN INTERVIEW WITH LUNGISILE NTSEBEZA

SEPIDEH AZARI

L ungisile Ntsebeza is one of South Africa's foremost scholars on land reform and democracy. He holds two research chairs at the University of Cape Town (UCT), the A. C. Jordan chair in African Studies, and the National Research Foundation Research Chair in Land Reform and Democracy in South Africa. As a political activist and scholar, Ntsebeza's relationship with UCT began with an Honours degree in 1987. Twenty years later, he was appointed as professor in sociology, and later as director of the Centre for African Studies, where he continues to work as professor emeritus.

Besides developing an exceptional body of work on the politics of land redistribution, traditional authorities, democracy and governance at UCT, Ntsebeza has been a keen observer of, and participant in, leadership at this university. There are few as well qualified to provide a first-hand, critical view into the recent history of the institution. Sepideh Azari interviewed Ntsebeza in Cape Town in August 2020. The interview provides a unique glimpse into the contestations and struggles that have unfolded at UCT as it has sought to transcend its moorings in colonial and apartheid South Africa. Ntsebeza reflects on UCT's liberal lineage, its fraught encounters with renowned scholars such as Archie Mafeje and Mahmood Mamdani, its attempts to recast itself as an Afropolitan campus, and the hopes and anxieties associated with the trajectory of African studies at UCT. His insights help us grasp how UCT became a site for discontent around transformation in post-apartheid South Africa, spurring student movements for decolonisation such as Rhodes Must Fall and Fees Must Fall in 2015 and 2016, respectively. His perceptions also enable us to understand UCT's character as an institution where, in the face of many challenges, teachers, students and staff members have been thoughtfully charting a course towards greater epistemic justice in a postcolonial university. The interview opens with Ntsebeza recounting his student years at UCT and at other South African university campuses.

Lungisile Ntsebeza (LN) I did my Master's and PhD while working at the same time. The last time I had the privilege of being a full-time student was during my Honours in economic history at UCT. People like Janet Cherry, Andrew Boraine, Victor Steyn, Max Ozinsky and Lennie (Leonard) Gentle were my fellow student activists at the time.[1] Then I moved to the University of Natal, Durban [UND] where my Master's was supervised by Bill Freund, who passed away recently, and, finally, I completed my PhD at Rhodes University in 2002.[2] While I was in Grahamstown, now Makhanda, I thought I would continue with my Master's work on urban youth, or urban politics, or urban economic history, in my doctoral work. But I ended up working with an NGO [non-governmental organisation] that was looking at land occupations, the Border Rural Committee in East London. I observed the tensions in rural governance: in the area where we worked, close to Queenstown, now Komani, there was a very strong component of SANCO, the South African National Civic Organisation.

This area, which fell under Ciskei at the time, was administered by chiefs and headmen. Every time I went there, young people would take me to the office of SANCO, but when I met elderly people, they would take me to the chief. Back in East London, I would ask my colleagues: 'Who governs in Thornhill?' (Thornhill was our research area). I asked this question because I could see that there was, on the one hand, contestation between young, former workers with trade union experience, high school students, and so on; and, on the other hand, mainly elderly people who still led the everyday governance of the area. The former workers and the youth were influenced by notions of democracy and shop floor worker organisation. Accountability was the watchword, and no leader was allowed to make decisions for the people. If you talked in a meeting, people would ask, 'Do you have a mandate?' In the rural areas of these former bantustans, the old traditional authority structure prevailed, with the power to allocate land.[3] People who wanted land needed to approach the traditional authorities. This tension between the authority of unelected chiefs and democratic thinking became central to my research and writings. The roots of this work go back more than 25 years, to 1994.

I left Rhodes in 1995 and went back to Natal where I worked for the Institute for Multiparty Democracy. It was like an NGO, but they paid me well; I bought the car that I still drive while I worked there.

Sepidah Azari (SA) Your car has lasted well if you have been driving it for 25 years. Were you still a PhD student, or a postdoctoral student at this time in 1995?

LN I had a car when I was at UCT as a student. Before that I had been arrested – I had a criminal record. I was running a very successful bookshop, selling virtually everything from the *South African Labour Bulletin* and *Staffrider* [an arts and literary magazine], to the Heinemann African Writers series. I sold books and publications that were banned in South Africa but I was actually living in the bantustan of Transkei at the time. Whenever the police raided my bookshop, I would ask them to show me their list of banned publications. They never produced such a list but they still harassed me. Through the bookshop, I had managed to buy a car and a couple of delivery vehicles.

UCT AS AN OPEN UNIVERSITY

LN I had left Transkei in 1987 following the murder of my cousin, Bathandwa Ndondo, by the South African security police, the 'death squad', on 24 September 1985. I came to UCT; that was my 'exile' period, running away from the Transkei.

SA Were the UCT residences at the time mixed or were they segregated?

LN The late 1980s were changing times. UCT was trying to project itself as a progressive, liberal – even radical – university. I remember being in Cape Town in the early 1980s and meeting students from UCT. The residences for Black students were in Gugulethu, in Malunga Park. At the time, there was no way they could stay in areas designated for non-Black people. It was the same at the University of Natal. However, by the late 1980s, UCT accommodated Black students in white designated areas. I stayed in Mowbray at the Glendower Residence [Glenres], a former hotel bought by UCT. We were mainly Black students, Black in the broader sense, the Black Consciousness sense of the word. Classes were open to everyone and there was no separation.

SA What made you come back to UCT in 2004, as an associate professor?

LN A couple of things. I am in love with Cape Town; I have spent most of my life here. I was born in the Eastern Cape, but I have many relatives in Gugulethu. Whenever I had the excuse, I would come to Cape Town. When I completed my Honours [in 1987], I worked for an NGO called SACHED [South African Committee on Higher Education]. It had a university project called Khanya College in which teachers tutored and mentored students from marginal communities who showed academic talent but who did not have sufficient points to be accepted at universities such as UCT.[4]

After a year at Khanya College, I left for Durban. In the late 1980s we thought that the revolution was around the corner but the intense, vicious crackdown [by the apartheid security forces] also made us feel defeated – we had to lick our wounds. A few of us thought we needed to regroup, rethink and restrategise. Natal was seen as the place to congregate. Steven Gelb[5] relocated to Natal, to the University of Durban-Westville. Alec Erwin[6] and Mike Morris,[7] then trade unionists, were also in Natal. Ari Sitas was also there. I went to Natal because there was a project that I was thinking of working on with Mike Morris. It was a project that was meant to assess the struggles of the mid-1980s.

After seven years [in Natal], I thought it was time to return to Cape Town. I had never quite settled in Durban, partly because there were violent conflicts involving the Inkatha Freedom Party (IFP), and the United Democratic Front (UDF) and African National Congress (ANC). I speak isiZulu, but with an isiXhosa accent. The IFP generally associated AmaXhosa as belonging to either the UDF or the ANC.[8] I felt that it was not so safe for me to live in Natal. I also realised how attached I was to Cape Town and would probably have returned even if there was no violent conflict in Natal.

Coming back to Cape Town, I had begun to think seriously about the issue of rural democracy and had read Mahmood Mamdani's [1996] book, *Citizen and Subject*. I must have been one of the first people to read that book. Mahmood was at the University of Durban-Westville in the years preceding the publication of his book. I cannot remember how I got in touch with Mahmood, but I got to know him. We even talked about the possibility of me doing my PhD under his supervision. In fact, I did not know until I came back to UCT in 2004 that Mahmood had actually registered me as his PhD student.

SA Was this before he left in 1999?

LN Yes, he was in the Centre for African Studies [CAS], holding the A. C. Jordan chair which I now hold. When I came back to Cape Town in 1996, I initially went to the University of the Western Cape [UWC]. Jakes Gerwel, then vice-chancellor at UWC, had declared UWC the intellectual home for the left. So, regarding myself as a member of the political left, I thought let me go to university of the left. But later in 2004, there was a job in the Department of Sociology at UCT which I applied for, and got; I have never regretted this decision. Although I chose to go to UWC, I never felt at home there. It turned out to be less the home for the left than I had expected. There was always something that told me that my home is at UCT.

THE LIBERAL UNIVERSITY AND AFRICAN STUDIES

SA Something about UCT which I find interesting is this subtlety around the different strands of liberalism. You wrote a piece in 2012, 'African Studies: An Overview', where you talk about similar issues.

LN It's an overview of African studies at UCT [Ntsebeza 2012, 1–20]. There is also an updated version of that article, published in 2020, in the journal *Social Dynamics* [Ntsebeza 2020]. African studies, in my view, captures the nature of UCT, going back to its view of the 'native problem' from the nineteenth century to the establishment of the School of Bantu Life and Languages in 1920 [Ntsebeza 2012, 4]. The dominance of anthropologists, from Alfred R. Radcliffe-Brown to Isaac Schapera, Monica Wilson, Martin West, is also notable. I think there were a few academics who were not anthropologists, such as Nikolaas van der Merwe from the Department of Archaeology. Archaeology, of course, had always been part of that thinking of African studies.

Up until 1948, African studies at UCT was a colonial project, with the view that if you want to control the 'natives', you must know them. In particular, Anglican missionaries of the nineteenth century like William A. Norton were of the view that you had to know their languages [Ntsebeza 2012]. In my article on African studies, I showed how Gerard-Paul Lestrade, who was head of the Department of Bantu Languages (as it was referred to then), was consulted by the architects of apartheid when they were developing the Bantu Education Act of 1953 [Ntsebeza 2020].

I think it is only with people like Monica Wilson that one starts to detect shades of liberalism, with UCT distancing itself from the apartheid government. At that time of course, the various schools of anthropology had split. There were the anthropologists, mainly at Afrikaans-speaking universities such as Stellenbosch and Pretoria, who believed in and identified with the apartheid ideology. And there were also those anthropologists who followed the Western liberal tradition; while they rejected the crude, brutal, naked racism of the ruling National Party, racism persisted among them too in more subtle and sophisticated ways.

Things got more sophisticated still from the mid-1970s when people such as Martin Hall and Brenda Cooper were at CAS.[9] African studies in those days was truly interdisciplinary. When I studied at UCT, I was registered in CAS, but my home department was economic history. Martin Hall was an archaeologist and Brenda Cooper came from the English department.

Some of the activities at CAS during this period are captured in Martin Hall's [1998] response to Mamdani's article on African studies as Bantu education [Mamdani 1998]. On the level of some factual details, Mamdani was off the mark. He made generalisations and Hall responded with details of specific activities, events, developments that were taking place in African studies, particularly in the 1980s [Hall 1998]. For example, CAS organised seminars that addressed the political struggles of the 1980s. There was a lot of creativity at CAS – people trying different models of teaching, curriculum reform and seminar topics. When there were States of Emergency, the university, and particularly CAS, offered a safe space for many students. There was a sense of protection on campus that was not evident off campus, where people were easy targets of the security police. Now and again police raided the campus, but it was not the norm. However, racism, at the everyday level, was very sophisticated. One couldn't just write a dismissive one-liner about these racists or liberals as one can do now on social media. One had to be equally sophisticated in one's analysis of what was happening at UCT at the time.

EPISTEMIC (IN)JUSTICE AND STUDENT ASSESSMENT

SA So, was Mamdani's contention lost?

LN Mamdani clearly had a point by raising the issue of African studies at UCT when there were tensions around how a course on African studies should be designed. But I think it is problematic to make generalisations or assertions that African studies was a form of Bantu education. Hall challenged Mamdani on that assertion. The issues were complex. It is important to remember that scholars, Black or white, are never homogeneous. There will always be progressive elements and conservative elements. Nevertheless, I would argue that white supremacy shows its ugly side in subtle ways when it comes to the curriculum. There has been an undercurrent of blame by staff members of Black students; teaching staff who would never consider that they themselves were part of the problem. When you cannot teach people, you blame them, theirs is the fault.

We dealt with these issues when I was at Khanya College and the University of Natal. I worked on an education development programme, TTT (Teach-Test-Teach). There, we avoided projecting the problem onto students but accepted that *we* needed to change in order to teach students for whom the concepts and methods were unfamiliar. UCT at the same time adopted an academic support programme where Black students would be separated from other students. They were taught separately in workshops that were meant to bring them on a par with their white counterparts. Once they had been 'workshopped', they would be brought back to join the white students. These are, in my view, versions of the kind of racism that you would find in South Africa's white universities; these range from crude racism as you would find at Stellenbosch University, and other kinds of white supremacy at liberal universities.

THE MAFEJE AFFAIR

SA Archie Mafeje was a student of and research assistant to Monica Wilson [Bank and Swana 2013]. In 1968, nearing the completion of his PhD, he was offered a job at UCT which was then rescinded. The university executive invoked directives from the apartheid state. The vice-chancellor, Richard Luyt, said that the minister of national education, Jan de Klerk [former president F. W. de Klerk's father], took offence at UCT wanting to appoint a Black scholar when government policy was to maintain apartheid education right through to higher education. This was after the appointment had been recommended, the letter to Mafeje had been written, and the vice-chancellor was supposed to inform Mafeje, who was then in Cambridge. Instead, he [Luyt] came back with explanations as to why he did not follow through with the decision to appoint Mafeje. Why did the university see Mafeje as a problem?

LN It was the state that had a problem with Mafeje's appointment. The National Party had a policy that established separate institutions along racial lines and saw the appointment of a Black academic in a white institution as being counter to their policy. However, there was no law that prevented UCT from making the appointment. There was no law that stipulated that a Black lecturer could not teach a white student.

Mafeje wanted to come to UCT, but the doors were closed. They were locked against him in 1968, ostensibly because of apartheid, just as they were locked again in the early 1990s when he again applied to UCT. In 1968, you could perhaps understand the excuse, but not in the 1990s when apartheid was on its way out. I have read threatening letters to UCT's Council from the minister of national education in 1968 [Hendricks 2008, 427–428]. If the university had had any principles, they should have stood by them and appointed Mafeje.

SA They took the easy way out?

LN Yes, I would say so. In the 1990s, they could not blame the apartheid system any longer. Mafeje was much better qualified in the early 1990s than he was in 1968. He was already a professor in his own right. The number of Mafeje's publications in the 1980s is unbelievable.

SA What do you think was happening at UCT in the 1990s?

LN In the 1990s, UCT's leadership was controlled by anthropologists and Mafeje had become very critical of the discipline. In the 1990s, the vice-chancellor was Mamphela Ramphele, who was a student of Martin West's, and he had become her deputy vice-chancellor.

Even though Mafeje started his career as an anthropologist, and early on had said that anthropology was his calling, he later became one of the discipline's severest critics. Martin West knew this and perhaps he thought that if Mafeje was brought to UCT there would be, intellectually speaking, blood all over the place. He would probably have turned the CAS into a Council for the Development of Social Science Research in Africa (CODESRIA) of some sort. He had many contacts across the globe and he would likely have made CAS a hub of *radical* intellectual activity. In fact, one of the plans of radical African intellectuals such as the Zimbabwean scholar, Ibbo Mandaza, was that Cape Town would be the next site of the Dar tradition. This was a group of radical African intellectuals based at the University of Dar es Salaam in the 1970s. Issa Shivji of Tanzania and

Mandaza were part of this group. When Zimbabwe became independent, that group moved to Harare. They established something called SAPES, Southern Africa Political Economy Series, run by Mandaza. The idea in the late 1980s was that with South Africa being one of the last countries to be liberated, SAPES should establish its presence in Cape Town. And the person who was going to lead that move was Mafeje. By then, Mafeje had written a booklet, *In Search of an Alternative* [Mafeje 1992]. You could see from his writing that he was gearing himself up to get back home to South Africa. This was also clear in his application for the A. C. Jordan chair in the early 1990s. In his application letter, he says something like: 'I have a mission, a mission of sharing experiences and insights not just with students but with my colleagues who have been disadvantaged by never having been in contact with the rest of their continent because of apartheid' [Ntsebeza 2014]. Mafeje thus held the view that everybody, Black and white, based in South Africa, was disadvantaged.

But what he would be bringing to UCT would be at odds with what African studies had been all those years; with what anthropology at UCT had been about. It would not just be a question of tension; it would be more like two rams butting heads. Those who ensured that Mafeje did not return to UCT in the early 1990s must have thought that he would bring down the established liberal tradition of anthropology at UCT.

It is clear in my mind that if Mafeje had been appointed in the early 1990s, we would have started debating issues of decolonisation then. Rhodes Must Fall and the entire Fallist movement would not have taken the form they did because people would have been familiar with those ideas.

SA You think UCT would have reached that point sooner than it did recently?

LN Yes, but it is clear that in the early 1990s, it was not urgent for UCT to claim to be an African university. They were still comfortable being part of the Western world and its academic canons.

SA Do you think that is why there was also a clash with Mamdani?

LN I do, and it started in his very first year. My guess – and this is only a guess – is that Mamdani was not as well known as Mafeje. He had published but *Citizen and Subject* only came out in 1996, *after* his appointment at UCT. UCT staff were probably not aware of the book or had not read it. It might have shocked them that Mamdani was not just your average Black or Indian who you could patronisingly take under your wing.

After I read his book, I was curious about Mamdani. But Mafeje's reputation was far ahead of him. I had the privilege of reading the notes from his interview, and you could see that members of the UCT committee were really keen to get an African scholar, but one whom they could control. They knew they would not be able to control Mafeje. So the easiest thing was not to employ him and suffer the pain of criticism, rather than bring him here to become a troublemaker. We talk about decolonialisation now, but Mafeje was deeply involved in discussions about decolonisation way back in the 1970s.

CENTRE FOR AFRICAN STUDIES

SA Shortly after 2009 you moved from sociology to African studies. One might say that you went to 'protect' African studies. Were you thinking of Mafeje's work and the things that he had envisioned for African studies when you went there?

LN CAS offered degrees and encouraged students to look for 'home' departments. My home department was, as I mentioned earlier, economic history. Economic history was a very small yet dynamic and interesting department of radical scholars and students. Ian Phimister was head of department, and there was a group of students, mainly activists. Some names that I have mentioned before like Steyn, Cherry, Boraine and Gentle come to mind. We all had our encounters with imprisonment, either as prisoners or as detainees, during the 1980s State of Emergency. And, importantly, we shared a vision about what should be taught.

When I was employed as lecturer in sociology, I knew that CAS existed but I had never tried to follow what was happening there after Mamdani left. I got a hint that CAS was in some trouble in 2009, when there were threats that CAS would be 'dis-established'.

When Max Price became vice-chancellor in 2008, he propagated the notion of UCT as an Afropolitan university. At the same time, there was talk about CAS being dis-established; it made no sense. My first reaction was alarm as to why they would be closing a unit that could potentially give expression and meaning to Price's vision.

I remember going to a special faculty board meeting in 2010 or 2011 where we debated the future of CAS. The key issue was finding someone to facilitate the discussions. The dean, Paula Ensor, thought we should consider an outsider. My view was that we needed an insider – a person who knew the issues – but I kept quiet. A day or two later, Paula Ensor asked if I would be willing to facilitate these discussions. I said I would, simply because I would be able to pursue the argument of the article I had just published in *Social Dynamics* on Mafeje and UCT, and its pretences [Ntsebeza 2014]. I saw this as an opportunity to bring this argument back to the table. I had studied the development of thinking at UCT, and its forms of inherent racism, from the early open collaboration with the colonial and apartheid governments to other, subtler forms of racism, later on.

DISCIPLINES, BOUNDARIES AND POWER

SN What do you think put you in a position to lead the discussion around the future of CAS?

LN I think I had the advantage of some seniority: when I came back to UCT in 2004, it was as an associate professor. By 2008, I had been promoted to full professor, and I had a National Research Foundation (NRF) chair too. That put me in a strong leadership position; no one could easily bully or pressure me. My view is that if I had stayed at UCT, completing all my studies at UCT and had worked there, things would have been different. It was a good move for me to leave and come back as a senior staff member. I bargained when I was first interviewed at UCT as they initially wanted to give me a senior lectureship, just as Mafeje had done in 1990. At the time, the dean was trying to merge anthropology and sociology. I believe I was seen as a person who could strengthen that move. Even though I was not a head of department, my presence as someone not enslaved by any discipline, could make a difference.

SA At the time, there were discussions about merging sociology and anthropology?

LN There were discussions about it. Anthropology eventually merged into the school that is now disbanding, AXL [School for African and Gender Studies, Anthropology and Linguistics]. But no, anthropology and sociology did not and do not seem to like each other.

SA There is something you wrote in your 2020 article, 'The Ebb and Flow of Fortunes of African Studies', that really struck me. There is a quote by Nic van der Merwe, who remarks that 'the way the universities operate is by catching you unawares' [cited in Ntsebeza 2020, 363], a remark you indicated struck a chord with you given your own experience. When you say you agree with the remark, do you mean in terms of the knowledge debates and racial politics that frequently play out at UCT, or were you referring to something else?

LN What Van der Merwe told me was along the lines that I should be careful, that people you think are on your side might turn out not to be. I had personal experience of this when I was facilitating the AXL discussions. People pretended they were with me when I presented the intellectual project of the school. We had worked on this for days, and I thought I had a group of allies. At the faculty board meeting, I stood up and boldly presented the concept note and fielded the initial questions, but no one came to my support when more questions were fired at me. Each time I looked around, people that I trusted were looking away and avoiding making eye contact. I was on my own, I realised, and was left out to dry. I have never felt so isolated. No one would support me, except those who were raising questions, and they were suspicious rather than supportive. I have to say that they were not really that hostile. If I had been white, perhaps, they would have been rude. Maybe my skin colour and who I am saved me from people who had the capacity to be outright insulting. They were asking really searching questions. These were questions we had debated within the school, which I could not field on my own, which would have been better fielded if all were involved. However, I stood my ground.

Ultimately, members of the faculty accepted the idea of the school. I came out of that meeting with no feeling of victory: I was thinking about how people can let you down. From there on I thought that academics in general do not have a backbone and are caught up in gossipmongering, something I detest. From then on, I stopped going to faculty board meetings; I stopped going to Senate meetings.

SA You said you won, and African studies is still there but you still felt excluded and alienated within the institution?

LN Well, yes. I worked well with colleagues within CAS who helped build it. Horman Chitonge, now a full professor, joined me in my chair in 2009 as a postdoc; Nkululeko Mabandla was my student and he is now a lecturer in the Department of Sociology. Ari Sitas had joined the department in 2009 and was very supportive of the work we did in CAS. At one level, CAS gave me the space and freedom to work with people I could rely on, especially when I had made up my mind that things like Senate and committees were not helpful and were energy-sapping. At CAS, I felt liberated. The programmes we designed, the people I worked with, were exciting and energising. But I had to control and protect my space from external attacks. In that way, I isolated myself, but it is precisely in that isolation that I created good company and friendships. My relationships with students were superb. We continue to run weekly seminars. Since the outbreak of the Covid-19 pandemic, we have established a study group with postdoctoral students. We debate everything, anything. I love it – they love it.

SA That must be very fulfilling. Most good ideas just fizzle away. Some people refer to UCT, or higher education institutions in general, as sausage factories, saying that they are just trying to produce as many graduates or publications as they can, but without substance.

LN There are people who are part of that system either through their parents, or their connections. For them, UCT makes sense. People who are trying to fight, to swim against the stream, *they* are the ones who really get punished. I think you are punished if you come with an agenda of changing the institution. I do not have those ambitions. I just want a small piece of UCT, access to their resources, to use those resources and to do things that I like to do. So far, that has worked. People have asked me to apply to be a dean or deputy vice-chancellor, or some other position in university administration: I have not. I am no longer the director of CAS but I still hold the two chairs. We are still waiting to appoint a head of the school. I do not know what is going to happen next. There are likely to be changes.

SA Are you worried about losing what is there?

LN The research projects are not going to change. But taking African studies a level higher: no one is going to change it in the short term. They might change some of the things we were trying to introduce but it is not going to affect the research that I am doing. It is not going to affect the network of students that I have, or the postdoctoral students, or the projects. However, if you have all these projects, you need someone to coordinate them and propel CAS to another level. I am not sure if that is going to happen, but it would be a good thing.

SA Can I ask you about Fees Must Fall, and the future of the university? Do you recall the debates about the School for African and Gender Studies, Anthropology and Linguistics, which were being brought together as AXL? Which aspects of the debate do you feel are crucial for understanding epistemic change at UCT?

LN There were several debates. The African studies unit worked closely with CAS and held seminars, conferences. If you look at any of our events posters you will see the CAS logo and African studies. Other units had their own activities. But what I cannot talk about with confidence are the debates involving all four units as a school. I am very familiar with the process leading to the establishment of the school; I led the process. I was determined to ensure a result. And there was a result of sorts, which may or may not have been satisfactory.

When the school was established, even its name was a big issue. Some people did not want the term 'African studies' included. Anthropology, for example, felt that they needed to have a clear stake in the school. Naming it the 'School of African Studies' gave rise to heated debates. I thought this would be an acceptable name, especially as there was once a School of African Studies at UCT. With time, I understood why there were these fierce debates. One issue was that departments such as anthropology lost their status as departments and were now referred to as units within the school. They had been a fully-fledged department earlier but with the merger, they became submerged as a unit while the school had the status of a department.

My view was that we needed more time to think through the implications of the merger, one to three years to clarify the intellectual foundations. This was over and above the administrative issue of establishing a school, which is what the dean, Paula Ensor, was interested in. I argued that there should be an intellectual basis that would justify four units coming together and operating as a school. However, there was so much pressure and the dean had her own deadlines: she wanted the school to be established by 2012.

We ended up establishing a school formally without constituting an intellectual agenda. The agenda could have been that we did not commit ourselves to one idea, but that there could have been projects within the school. This was before decolonisation was uppermost in the discourse, but already the issue of the need for a thoroughgoing decolonisation project was arising in our debates. If you read my work [Ntsebeza 2012, 2020], I raise the failure to embark on decolonisation post-1994, well before Rhodes Must Fall and Fees Must Fall.

We are in Africa; UCT is in Africa. We should promote UCT as an African university, not just in geographical terms. It must be seen as an integral part of the intellectual life of Africa. I saw AXL as providing an opportunity for each of the units responding to the need for decolonising higher education at UCT, and beyond. We needed this vision.

What happened was that CAS was relaunched and the A. C. Jordan chair, which had been frozen in 1999, was re-advertised. I was very happy with these developments. I ended up being the director of CAS in June 2012, but the school needed its own head, notwithstanding that there was no money to appoint a director of the school. The decision was that one of the heads of the school should be the acting director for AXL. That became the history of AXL until Shahid Vawda was appointed to the Archie Mafeje chair in 2018.

In that period, I am not aware of any intellectual activity of note that was undertaken by the school as those four units working together. This is my perception of the school, and I may be wrong. I have not actively participated in the activities of the school since it was established in 2012. I had my own responsibilities in CAS.

The fact that the school disbanded did not surprise me. The fact that African studies and linguistics ended up in a partnership did not surprise me either; they collaborated on important intellectual endeavours. The undergraduate course in African studies was designed with the full participation of linguistics. Linguistics has been part of a committee that we set up to explore the possibility of a university-wide course in African studies. That was one of my very first projects when I became director of CAS.

In short, the units were very active in their own capacities, but we were not even able to have seminars together. We would organise a seminar and on the same day you would hear that anthropology or gender studies had their own seminar.

SA Is it because of a disciplinary clash of some sort, or in order to maintain individual and epistemic autonomy?

LN I think it is both, and I think personalities get in the way. There were so many things I thought we would do together with gender studies, for example, around the issue of land, the land reform programme, masculinity, and so on. The key thinking on the land question is currently dominated by men, both Black and white, including myself. I am very conscious of that. I failed to convince colleagues in gender studies that we needed to put a course together on land, where gender issues would be highlighted.

FEES MUST FALL AND DECOLONISATION

SA What changes are we seeing since the Fees Must Fall movement, the Black Academics Caucus, and all the conversations that are going on? And what do you make of the heated debates around the curriculum?

LN Some of these issues are coming up even in our conferences where people still complain that despite everything the curriculum is still Eurocentric, with one or two books by African scholars. In some instances, these texts are only prescribed to prevent complaints about the absence of African scholars in the curriculum. The issue of course is that Eurocentrism can be practised by both white and Black people. Colonialism divided Black people. There were the converts: people who believed in Western values and wanted to be like white people to be accepted as 'civilised'. So they could be Black, but their thinking is white. Fanon's [1967] title, *Black Skin, White Masks,* says it all. To open a book by Ntsebeza, for example, and *not* to see a difference between Ntsebeza's thinking and that of colonial-trained scholars, is just not good enough.

Still on the issue of the curriculum, we tend to overlook the power lecturers have. My view is that there are no major obstacles to lecturers prescribing texts they think are relevant, and deciding how they will teach. If you are a lecturer, you design your own course. Why should you teach according to Oxbridge approaches? What matters is quality, whether it meets a certain standard; and that standard is also up for debate. This is something that you ought to be able to defend in staff meetings, right up to faculty board level when we all look at course outlines to determine whether the course is worth the level at which it is pitched. It is easier now after Rhodes Must Fall, Fees Must Fall, the entire Fallist movement, than it was before.

We tried to do that in the African studies unit, in our undergraduate course. We brought senior people to teach there, the late Harry Garuba was one of them.[10] Students are introduced to the various ways in which Africa is understood. Some individuals in sociology and history are doing this. Our department, though, knows no disciplinary boundaries.

SA What about the tension between questions of academic freedom and curriculum transformation? Do you think the former is sometimes mobilised to prevent the latter?

LN I think there are cracks in the old edifice, among people who had authoritative voices in the past. We must exploit those cracks. If we do not use those openings to bring substantial changes, we are going to be defeated. People who were arrogant and vocal before Fees Must Fall are quiet now; they appear to be lying low. We must, however, ensure that by the time this is over, a new ethos, a new intellectual climate, is established. Those who are waiting for the tide to subside should realise that there are other actors now who cannot be wished away.

The space we have obtained is a fraught one. Things have become more complicated since the Fallist movement. The forces that had to retreat at the height of the Fallist movement might be getting stronger and are trying to gain lost ground. It is not going to be easy. But I think that the work that is done in African studies, linguistics and some departments such as sociology, history and anthropology, is equally gaining ground. You may find that in all these departments, indeed in other faculties too, there are individuals who are fighting battles, but in isolation. What I was trying to do in CAS was to identify those elements and create a hub. CAS is a place that does not have any claim to any of these disciplines: it is truly non-disciplinary. You could be a philosopher, or a mathematician, or a heart specialist. For example, we work with the Bongani Mayosi Programme in the health sciences. That was a breakthrough because it shows that African studies is not a departmental issue, it does not belong to a faculty, it cuts across the university and beyond.

SA You mentioned that you are looking at the history of the Unity Movement. It made me think of Crain Soudien's [2019] book, and about Isaac Tabata.

LN This is one of the projects that I am still involved in through the A. C. Jordan chair. I may no longer be the director, but I am still very much involved with the intellectual life of African studies. One of the key projects we are working on with Shahid Vawda is a project that looks at intellectual activity outside the academy. There are great intellectuals whose work is not known by most of us in the academy, simply because these texts are not 'peer-reviewed' in the standard academic fashion. This is how books by the likes of political activist, author and founder of the Unity Movement, Isaac Bangani Tabata, and others, are excluded, yet scholars such as Mafeje were trained by these intellectuals. Crain Soudien's [2019] book *Cape Radicals*, about a group of young, socialist intellectuals who formed the New Era Fellowship (NEF) project in Cape Town in 1937, highlights the importance of this intellectual tradition. Discussions are under way in CAS about the relationship between the university and other spaces. We hope colleagues in other departments will join us. They should join hands with CAS in this endeavour, from within their disciplines but also across disciplines. They do not have to be employed by CAS: they can come from any discipline and share what they are doing and, at the same time, listen to other academics from other disciplines, and talk together about their work. In this way, the project of transforming curricula at UCT can grow.

NOTES

1   These student activists went on to play important roles in 1980s anti-apartheid politics in South Africa, and in the development sector, government, academia and trade union organising after 1994.

2   Bill Freund was an influential economic, social, political and developmental historian who was professor emeritus at the University of KwaZulu-Natal in Durban at the time of his death in 2020.

3   Bantustans were a creation of the apartheid era, designed to establish separate 'homelands' for Black Africans. Assigned on arbitrary ethnic and linguistic lines by the South African government, there were ten 'self-governing' and mainly independent states set up on insufficient land in largely rural, impoverished and underdeveloped areas, between 1976 and 1994. Transkei and Ciskei were among those, in what is now the Eastern Cape.

4   A points system was in place at the time at most South African universities as a mechanism to score applicants based on school examination performance for admission to university programmes.

5   Steven Gelb, an economist by training, was associated with the Canadian anti-apartheid movement in the mid-1970s and early 1980s. He has been an academic, an economic advisor to trade unions, and a consultant employed in Thabo Mbeki's government.

6   After many years of close association with the trade union movement in Natal, Alec Erwin was elected as general secretary of FOSATU (Federation of South African Trade Unions) in 1979; in the following decade, he occupied key executive positions in other major unions; became a deputy minister of finance in Nelson Mandela's presidency; minister of trade and industry, and subsequently minister of public enterprises in Thabo Mbeki's government.

7   Mike Morris is a unionist and was actively involved in supporting the labour movement during apartheid. Morris has also held academic positions in many countries.

8   The history of the de facto civil war that played out in KwaZulu-Natal and the East
     Rand in the late 1980s and early 1990s is well documented. Nearly 21 000 people
     died in that violence in KwaZulu and Natal (Bonnin 2007, 21). Factors ranging from
     the contributions of youth membership, divergent ideological and social visions, and
     the insertion of military capacity by the apartheid state, all contributed to the conflict
     between Inkatha Freedom Party (IFP), Azanian People's Organisation (AZAPO) and
     United Democratic Front (UDF) cadres (Sitas 1992; Bonnin 2007).

9   A historical archaeologist, Martin Hall developed interest and expertise in higher
     education management, serving at various points in his career as director of CAS;
     director of the Multimedia Education Group and deputy vice-chancellor at UCT (2002–
     2008, 2020–2021); as well as vice-chancellor of the University of Salford, Manchester
     (2009–2014). Hall is currently an emeritus professor at the Graduate School of
     Business, UCT. Literary studies scholar Brenda Cooper has a long history of association
     with UCT and the CAS. Cooper was the director of the centre from 1992–2008. She is
     currently an emeritus professor of CAS.

10   Harry Olúdáre Garuba (1958–2020) was a Nigerian poet and professor of English and
     African studies at UCT (Omoyele 2020).

REFERENCES

Bank, Andrew and Vuyiswa Swana. 2013. '"Speaking from Inside": Archie Mafeje, Monica
     Wilson and the Co-Production of Langa: A Study of Social Groups in an African
     Township'. In *Inside African Anthropology: Monica Wilson and Her Interpreters*, edited
     by Andrew Bank and Leslie J Bank. The International African Library. Cambridge:
     Cambridge University Press. doi: 10.1017/CBO9781139333634.009.

Bonnin, Deborah. 2007. 'Space, Place and Identity: Political Violence in Mpumalanga
     Township, KwaZulu-Natal, 1987–1993'. PhD diss., University of KwaZulu-Natal.

Fanon, Frantz. 1967. *Black Skin, White Masks*. New York, NY: Grove Press.

Hall, Martin. 1998. '"Bantu Education"? A Reply to Mahmood Mamdani'. *Social Dynamics*
     24 (2): 86–92. https://doi.org/10.1080/02533959808458651.

Hendricks, Fred. 2008. 'The Mafeje Affair: The University of Cape Town and Apartheid'.
     African Studies 67 (3): 423–451. https://doi.org/10.1080/00020180802505061.

Mafeje, Archie. 1992. *In Search of an Alternative: A Collection of Essays on Revolutionary
     Theory and Politics*. Harare: SAPES Books.

Mamdani, Mahmood. 1996. *Citizen and Subject: Contemporary Africa and the Legacy of Late
     Colonialism*. Princeton, NJ: Princeton University Press.

Mamdani, Mahmood. 1998. 'Is African Studies to Be Turned into a New Home for Bantu Education at UCT?' *Social Dynamics* 24 (2): 63–75. https://doi.org/10.1080/02533959808458649.

Ntsebeza, Lungisile. 2012. 'African Studies at UCT: An Overview.' In *African Studies in the Post-Colonial University*, edited by Thandabantu Nhlapo and Harry Garuba, 1–20. Cape Town: University of Cape Town in association with the Centre for African Studies.

Ntsebeza, Lungisile. 2014. 'The Mafeje and the UCT Saga: Unfinished Business?' *Social Dynamics* 40 (2): 274–288. https://doi.org/10.1080/02533952.2014.946254.

Ntsebeza, Lungisile. 2020. 'The Ebb and Flow of the Fortunes of African Studies at the University of Cape Town: An Overview'. *Social Dynamics* 46 (2): 356–372. https://doi.org/10.1080/02533952.2020.1815335.

Omoyele, Idowu. 2020. 'Harry Garuba Obituary'. *The Guardian*, 7 May 2020. https://www.theguardian.com/books/2020/may/07/harry-garuba-obituary.

Sitas, Ari. 1992. 'The Making of the "Comrades Movement" in Natal 1985–91'. *Journal of Southern African Studies* 18 (3): 629–641. https://doi.org/10.1080/03057079208708329.

Soudien, Crain. 2019. *The Cape Radicals: Intellectual and Political Thought of the New Era Fellowship 1930s–1960s*. Johannesburg: Wits University Press.

University of Cape Town. 2022. 'Celebrating the Bongani Mayosi Legacy'. 28 May 2022. http://www.mayosilegacy.uct.ac.za/.

THE AFRICAN GENDER INSTITUTE: A JOURNEY OF PLACEMAKING

KEALEBOGA MASE RAMARU

This chapter is a multigenerational account born of three feminists' reflections on our respective and collective journeys of placemaking at the African Gender Institute (AGI) at the University of Cape Town (UCT). The feminists in question are Jane Bennett, Yaliwe Clarke and myself, Kealeboga Mase Ramaru, all of whom have been located in the AGI at various times and have contributed to the political project of the space.[1] The reflection is based on virtual discussions conducted with Yaliwe and Jane, who shared their reflections of journeying through the AGI, as well as my own personal accounts of placemaking in the AGI. This piece synthesises our different accounts to offer insights into the AGI's history. It describes what it means to make and inhabit a place that mobilises feminist thought, activism and solidarity while contending with institutions and individuals who question the legitimacy of its work.

The AGI's journey at UCT has been dynamic. Too often, African feminist work on the African continent is co-opted into narratives of Western feminism or referred to as an import from other (usually Western) spaces. It is hence important to retell its history. In this chapter, Jane Bennett (AGI director from 2002 to 2016) recounts how the AGI became a node for conversations on pan-African feminism in the 1990s, around the time the institute was founded, and served as a space for feminists on the continent to collectively build an archive of African feminist knowledge. She recalls vibrant conversations in which the institute engaged through the journal *Feminist Africa* and the Gender and Women's Studies (GWS) listserv, an email-based forum, which were instrumental in growing continental and diasporic networks of pan-Africanist feminists, and which facilitated access to scholarly publications and learning resources. The story of the challenges and changes the AGI underwent due to limited institutional support, shrinking funding and its fight for survival are central to both Bennett's and Clarke's accounts. Interestingly, that fight for survival led them (together with other feminist colleagues) to produce an academic programme which has been thriving for many years. Yaliwe Clarke (AGI director from 2017 and current incumbent) also maps the shifts in leadership and strategies that AGI adopted in the last five years, as the institution itself entered a particularly eventful period with the intensification of student movements.

I reflect on this part of the AGI's recent history as I share my own experience of being a student and, later, a member of staff at the institute. Drawing from the 2015 student movement moment, this section of the chapter discusses how gender studies and the AGI's academic programme were instrumental in giving the students a language to inform the three critical pillars of the movement: Black feminism, pan-Africanism and Black Consciousness. This section also evokes the AGI's more recent work (since 2018 through the Queer Feminist Film Festival (#QFFF), the conversation series Dreaming Feminist Futures, and the Global Grace Research Project, and the ways in which these programmes strengthened the institute's connection to feminist organisers, activists, scholars and practitioners in the region.

Finally, the chapter documents the AGI's first director, Amina Mama's (2020) reflections on her journey at the AGI and the development of the journal *Feminist Africa* as a key publication that galvanised the thought and work of African feminist scholars outside of mainstream academic publishing. Mama (2020) argues that mainstream publishing 'was not suitable' (and was arguably closed off) 'to the circulation of knowledge on the continent, no matter how much research was carried out' (cited by Bennett 2022). The AGI's epistemological framing was unapologetically pan-African and feminist, two schools of thought often met with great unease, especially when brought together like this. The AGI's political work should be considered decolonial because it pushed back against an academy that has historically invalidated African and feminist perspectives. It demonstrates that embracing the knowledge and experiences of African women who build communities through activism, care work, written and oral histories and art, is valid and deserves to be engaged with and cited more broadly.

ORIGINS OF THE AFRICAN GENDER INSTITUTE

The AGI was founded in 1995 under the leadership of then deputy vice-chancellor Dr Mamphela Ramphele under a mandate from the pan-African Forum for African Women Educationalists (FAWE). The institute was initiated, in part, to facilitate greater employment equity and make more positions available to women at UCT. The hope was that the institute would become an important place for women from the African continent to convene, share ideas, write for publication and build solidarity. The space was envisaged as a soft-funded scholarly hub that would bring together women from the African continent, from a range of disciplines. While gender at the time was narrowly defined within a binary framework, centring on women (arguably, cisgender and mostly heterosexual women's experiences), the space was necessary to grapple with the intellectual, political and cultural realities of women on the continent and connect their varied struggles.

In 1995, South Africa was transitioning out of apartheid and most of the political discussions in the country were inward-looking. The skewed relationship between South Africa and other African countries has a complex history. Many other African countries achieved independence years before South Africa's transition to democracy and were not necessarily occupied with the same political questions and challenges. Regardless of the scepticism expressed about South Africa's position and political moment, the Rockefeller Foundation supported the institute and the establishment of the associates' programme.

The associates' programme played a formative role in linking South African struggles with continental ones. It was a scholarly structure that attracted feminists and gender activists, practitioners and scholars from across Africa who were interested in researching and documenting knowledge(s) from the continent. The programme was open to all African women from professional backgrounds. It became a space to share ideas, develop new tools, share strategies, and produce research and publications that contributed to the archive of African women's and African feminist experiences on the continent. The programme, however, required participants to produce work in English only. This limited the participation of women from non-anglophone countries. The associates engaged in various workshops, exchanges and networking sessions with other feminists and gender practitioners, who shared their skills and knowledge and trained different groups on gender-related issues that they were grappling with in their respective organisations and communities. Both Mama and Bennett played key roles in the associates' programme. Mama extended her network of feminists on the continent by supporting the recruitment of participants, particularly those in West Africa and East Africa. Bennett offered her expertise through the development of the Sexual Harassment Network, which functioned primarily in southern Africa. The associates' programme continued to contribute to the growing community while the Ford Foundation supported this work financially.

The AGI's commitment, especially under Mama's leadership as the institute's chair from 1999, was to create a network and establish links between feminist work, thinking and organising on the African continent. Bennett argues that this was particularly important since UCT had limited continental links. Mama was hugely influential in building the AGI's continental identity and extending its reach because of her vast networks and connections. Her vision and energy were instrumental in transitioning the AGI from a space that engaged with feminists only through an associates' programme, to a space with deep connections to various continental networks of feminist communities, which constantly engaged with each other through the GWS listserv and *Feminist Africa*.

FEMINIST AFRICA AND THE CHALLENGE TO THE KNOWLEDGE 'ARCHIVE'

Feminist Africa is a continental gender studies journal that provides a platform for feminist intellectual and activist research, dialogue and strategy (Mama 2020). Bennett (2022) describes the work of *Feminist Africa* as a decolonial practice because of its intentional focus on voices from the continent, and its prioritising of the voices of African feminist scholars and activists. First published in 2002, the journal was located at the AGI. The institute provided administrative and fiscal support for the journal while the editorial functions remained the responsibility of the editorial collective comprised of members from different parts of the continent. The AGI's input in the curatorial process of the journal was mostly through Bennett's and Mama's (before her departure in 2012) roles as members of the editorial collective. The journal produced 22 issues in its time at the AGI.

Initially, *Feminist Africa* was organised through workshops and collective learning spaces, and different communities of people convened in various African countries to engage in broad thematic areas such as culture, sexuality, militarism, higher education and feminism. This work was important not only because of the opportunity for knowledge sharing and building an archive of pan-African feminist knowledge(s) across the continent, but also presented an epistemic challenge to traditional archives that were obsessed with mainstream, often Western-centric knowledge, with no interest in engaging with knowledge(s) from the African continent. Bennett describes it as a 'commitment to an ungrounded university' (Bennett 2022) where knowledge lived within communities and movements and not within a single institution.

The impact of *Feminist Africa* is undoubtedly essential as an archive of pan-African feminist knowledge, thinking and scholarship that exists beyond universities and bureaucratised institutions. It presents movements, communities, individual activists and grassroots networks as keepers of knowledge that should be shared and available for all people to learn from, regardless of institutional location and economic access. Hence, the publication is open access, in keeping with the principle of distributing knowledge and research outputs online, free of access charges.

GENDER STUDIES UNDERGRADUATE AND POSTGRADUATE TEACHING PROGRAMMES

The gender studies academic teaching programme developed much later than the AGI itself. The teaching programme has a fascinating history since it was an unintended consequence of the institute's precarious institutional location. In its early years, the AGI was primarily focused on building a research community and corpus. The institute was one of several soft-funded groupings and research units at the university, with no intention of developing a teaching programme. Growing pressure from the university to develop teaching programmes for continued support meant that institutes like the AGI needed to expand their scope to survive and secure their place at the university. Bennett started the first undergraduate teaching programme and, in the wake of its success, a postgraduate programme followed, initiated by

Mama. The postgraduate programme focused on gender and the politics of development and militarisation. Despite limited resources, the institute was able to bring on several other scholars and academics, including Elaine Salo, Adelene Africa and Helen Scanlon, as teaching staff.[2] The academic programme allowed the AGI's 'real' work to continue, that of advancing Africa's gender and women studies network. The academic programme continues to grow and has seen tremendous success, as well as some changes in recent years. In 2021, the teaching programme and research institute were merged again after the disbanding of the AXL (School of African and Gender Studies, Anthropology and Linguistics). The department has also changed the name of the programme to African Feminist Studies (AFS) to reflect the deepening feminist scholarship reflected in the curriculum.

CHALLENGING TERRAINS AND NEW TRANSITIONS

The community and solidarity the AGI managed to build on the continent with African feminists were not quite replicated at UCT. Bennett (2022) and Clarke (2022) both reflect on the absence of support from feminist scholars at UCT, especially some white feminists, as well as from faculty leadership. Many UCT feminist academics felt marginalised by a space that foregrounded pan-Africanism, and by continental feminist politics that intentionally carved out spaces for Black African women. Many feminist researchers at UCT felt that the AGI was exclusionary and did not represent 'all' feminists, resulting in a lack of solidarity and even antagonism.

Faculty leaders who regarded the institute's work as too ideological and un- or mis-aligned with what they saw as the academic project, similarly failed to support it or to make available resources that were extended to similar initiatives. Bennett (2022) argues that the lack of institutional backing put a great strain on Mama's ability to mobilise institutional support for the AGI. This, together with a combination of other factors, which Clarke characterises as the intersection of patriarchy, misogyny, racism and isolation, informed Mama's decision to take unpaid leave from UCT from 2008 to 2011 (Clarke 2022). Mama officially resigned from her role as chair of the AGI, and left UCT entirely in 2012.

Bennett took over as director of the AGI after Mama's departure. In 2012, after nearly four years of discussion, the Faculty of Humanities had launched the AXL. Faculty leadership had perceived the AGI, the Centre for African

Studies (CAS), anthropology and linguistics as being too small to function as separate entities, and sought to merge them into a single school offering interdisciplinary research and teaching opportunities. These different entities now all became units within the school, permitted to have their own websites and teaching programmes but administratively functioning as a co-constituted department. The formation of the school required the AGI to separate its research and teaching programmes, the latter coming under the banner of gender studies. In many ways, however, this separation was more bureaucratic than epistemic or political. The teaching and research programmes continued to challenge the university's limited engagement with and promotion of knowledge(s) rooted on the African continent. The academic programme maintained its focus on questions of decoloniality, power, equity, justice and building institutions that reflected the diversity of African experiences and knowledge(s). The AGI and CAS remained soft-funded research groupings with little institutional standing during this time.

The AGI and gender studies team at the time comprised Bennett and Clarke, and both were severely stretched. They needed to reconfigure the institute's programming in a climate where funding was scarce and they had little institutional support. *Feminist Africa* and the Sexual Harassment Network, which later became the Young Women's Leadership Project (YWLP), were the only projects that were able to continue, as both were funded and managed by feminists outside of the AGI, or by part-time AGI staff. Due to the financial, staffing and capacity issues that the AGI faced, *Feminist Africa* could no longer be convened in the same participatory way as before and, in 2019, the journal moved out of the AGI due to a decision taken by the journal's editorial team after a meeting in Legon, Ghana, in 2017. The team was of the opinion that *Feminist Africa* should be moved to another institution on the continent with more capacity to dedicate to the journal. The decision was also made in honour of the founding agreement of the journal, which encouraged the rotation of editorial and publishing responsibility among different feminist academic institutions on the continent. This decision is known as the Yiri Consensus: it was a disappointment for the institute and the vibrant continental connections it had forged, especially as YWLP was focused more narrowly on the Southern African Development Community (SADC) region. The AGI thus became a regional or local feminist node rather than a continental one.

THE SHIFTING POLITICAL LANDSCAPE AND RECONFIGURING THE SPACE

In 2015, student movements such as Rhodes Must Fall (RMF) and Fees Must Fall (FMF) began organising around the idea of a decolonised university. The student movement posed crucial questions about the kinds of knowledges celebrated in African universities, including UCT. In addition to the challenges they posed to public universities in South Africa, RMF and FMF also developed an internal politics that challenged historical cultural exclusion by claiming Black feminist politics as part of its political identity (Ramaru 2017). This framing was important because it placed the labour and contributions of Black women and queer students front and centre.

The decision to include Black feminism as a pillar of RMF, which also informed some formations of FMF, was championed by students and scholars who were engaged in the gender studies department and the AGI. The vibrant and often challenging debates in the classroom and discussion spaces, such as the African Feminists: Talking the Walk series (a seminar series for feminists within and outside of the academy to share their research and intellectual activist work) and many other platforms initiated by gender studies and the AGI, provided students with an outlet to discuss political and epistemic standpoints, share their lived experiences and gain language that described their experiences. The academic programmes and teaching provided a language for and understanding of what feminist organising meant in settings that were historically patriarchal, heteronormative, cisnormative and sexist. Platforms such as African Feminists: Talking the Walk, Mama's seminal 2015 presentation, titled 'Decolonising Knowledges 101: In the Master's House' (Mama 2015), and the YWLP, provided a community to workshop thoughts, share knowledge and build solidarity with other feminists who were similarly invested in building networks of care and support. The AGI and gender studies also became, and remain, a safe landing for students who were engaged with a university that continues to shrink the available spaces for honest, meaningful engagement on issues relating to decolonisation.

LOCALISING THE CONTINENTAL DISCUSSIONS

In 2017, Clarke took over the directorship at the AGI. She came into the leadership of the AGI at the height of the FMF movement and during a time when the university was buzzing with conversations about decoloniality and transformation. Under this new directorship, the challenge was how to reconvene structures such as the institute's advisory board, and how to redefine the AGI after two decades of holding space in an institution that was often unsupportive of its vision. According to Clarke, 'the time was about re-evaluating the political work of the AGI and understanding itself in the broader university context ... [furthermore] the institute's identity had [also] evolved from its earlier political work' (Clarke 2022).

During this period (2017–2020), the AGI's work began to focus more on building relationships with local activists, organisers, academics and scholars who worked in South Africa and the SADC region. The Dreaming Feminist Futures conversation series (Oxfam South Africa 2018) provided building blocks. The series brought together over 500 feminists from across the country, the continent and the diaspora to share ideas on the future of feminist politics post-FMF. Together they sought to envision a decolonised space and community.

The institute continued its work with the YWLP, which sustained the AGI's southern African connections through cooperation with six other universities in the region (UCT, University of Botswana, University of Zimbabwe, Eduardo Mondlane University in Mozambique, University of the Witwatersrand and the University of Namibia). All members were activist scholars engaged in action research on sexual health and reproductive rights. Other projects that bridged the divide between grassroots organising and the AGI as a knowledge hub were the QFFF and the Global Grace-supported Sex Workers Theatre. Both these projects fostered collaborations and partnerships with local non-governmental organisations (NGOs) and grassroots movements like the Triangle Project, the Sex Worker Education and Advocacy Taskforce (SWEAT) and Free Gender, to explore the use of performance art and film as mediums for dialogue and knowledge-making. These projects successfully expanded the AGI's local and regional networks.

As noted earlier, in 2019 the AGI ceased to be the institutional home of *Feminist Africa*. The decision to move the journal was taken at a 2017 workshop that included the editorial collective of *Feminist Africa*, the University of Ghana and the African Women's Development Fund (AWDF) in Accra, Ghana. The Yiri Consensus, named after the workshop venue, Yiri Lodge, in Legon, Ghana, was the collective's decision to relocate and re-establish the journal in a 'favorable intellectual and institutional home' (Mama 2020, 159). The Institute of African Studies (IAS), Accra, took over the responsibility of housing the next phase of publishing *Feminist Africa*, while the journal's archive (2002–2017) is hosted by the AGI and IAS.

FINDING ITS PLACE: THE AGI NOW

In 2019, the Faculty of Humanities reviewed AXL. The faculty resolved to dissolve the school on the grounds that the different units had grown substantially and could function as separate departments. The dissolution was finalised in 2021. For the institute, this has meant an institutional and political realignment with the broader university academic programme. The Gender Studies Department and the AGI had embarked on a curriculum review process in 2016, engaging in a series of talks, workshops and knowledge exchange spaces with feminist organisers, academics and students. Recently, the academic programme changed its name to African Feminist Studies, reflecting both the current thinking and political energy of the department and the institute, and the changing political climate within the university and the student body. This represents a return to the core values and politics of the AGI and the African Feminist Studies programme, presenting an opportunity to shape a vision for the future that is radically feminist in its ethos and determinedly pan-Africanist in its scope.

NOTES

1   The interviews with Bennett and Clarke used for the development of this chapter were conducted by Ruchi Chaturvedi, Amrita Pande and Kealeboga Ramaru over a number of months throughout 2022 in Cape Town, South Africa. The opinions shared do not purport to represent the vast experiences of all the people who engaged with and contributed to the intellectual grounding of the AGI.

2   Over the last two decades, Elaine Salo emerged as a highly regarded and much-loved feminist anthropologist activist who went on to teach at the University of Pretoria and the University of Delaware, USA. Salo passed away in 2016. Adelene Africa is trained in clinical psychology, feminist theory on the criminalisation of women, and is an expert in feminist and social pedagogies. Helen Scanlon is the convener of the Justice and Transformation Programme in the Department of Political Studies at UCT.

REFERENCES

Bennett, Jane. 2022. Interview by Ruchi Chaturvedi, Amrita Pande and Kealeboga Ramaru. 27 June 2022, Cape Town.

Clarke, Yaliwe. 2022. Interviews by Ruchi Chaturvedi, Amrita Pande and Kealeboga Ramaru. March–October 2022, Cape Town.

Mama, Amina. 2015. 'Decolonising Knowledges 101: In the Master's House'. Filmed by Wandile Kasibe, 6 May 2015 at Centre for African Studies, UCT. Video, 1:38. https://www.youtube.com/watch?v=pXoisspygxU.

Mama, Amina. 2020. '*Feminist Africa*: A Pan-African Feminist Publication for the 21st Century'. *Storia delle Donne* 15 (15): 141–163. https://doi.org/10.13128/sd-9044.

Oxfam South Africa. 2018. 'Dreaming Feminist Futures'. Filmed 21–23 March 2018 in Cape Town. YouTube Video, 6:55. https://www.youtube.com/watch?v=-S1UbDpdEkg.

Ramaru, Kealeboga. 2017. 'Feminist Reflections on the Rhodes Must Fall Movement'. *Feminist Africa* 22: 89–97.

THE ETHIC OF RECONCILIATION AND A NEW CURRICULUM

0

ARI SITAS

n 2007, I argued to some applause the vitality of an ethic of reconciliation. Having served in the South African transition's peace processes after Nelson Mandela chastised us all to throw our guns into the sea in 1990, and, fresh from an encounter with Cyprus' failed attempt at reunification, I penned a slim volume on the ethic, its moral and philosophical dimensions, and its sources (Sitas 2007).

The Cyprus debacle started with Djelal Kadir, the Iowa-based pundit and editor of the *World Literature Review*, and me being invited to share a platform on reunification and reconciliation to mark the expected victory of Transcendence after the Annan referendum. Both of us were of Cypriot extraction but with enough distance from the everyday to play some constructive role, people felt. Alas, we arrived a week after the United Nations (UN) secretary general Kofi Annan plan was defeated by Greek Cypriots in a volatile electoral atmosphere. As is now known, Turkish Cypriots voted overwhelmingly for the plan. I remained on the 'scene', as it were, to coordinate a study on the prospects of reconciliation, and continued thereafter as part of the ever unsuccessful and often quixotic reunification initiatives.

The reception of the volume, *Ethic of Reconciliation* (Sitas 2007), found keen audiences in Palestine, in Colombia and on the rest of the African continent.

I found myself on panels that brought together Israeli and Palestinian, Greek and Turkish Cypriot, Rwandese and Congolese thinkers, all discussing aspects of the book. Before long, *Current Sociology* organised a special issue (Sitas 2011) on its basic tenets. However critical, all commentators found some importance and some resonance in and through my arguments.

A decade later, radical circles in South Africa, in the midst of protests and of largely Black student insurgency, thought poorly of my contention. The very same arguments were met with gruff and brazen responses: take your truth and reconciliation commissions (TRCs), your Mandela sell-outs and your pacifist nonsense, and chuck them in some sea. A sense of this energy is conveyed in the 2018 collection that attempted to bring the voices of the Black student insurgency together (Anonymous 2018).[1] The consensus that it conveyed was this: violence was the inevitable and necessary condition for things to fall – colonialism, settler racism, capitalism, patriarchy. The insurgent's violence was nothing compared to the symbolic and epistemic violence experienced by Black people and by Black children even in a post-apartheid South Africa. The Black student participants of Rhodes Must Fall and Fees Must Fall argued in seminars that such thoughts of reconciliation belonged to a museum, and the very museum itself belonged in the trash can, together with the colonial idea that spawned it. Frantz Fanon (1974), Steve Biko (1978) and Jacques Derrida (2001) were rolled onto the stage to announce that the native's violence was cathartic and that 'forgiveness' was impossible, a religious folly said Derrida, the French doyen of deconstruction of the Abrahamic tradition.

The heated exchanges were mostly extra-curricular and were only brought to the seminar room because of student insurgency. I would like to call them 'contingent' rather than substantive however much in retrospect they could be seen as fundamental, and that they had changed ways of thinking and being. The educator's task surely was to take a leap towards the future by making them substantive by, in short, creating a transformed curriculum. I will return to ways of doing that at the end of the piece, and remain now with the idea of 'contingency'. In my way of thinking, such a contingency involves a rupture in the relationship between lecturer and student, the taught and the learnt, and the process of teaching and learning.

These ruptures are brought about by the energies unleashed by movements within and outside institutions: the Durban worker strikes created such ruptures at the University of Durban-Westville and the University of Natal in 1973;

the independence of Mozambique in 1975; the Soweto uprising was animating such exchanges in 1976, and facilitated the spread of Black Consciousness ideas; the 1990 'Knowledge Affair' at the University of Natal around academic exclusions; in short, every academic institution had its own unique experience of such irruptions. A new cycle of them started at the University of Cape Town in 2011 when African studies students started a protest surge around the proposed closure of the Centre for African Studies (CAS). It took another four years before these protests turned into the Rhodes Must Fall movement. The challenges created a context for contingent responses. During the first year or so of the protests, the word 'reconciliation' was taboo. By 2016, the very students started demanding a truth and reconciliation process, and insisted on forms of pardon and restorative justice ideals.

In response to my critics, I first retorted that the ethic I presented was not brewed out of a pacifist recipe book but out of a deep historical lesson fresh from the experience of liberation movements, and often very violent struggles and civil wars, since the 1970s. It was not something derived from a Platonic idea of moral perfection once we ascended from our cave, but something fragile, proximate, emergent.

To the students' reminders that violence was the midwife of history, I claimed that we are sufficiently well read to know that Marx declared all that, and even in *Capital* we read keenly that 'force is the midwife of every old society which is pregnant with a new one' (1986, 916). But, I returned, look at what kind of creature such midwifery had produced. The violent entanglement that brought the modern world system into place through European foraging, settlement, enslavement and colonisation and its resistances later, have brought us by the late twentieth century into a normative cul-de-sac. You could no longer blast yourself into moral rectitude. There is a potential Syria in all of us.

Of course, the arguments were quite complex, and emotive to boot: students claimed that it was the readiness to die for a cause that was cathartic but admitted finally that such readiness could be shared with non-violent resistance and militancy. Some insisted that Fanon had to be right and that the killing of whites would bring a sense of power back from degrading powerlessness. When pressed about the limits of such readiness, they admitted that they differed from the idea of a kamikaze or a suicide bomber as such forms of self-sacrifice were 'foreign' to them. Even though one's death could strictly not be experienced as cathartic, the self-sacrifice was a cathartic moment for the collective. Indeed, that was not untrue: the role of such funerals in the South African struggle have been noted and so had their symbolic overcoming of death, the recreation in such gatherings of the spirit of the *amadelakufa*, the spirit of the death-defiers, emerged through the threnodies and martial songs stronger than ever. Yet, the new generation had no memory of the insurgency of the 1970s and the 1980s, the counter-revolution, the civil war, but shared an imagined narrative of what it ought to have been.

What did I argue then? It was quite simple: 'one of the most significant phenomena of the recent history of our species [was] the emergence and con-solidation of an "ethic of reconciliation"' (Sitas 2007, 9). Since the Second World War and decolonisation mainly of Africa, gradually at first but with remarkable speed since the 1970s, and with a breathtaking acceleration after the collapse of the Berlin Wall in 1989, its resonance has been deeply felt (Sitas 2007, 9). I argued too that the ethic was not about TRCs – they may be an aspect of it, but that depended on context and issue. I argued that its features were three: that the 'Other' (however defined) was not surplus and therefore s/he was not eliminable – and if such an Other was defined so due to 'inherent' and 'immutable' attributes, such a notion would be racist as well; that the Other (again racism might be part of the definition) was not a reified thing, a potential beast of burden to be compelled into servitude, an object, and therefore s/he was non-enslaveable and non-exploitable; and that the Other, finally, was not a 'non' (as in the 'non-Us') and therefore is non-ex-cludable or marginalisable from social norms or rights despite gender, race, sexuality, ethnicity or caste-like group (Sitas 2007, 11).

Furthermore, the very 'Us' that created so many regimes of derogation and Other-ness was a product of regrettable historical constructions based on false essentialisms. It did not exist *ab initio* – we have all been converted to Christianity or Islam, we have all been inscribed into the Vedas, we have been Us-ed into collective ensembles as much as we have Us-ed ourselves. Even in the most progressive of anti-colonial nationalisms which were a genuine search after their rejection of the Other-ness defined through the category of the 'Native', inaugurating a search for a move from Other-ness to 'selfhood', the borders of the nation-state were always in question. Any careful reading of history shows how the 227 geopolitical barbwire borders that enshrine the Us in our contemporary world do not reflect the boundaries of an essence but are absurdities enshrining interests and power. If you doubt that, look carefully at the work of archaeologists and geneticists on human dispersions and diasporas, and situate for yourself the difference between the antiquity claimed by nationalists versus the emergence of nationalism and the nation-state.

I argued therefore that an ethic of reconciliation was as necessary for the life of social ensembles within borders but across them too. It is not only the necessary lens to stare across the India–Pakistan border, the Cypriot barbwire, the Palestinian wall, or Trump border walls and the well-measured response by Mexican president Andres Manuel Lopez Obrador, but also about deep historic rends within the contours of the wire. I added that any ethic of this kind needs the self-understanding by social ensembles of a past that was regrettable and it needed to shove away its closeness to any imperial idea, from Cyprus to Patagonia, and Vladivostok to New Mexico, because we are *all* to the last one of us, *Others*. It is no longer plausible to construct a claim 'that the right to subjective freedom, is the pivot and the centre of the difference between antiquity and modern times' as Hegel did, calling it both 'Christian and the universal effective principle of a new form of civilization' (Hegel 1975, 84). In short, the pivot and the centre of Eurocentrism: it is over.

For a while the borders were deemed an anachronism: what with the currents of globalisation, the new digital flows, the openness of markets, the transnational corporations (TNCs), the network society, the global civil society, the transnational sense of cosmopolitanism, the global social movements (Cohen and Rai 2000). All seemed fine in theory until Cancun 2003.

Giovanni Arrighi, in his *Adam Smith in Beijing* (2007), noticed the shift that caused the fallout early, describing it as a new Bandung, and found its sources in the economic rise of China:

What is truly stunning is the lack of awareness – in the South no less than in the North – of the extent to which the monetarist counterrevolution of the early 1980s has backfired, creating conditions more favourable than ever for a new Bandung to bring into existence the commonwealth of civilisations that Smith envisioned long ago … For a new Bandung can do what the old could not: it can mobilize and use the global market as an instrument of equalization of South-North power relations. The foundations of the old Bandung were strictly political-ideological and as such, very easily destroyed by the monetarist counter-revolution. The foundations of the Bandung that may be emerging now, in contrast are primarily economic and as such much more solid (Arrighi 2007, 384–385).

Why was Cancun in 2003 at all relevant? The World Trade Organization (WTO) talks had failed (Deutsche Welle 2003) and Brazil, India and South Africa found themselves the unofficial spokespeople of the developing world. Economic globalisation met its first serious hiccup. Before long, China and Russia found themselves discussing the possibility of a growth alliance, titled BRIC. China insisted that South Africa should be invited, and BRICS became history. What brought these countries together was not Goldman Sachs but the discovery that economic globalisation was to work only in the interests of the dominant economies of the so-called West. The reason why these countries sought each other was that they had bought into an open world economy because their economies had reached peculiar internal limits that could benefit from export-led growth. They were all already industrial societies and regional powerhouses. There was also a sense that such relationships should move beyond the Washington Consensus, and beyond the 'economic sphere'. Difference was seen as a virtue. Equality of voice was seen as a non-negotiable principle. They were, by 2019, in a formal reciprocity, something like: 'I am not satisfied with what you say or do but it is within our common interest to enhance each other's and our region's development.' There is not only a reconfiguration of the world economy but also a realignment of thinking. Roberto Unger's (Rathbone 2014) put-down that it has unfortunately been about 'compromises', 'qualifications' and 'evasions' rather than helping one another develop sturdy national projects, was inaccurate. Speaking to the *Financial Times*, he chastised the failure of BRICS 'intelligentsias' and its 'power elites'. This failure was due to a timidity, a 'servility' and a 'submissiveness' to the West, a kind of colonial mentality. These are serious criticisms but if they are true, and some of them are becoming true due to the new Indian and Brazilian governments, this has occurred despite intentions. Somewhere in there, fragments of the ethic survive, at least in the serious emphasis on the methodologies of achieving a pacific world.

I did not make a claim that this ethic was dominant or hegemonic but simply that it was emergent: I even created a neologism that it was 'ideomorphic', stretching the Greek language to some new limit. It is about a value system that may only gain real traction if other transformations occur in the socio-economy, in gender, in voice. It was not even dominant in South Africa where it had a very solid innings during the Mandela stewardship. It was a post-1970s phenomenon and its sources were fascinating. It belonged to no party or specific movement but that it should start defining what kind of a moral code ought to be guiding international, intranational and local relations.

The response to my detractors was that they were duped into thinking that a Fanonian catharsis through violence, or an armed struggle, was any longer the path to emancipated humanity, and there was no virtue in arming up for 'just wars' or the defence of some home and hearth. Even though the military defeat of fascism was a major step for our known world, it drove it underground, ever ready to re-emerge with vigour. It has.

Listen, I pleaded, we had learnt the hard way on the continent. This Africa too was a racial construction simplifying and reducing the sheer diversity of the continent into a singular tribal mush. For example, look at both the diversity and similarities within and across the 17 countries that constitute West Africa, but also look at their commonalities due to deep historical connections. What was and is the logic of arming that very diversity? Mauritania is not Senegal, the Fulani pastoralists are not the Wolof, the liberation movement in Guinea-Bissau (Cabral) was not the same as the Azikiwe-led nationalism in Nigeria, and Sierra Leone is not Ghana, Ali Farka Touré is not Fela Kuti. The borders were arbitrary, the forms of indirect rule were complex but the fact remains, cultural formations traversed national boundaries. Whatever the complexities, the Biafran war in Nigeria (1967–1970) was not inevitable – it was avoidable and preventable; on the other side of the continent, the Ethiopian conflagration was not inevitable nor was Mengistu Haile Mariam's rule a logical consequence of anything; and as for the Congo and the Great Lakes region with bloodshed continuing to these days, all were and are deeply regrettable. I agree in principle with Adama Samassékou (2017), the Malian philosopher and visionary, that we should be thinking through his concept of 'humanitude' and prioritise 'being' over 'having', plenitude and compassion over accumulation. In the words of the late Samir Amin (1973), such a humanitude can only flourish when conditions for autochthonous development away from the grip of neocolonialism have been realised.

I never argued though that violence should or could always be avoided. There were and are moments in history when the defence of a movement's integrity or the ultra-violence of a collapsing regime should be dealt with. In the latter case, most settler-thick societies of the colonial era seemed to have spawned violent armed struggles – Algeria, South Africa, Mozambique, Angola, Zimbabwe. But in most it was not about making a fetish of it, but rather regretting the necessity of it as Mandela did both in his famous trial that could have seen him strung up with a sturdy rope, and again after his release from prison.

But if the ethic was seen as problematic by serious colleagues, so were various aspects of my argument about its sources: there were four I had presented then and, despite their discrete origins, I argued it was their contemporary coincidence that mattered. They were: the increasing predominance of neo-Gandhian ideas and practices of militant non-violence in the so-called Third World and the global South; the self-reflexivity of modernity in the West; the increasing convergence between socialist (read anti-Stalinist) and human rights discourses; and finally, the subterranean and usually underrated work of the 'arts' and 'literature' (Sitas 2007, 12). 'After Márquez,' I enthused 'you could never bomb Macondo.'[2]

My first source, which asked of us to take some of Gandhi's philosophy of praxis seriously, met with vociferous criticism from Naxal[3]-supporting students and youth at the Jawaharlal Nehru University in New Delhi, India, but also from the Dalit movement which had been on the rise since the late twentieth century. The former pointed to the necessity of an armed insurgency as the only way to a people's republic. I was told to wake up to the fact that Gandhi's chakra was dead and the Nehruvian vision, a modernist mistake. I tended to agree with Aijaz Ahmad's (1996, 278) take: 'we need a far more careful look at those positions – frequently overlapping positions – that Gandhi and Nehru have represented within that history, even though the fashion these days, on the Right certainly but also in some sections of the radical intelligentsia, is to pitch them as opposites'. The students were not convinced. I was convinced by Nandini Sundar's (2016) nuanced argument in *The Burning Forest*, and I have my doubts of the emancipatory potential of the continuing carnage in the forests.

Similarly, vocal Dalit intellectuals concurred with Gandhi's demotion while elevating B. R. Ambedkar as the true thinker for any discourse of emancipation. They pointed to Gandhi's upper-caste patronising ideas, and as some South African historians have verified, he was a racist to boot. *The South*

African Gandhi: Stretcher Bearer of Empire (2015), written with some finesse by Ashwin Desai and Goolam Vahed, takes us to Gandhi's role on the side of the British against the Zulu insurgents and it demonstrates a racist attitude to non-Indian Blacks. This point is taken up by Arundhati Roy and in her lengthy introduction to Ambedkar's new edition of *Annihilation of Caste* (2014). She claims that Gandhi in 1923 is watering down his prior racism, making himself appear as a supporter of African nationalism. This disturbed me because I was close to the Gandhi family and to his protégées like Ella Gandhi and Fatima Meer. The Gandhi Must Fall movement seemed rather rash but growing in popularity. There is a turning point in 1911 during and after Gandhi's attendance of the famous London Universal Races Congress. After his attendance, his newspaper *Indian Opinion* started publishing a range of critical and strident pieces on race: 'Dr. Du Bois on Race Prejudice' (Du Bois 1909), 'The Crime of Colour' (1911) and another 16 pieces, in three months alone. Gandhi was beginning to open up to the 'race question'. So, by 1923, he could have developed a serious re-evaluation of African nationalism, especially since the South African Native Congress (later the African National Congress, or ANC) was in serious dialogue with him and his networks.

That Gandhi Must Fall has also become a serious preoccupation. I had not at that stage worked through the challenging writings of Gopal Guru (2009) and his compeers on 'humiliation', which was under way at more or less the same time as the 'ethic'. The reduction of a people to a 'walking carrion', to 'mobile dirt', to that nauseating distance that animates a caste order needed serious engagement. And the stark reality that what was promised in the political order was denied in practice demanded a serious take on the dialectics of humiliation, rejection and emergence (Guru 2009). That Gandhi's views on the caste system were problematic there is no doubt. Surinder S. Jodhka's (2014) overview summarises the contours of this dilemma and the emergence of a powerful Dalit movement out of the so-called untouchable castes. He also accounts for the shifting character of the very functioning of caste. A close reading of all this ought to make us critical of the sanctity of a real or imaginary Gandhi.

Because of the sacralisation of the Mahatma, many Indian colleagues cannot separate his philosophy of being from his philosophy of praxis. It is much easier in South Africa where non-violent struggle preceded cosmological argument and within those scattered pieces of writing that constituted the

South African Gandhi, five principles are easily uploaded to a broader conception of morality (Meer and Seedat 1996): social voluntarism – that time is not money and that the free giving of it for other people's well-being is a mark of distinction and self-worth; the cooperative idea, which is a rather obvious socialist principle; the idea that the means of struggle are as important as the ends; the notion of the refusal to think in instrumental terms and an empathetic relationship to people and nature; and, that cultural synthesis was vital but never on the terms of the powerful – a synthesis on the basis of the colonised people's 'cultural dignity and contribution' (Meer and Seedat 1996, 19–20). It is the 'praxological' that I emphasised and not his very Hindu-centric sense of the virtuous life, however deviant and feminine it was, as Ashish Nandy (1983, 52) made us think of it.

It is the praxological that came to influence a struggling humanity on the African continent through vital thinkers like Julius Nyerere and Kwame Nkrumah, Albert Luthuli and Kenneth Kaunda, and many others. It was perhaps wrong of me to juxtapose Nyerere to Fanon instead of juxtaposing him to more hawkish militarists of the continent. I should have pointed out that I was taking issue with a kind of Fanonism that had become paradigmatic in some Black radical intellectual formations. I understand the psychological sources of the need for such assertions, but I tend to agree with Immanuel Wallerstein (1979, 251) that 'if Marx was not a Marxist; then surely Fanon was not a Fanonist'. Wallerstein (1979, 251) continues:

> Fanonism, if I seize the essence of the now countless pejorative (and even some favorable) references to it, is said to be a belief that peasants are more revolutionary than urban workers, that the lumpenproletariat is more revolutionary than the proletariat, that the national bourgeoisie of the Third World is always hopeless, that violence is always purgative, and not only intellectuals but even cadres cannot be relied upon to make the revolution, without spontaneous explosions from the base.

The brutalisation of much of the continent through the forays of armed columns of (primarily) men has devastated vast numbers of people. Neo-Gandhian ideas proliferated as a critique of the bruising nature of the violence that took root. And it is much of this that is appreciated in Africa, and anywhere from Latin America to the furthest East.

I was also challenged by European friends who misunderstood my take on the self-reflexivity of modernity. It was not about the 'spirit of 68' moving us beyond the partial universalisms of the Enlightenment and European imperialism. It is not about the countless, neo-Nietzscheans who have found in his authoritarian postures a precursor of the postmodern, ignoring his derision of anything resembling freedom or equality – remember always that 'with dialectics the rabble gets on top' (Nietzsche 1985, 34). Friedrich Nietzsche, the hero of the philosophers of the 'new', was already bemoaning in 1888 the 'victory of Chandala values, the evangel preached to the poor, and lowly, the rebellion of everything downtrodden, wretched, ill-constituted, underprivileged against the race – undying Chandala revenge as the religion of love! A perpetual rage against the herd, democracy, the feminine – and the well-being dreamed of by shop keepers, Christians, cows, women, Englishmen and other democrats' (Nietzche 1985, 92).

It is not only about the kind of thinker that wins the Adorno prize, from Derrida to Zygmunt Bauman, from Jürgen Habermas to John Butler, heirs of a critical tradition, or even Alexandre Kojève with his design work of a Rome statute in 1962 that gave birth to the European Union. Had it been a debate about instrumental rationality or the critique of enlightenment, the Frankfurt School would have occupied centre stage (Adorno and Horkheimer 1979). It is something more specific that I emphasised, something that deals with Other-ness: about the critique of war and of the bomb, the very notes on 'exterminism' that Edward Thompson (1978) tabled and the need for a post-imperial Europe and a post-racist world. The space where Jean-Paul Sartre met Bertrand Russell to create a People's Tribunal, where Stuart Hall met the anti-apartheid movement, and where feminism met the CND (Campaign for Nuclear Disarmament) on Greenham Common. A self-reflexive modernity that is convinced that might is not right and that Europe or the West is not their neighbours' keeper. A modernity that, after Black people's and migrant communities' struggles, has moved to a sense of the 'post-racial'.

Now to my claims about a multifaceted, democratic socialism: much of the reassertion of socialism does not only owe its presence to the admirable Bernie Sanders and Alexandria Ocasio-Cortez. Much of its normality has also to do with China's ascendance. Its idiomatic expressions of socialism with Chinese characteristics, or the creation of a harmonious society, the Belt and Road Initiative of 'win-win' cooperation make much of what is being invested, moved and claimed palatable. The Chinese emergence and the development model are underpinned by ghastly silk roads with dangerous excesses in Africa. Yet I agree, who wouldn't, with Xi Jinping's (2017, 221) assertion for the need for a new concept of development that is innovative, coordinated, green, open and inclusive. His take on the necessity of greening the economy has been strident: 'eco-environment has no substitutes. We are not aware of this when we exploit it, yet it is irreversible once lost. As I previously mentioned, environment is livelihood, green mountains are beauty, blue sky is happiness, and clear water is wealth. Protecting the environment equates to developing productive forces. We must develop a broad, long-term and holistic perspective' (Xi Jinping 2017, 231). But his pragmatic vanguardism is of a top-town, centralised apparatus of thinking. The 'success' story hides the problematic nature of an undemocratic and a univocal socialism.

Chinese colleagues, enamoured with the vision of Xi Jinping, found my critique of the reified socialism of vanguards ungenerous and they insist that Mao was, as the slogan has it, '70% correct'. They are not alone. There is a reassertion of the correctness of Marxism–Leninism in many parts of the planet. I find that these reassertions of Marxism–Leninism by many in the communist movement are fine as long as they do not mark a return to the monochrome, diamat-inspired socialism of the Stalin era. It seems to me that we have moved from an Ostalgie to a Stalinalgie because most of the existing communist parties are not daring any new ideas. Dogmatisms also continue unabated in many Trotsky-inspired networks as well. No one disagrees with the centrality of class struggles and polarisations, which will continue even without a political form. Even Adam Smith (1974, 169) said as much when he intoned way back in the eighteenth century: 'the workmen desire to get as much, the masters to give as little as possible. The former are disposed to combine in order to raise, the latter in order to lower the wages of labour'. The next step with such a reassertion is the link of this tradition with violent insurrection. Yet, it is only a misreading of Lenin that sanctifies the art of violent insurrection: 'it is impossible to remain loyal to Marxism, to remain loyal to the revolution unless insurrection is treated as an art' (Lenin 1974, 358). Written barely a month before the storming of the Winter Palace, he could not have argued otherwise in 1917. Lenin was never a follower of Louis Auguste Blanqui.

On this too, many luminaries of Western Marxism from, for example, Georg Lukács, Max Horkheimer, Herbert Marcuse, Antonio Gramsci,

Jean-Paul Sartre, Louis Althusser (although his chapter on 'humanism' in *For Marx* [1974] is a peculiar tap dance away from the issue), to Lucio Colletti, would have had different takes on Soviet Marxism. In justifying its existence or abhorring its excesses, not many called it by its proper name, a dictatorship over the proletariat exercised in its assumed interests (Stedman Jones 1977). And its unscientific corollary that only a small vanguard was entitled to define 'its' interests. Even though I am discomfited by the constant reassertion of Marxism–Leninism even in the CPIM (Communist Party of India [Marxist]), the analytical choice for a democratic road to socialism, articulated and re-articulated by E. M. S. Namboodiripad (2005), its breakthroughs in Kerala and so on, must be held in high esteem as it was a demonstrable popular majority that undergirded major reforms. I tend to side with Perry Anderson's (1980, 156) praiseworthy realisation that 'there will never be, and there ought never to be, one single format of socialist internationalism. Here, as elsewhere, variety of tenor and emphasis is not a drawback but an asset for the growth of a vital political culture of the Left'.

In South Africa, for a moment, a year after Joe Slovo (1990) ventured to provide a democratic critique of the reasons why the Soviet Union collapsed, promising a non-vanguard future remained what it was: a moment. The South African Communist Party (SACP) seems to have put his ideas to rest and continued with its belief and commitment in the national democratic revolution as a first stage before the transition to a socialist society.

My argument was different, that there was a return to what was 'lost': 'the universalism of the First International, made up of strands of socialist and communist leaders who articulated that there was only one race, the human race – Chartists, Proudhonists, Manzinians, social democrats, brilliant dogmatists like Marx, and many others who saw the recognition of human equality as a precondition to human freedom' (Sitas 2007, 33). Since the collapse of the Soviet Union, it is the balance between equality and freedom that animates calls for social justice and social rights, and not the one acting as a precondition to the other.

The only constituency that applauded my arguments unequivocally was made up of thinking artists and writers, performers and composers. My discourse on the vital role of their craft as going deeper than 'human rights' or rhetorical abstractions, but creating a polysemic universe in the North and in the South through which the Other disappears into a dignified difference, was well taken. 'What artists bring to consciousness is a unique attention to the "particular", to life forms, to living rights,' I argued (Sitas 2007, 47). In 'inscending' into our civilisational detritus, in refusing to deal with the 'human abstract', they have etched a new landscape of 'humanitude'. Rather than creating an 'artistically faithful image of a concrete historical epoch' (Lukács 1976, 15) as a kind of old school take on the arts, the best exponents since the 1970s have dissected the elements that made up the admixture of the concrete and often the concrete's pretensions.

Among them I found a ready audience that understood how forms moved, how the timbre let us say of South African writing that it is intimately linked to a musicality and infected by jazz, and its transformation by local musicians into a life-defining genre. Had I not had the experiences of the kind of work we spawned in the South African anti-apartheid movement, I would have remained at a level of useless generality. It was not always easy: the Culture and Resistance Conference of 1982 in Gaborone, Botswana, orchestrated by the ANC, involved a very serious fightback by many of us against social-ist realism. The rest was history as 'diverse forms of cultural artefacts and practices emerged during this period, especially in literature, theatre and performance, the plastic arts and the revival of traditional modes of dance (including orature, movement and performance). The development of this counter-hegemonic discourse and practice was welded to the political resist-ance movement ("the struggle"). All this had its repressive consequences too' (Kriger and Zegeye 2001, 2). The Congress of South African Writers we formed with Nadine Gordimer, Achmat Dangor, Mewa Ramgobin, Njabulo Ndebele, Mafika Pascal Gwala, Lance Nawa, Nise Malange, and many others, had a more heterodox view of self-expression. Our work in labour and com-munity performance movements (Von Kotze 1985) used and transformed aspects of a powerful indigenous orature. The entire 1980s and early 1990s was defined primarily by oral debates that have not been collected yet – the Ngũgĩs (wa Mirii and wa Thiong'o), Ayi Kwei Armah, Chenjerai Hove, Nawal El Sadaawi, Wole Soyinka, Ben Okri, and many others, were in fre-quent conversation with us and the worlds ranged from the magical realist to the hyper-realistic.

Alas, I had started my serious discussions on aesthetics and politics with a range of remarkable creators in AfroAsia a year after drafting the *Ethic*. The idea of an international of the imagination came through lengthy discussions with Sumangala Damodaran (2017) in India whose *Radical Impulse* – a study of the complexity of the Indian People's Theatre Association's musical legacy – depended on intensely local and trans-local connections, and the nurturing of an affective and varied universe of expression. Since then, our award-winning work in music through the *Insurrections Ensemble* and musicological research, ancient and contemporary, has brought out commonalities of affect and sorrow over vast swathes of terra firma. Whereas our work has been quite political, there are plenty of examples of how this has taken a deep cultural turn: it is a similar animus that propels Yo-Yo Ma's *Silk Road Ensemble* and Jordi Savall's reconstruction of neglected soundscapes from medieval Europe, Byzantium, Granada, Istanbul and Jerusalem, and lately, of the Slave Routes.

So, to my critics: I still stand by my argument that give or take some corrections, an ethic of reconciliation is very much with us, despite the waves of authoritarian and quasi-fascist forms of restoration. Perhaps it is one of the few weapons left for many of us during this weakening period of drift.

It has been hard to define an ethic that envelops human relations in an emancipated society. It has been very hard even for positivists to derive an 'ought' from what 'is', let alone a notion beyond distributive or restorative justice, or a fairer version of individual/human/social rights.

The closest in Marx is to be found in a radical contrast: the notion of alienation in capitalist society on the one hand, versus a dis-alienated reciprocity where 'the free development of each is a condition for the free development of all' (Marx and Engels 1974, 35). The latter has been common fare in African philosophies of coexistence, the very 'humanitude' that Adama Samassékou (2017, 2) alerted us to: 'I use this concept of *humanitude* to translate what, in Africa,' he argues, 'we call *maaya* (in Bamanankan, the Bambara language), *neddaaku* (in Fulfulde, the Fula language), *boroterey* (in Songhay, the Songhay language), *nite* (in Wolof), *ubuntu* (in the Bantu languages), and many more.' Even if the concept of alienation is quite restrictive, it hints heavily in this direction. Defined as it was in Marx's Paris Manuscripts as fourfold, alienation was about the experience in and around the worlds of capitalist work. There are other senses of oppression and powerlessness that need to come into the equation like senses of degendering, this inchoate sensation out of the pressures of sexed and gendered role performances; there are senses of disoralia, through which voice, speech, expression and language are sources of suffering and senses of dis-valuation – an incapacity to arrive at any moral certitude about good or bad, right or wrong. Although the pressures of capitalist society may influence all, they demand different levels of attention because they operate in relative autonomy from each other.

Part of the problem is the couching of all this in the elegance of a Hegelian dialectic of recognition, otherwise known as the dialectic of mastery and slavery (Honneth 1995). It operates as a cryptocurrency in all accounts of emancipation. It presupposes two equal wills or desires facing off in a duel unto death. The one cowers to become the slave, the other triumphs into mastery, and thus starts the story of their reciprocal contradictions that lead to the emancipation of bondage and mastery. Slave consciousness emerges as the true impulse for its overcoming. This fable of historical thinking obfuscates what the crux of historical encounters entails.

It was never about two equal wills in the arena of battle. There were those who were seen as non-beings and exterminable from the Americas to the southern Cape, from Africa to Australasia.

In 1992, I met up with Aboriginal leadership in and around Perth, Australia, and then later artists who were from the forcefully adopted mixed-descent children. I was part of the South African labour movement's delegation that was to inaugurate what became SIGTUR (Southern Initiative on Globalisation and Trade Union Rights), linking the movements of Brazil, India, Vietnam, Philippines, Indonesia, Australia, South Korea, among others, and South Africa. We spent hours asking questions from our perspective of land expropriation and colonisation. We soon realised that we were coming from another galaxy of issues and grievances. First, they were a contemporary minority; second, they were not supposed to exist; third, they had survived but were forced into the remotest and most fallow spaces; fourth, the idea of Australia, its very indigeneity, excluded them. Finally, their very unassimilable Other-ness disturbed the essence and narrative of 'Aussiehood'. We also talked about dreaming and songlines.

I was fortunate, too, to be partly responsible for the 2001 civil society testimonies – the shadow gig of the World Conference on Racism, in Durban, where I had the privilege of meeting delegates of First Nation formations from Central and South America, Marshall Islanders and Dalit movement leaders. The Central and South Americans and Marshall Islanders taught me what I had named later as 'ecoality' – the unmediated relationship to all other sentient beings and ecosystems. The Dalit movement leaders taught me about their need to equate Indian caste-ism with apartheid racism. In-between, I was more than lucky to meet leaderships of Latino movements in Berkeley, and a major figure of the Sandinistas in Mexico (she insists still that she remain anonymous). My interactions with the leadership of the National Association for the Advancement of Colored People (NAACP) and my fathoming of contemporary African American politics had to await their visit to Durban as part of the African Renaissance Initiative that I co-led with ANC minister and later premier, Sbu Ndebele, and my mercurial philosopher artist friend Pitika Ntuli, and quite a few others – the crux of it was to move the province of KwaZulu-Natal beyond conflict and the ravages of the civil war it had endured in the 1980s and early 1990s.

To commit to the other as non-exterminable drags two monstrous experiences back into the arena: the experience of First Nations as they are known today, and later all instances of existential deviants – where who you *are*, has been or is the problem. Your extinction, extirpation, removal was and is the obvious sequel. The problem with 'the' dialectic (and its assumptions of progress) was that such non-people survived and are finding their voice. Their sense of Other-ness and self-abjection, solidarity and transcendence are very different from the classic cameo. First Nations will remain minorities in our modern world, as have their historical traumata of near extinction inside their meaning-worlds. Their mnemonic constellations, the result of prior processes of grief-work, can never be invoked to construct a hegemonic trauma, a collective memory in the societies they live in. Their experiences and actions remain inassimilable. Later there were those who were seen as existential deviants – not because of what they did or said, but for who they were or are. They survived holocausts and genocide. They too have voice.

Then there were those who were derogated but deemed to be useful as slaves or colonial subjects, who were seen to be full of 'the moral efficiency of savage beliefs', as Bronislaw Malinowski (1948, 12) mused. They were 'othered', broken into, classified, excluded, defined and redefined, and they resisted, fought, expressed, counter-argued. And then, there are our 'nons', the undesirable Others in our proverbial midst, the migrant and the refugee, the various not-us that could be at any moment the very 'us' as well: there is a potential Syria everywhere.

Indigenous movements have added a fourth: sentient beings and the very axis of this planet is also a non-us, they are very much us to the last molecule.

If Black slaves in rebellion brought the meaning of freedom into the modern entanglement, if levellers, women and workers brought the notion of equality into sharp focus, the people of the forests and arid pampas, those who have survived the sharp metallic splinters of progress, brought ecoality as part of the pulse of freedom and transformation.

The ethic I thought is a small tentative beginning in sorting out this historical, regrettable mess of so-called progress. Is reconciliation possible? Is coexistence possible? Is regret ever enough? Recognition and morality have to be much more complex than a simple dialectic. I do think that the moment of Fusako Shigenobu (Al Jazeera 2022) has passed.[4] It will have to be a complex and quite differentiated society that we dream of united in difference and diversity, and there to facilitate individual, group and collective forms of flourishing. And the borders must go.

The implications of all this for the need for a new curriculum in the social sciences should be obvious. One needs a clear redrafting of the emergence of social formations in southern Africa before European foraging and settlement. Then one needs the stories of the violent entanglements that followed, and the processes of settler colonisation. The constructions of the European and the African as well as the creation of phenotypes, religious insiders and outsiders, will be found there. The Cape Town encounters were as key a contributor to the development of the Calvinist/Protestant ethic in Europe as North American encounters were key to the development of Wesleyan Methodism. Slavery, indenture, forced labour and tenancy had their seminal and world-defining frontiers there.

Whereas Great Zimbabwe, Mapungubwe and what is now Limpopo province were important nodes of the world system until the sixteenth century, through the East African coastlines with gold being one of its prized exports, their importance recedes once the Potosi mines in the Americas start stockpiling silver, and the Chinese decide that silver's shine was more suitable to their taste. Gold re-emerges as a blessing and a curse for southern Africa via imperial Britain's decision to establish a gold standard and force hundreds of thousands of Black miners underground. All that is indicated here is that the local can be a way through which the entire entanglement that constituted the so-called modern world system can be elucidated.

More than that is what constitutes the anti-colonial – that search from Other-ness to Self. By this I mean the search that arises once the externally imposed categories of the 'Native' as Other are rejected by the colonised. This search took many turns in southern Africa, as much as it did in the Congo, Tanzania, Nigeria, Senegal or Egypt. The same impulse produced a multiplicity of claims; they can be compared, outlined and extended. One could stretch East and West and say wait a minute, the prior acts of independence in the Americas were settler-led rebellions as opposed to the ones in South East Asia.

One can even script the drama of epistemic encounters in the 1911 Universal Race Congress in London which had Abdullah Abdurahman, Alfred Mangena, Mohandas Gandhi (alas, Olive Schreiner fell ill and could not attend) meet sociologists W. E. B. DuBois, Ferdinand Tönnies, Émile Durkheim, Max Weber, eugenicist Eugen Fischer (later a Nazi guru), anthropologist Franz Boas, as well as Fabians, socialists, Christians, Moslems, Hindus, Jews, theosophists, colonial administrators, and so on. One could ask why it failed, despite its anti-racist resolutions, to ever reconvene again.

In doing this we will start moving from the 'contingent' to the 'substantive', to a new curriculum. Such an effort is being encouraged by institutions like the National Institute of Humanities and Social Sciences, and by the UNESCO (United Nations Educational, Scientific and Cultural Organization) initiatives to create substantive recognitions of tangible and intangible forms of heritage. It would be prudent to look back at what emerged during other 'rapturous periods' so nothing is lost in the story of scholarship and resistance on this tip of the African continent.

Through all of the contextual nuances one could be studying regimes of derogation, environmental and epistemic forms of violence, archaeology and musicality. Yet whichever content is chosen, the subterranean moral formation and its implications remain: what kind of non-derogatory ethic animates scholarship?

NOTES

1   The collection, 'This Here Collection Is Incoherent', was published as a newspaper incorporating leading student voices of the movement and circulated widely.

2   Madondo is the fictional town, home to the Buendía family, in Gabriel García Márquez' novel *One Hundred Years of Solitude* (1967).

3   Indian communist groups, of the Naxal movement.

4   In May 2022, 76-year-old Fusako Shigenobu, co-founder of the armed group Japanese Red Army, was released from prison in Japan after serving a 20-year sentence. In 1971,

Shigenobu had set up the Japanese Red Army in Lebanon to link up with Palestinian fighters against Israel. The group was responsible for plane attacks and hostage-taking throughout the 1970s.

REFERENCES

Adorno, Theodor W. and Max Horkheimer. 1979. *The Dialectic of Enlightenment*. London: Verso.

Ahmad, Aijaz. 1996. *Lineages of the Present*. Delhi: Tulika Press.

Al Jazeera. 2022. 'Japanese Red Army Founder Shigenobu Freed from Prison'. *Al Jazeera*, 28 May 2022. https://www.aljazeera.com/news/2022/5/28/japanese-red-army-founder-shigenobu-freed-from-prison.

Althusser, Louis. 1974. *For Marx*. London: New Left Books.

Ambedkar, Bhimrao Ramji. 2014. *Annihilation of Caste: The Annotated Critical Edition*. New Delhi: Navayana.

Amin, Samir. 1973. *Neo-Colonialism in West Africa*. Harmondsworth: Penguin.

Anderson, Perry. 1980. *Arguments within English Marxism*. London: New Left Books.

Anonymous. 1911. 'Record of the Proceedings of the First Universal Race Congress, July 26–29, 1911'. London: P. S. King & Son.

Anonymous. 2018. 'This Here Collection is Incoherent'. Special Edition by the Fees and Rhodes Must Fall Students.

Arrighi, Giovanni. 2007. *Adam Smith in Beijing*. London: Verso.

Biko, Steve. 1978. *I Write What I Like*. Johannesburg: Heinemann Educational Publishers.

Cohen, Robin and Shirin M. Rai, eds. 2000. *Global Social Movements*. London: Athlone Press.

Damodaran, Sumangala. 2017. *The Radical Impulse: Music in the Tradition of the Indian People's Theatre Association*. Delhi: Tulika Press.

Derrida, Jacques. 2001. *Cosmopolitanism and Forgiveness*. London: Routledge.

Desai, Ashwin and Goolam Vahed. 2015. *The South African Gandhi: Stretcher Bearer of Empire*. Stanford, CA: Stanford University Press.

Deutsche Welle. 2003. 'WTO Talks Collapse in Cancun'. *Deutsche Welle*, 15 September 2003. https://www.dw.com/en/wto-talks-collapse-in-cancun/a-970989.

Du Bois, William Edward Burghardt. 1909. 'Dr. Du Bois on Race Prejudice'. *Indian Opinion*, 28 August 1909.

Fanon, Frantz. 1974. *The Wretched of the Earth*. Harmondsworth: Penguin.

García Márquez, Gabriel. 1978 [1967]. *One Hundred Years of Solitude*. Translated by Gregory Rabassa. London: Picador/Pan Macmillan.

Guru, Gopal, ed. 2009. *Humiliation*. Delhi: Oxford University Press.

Hegel, Georg W. 1975. *The Philosophy of Right*. Translated by T. M. Knox. London: Oxford University Press.

Honneth, Alex. 1995. *The Struggle for Recognition: The Moral Grammar of Social Conflicts*. Cambridge: Cambridge University Press.

Jinping, Xi. 2017. *The Governance of China II*. Beijing: Foreign Languages Press.

Jodhka, Surinder S. 2014. *Caste*. Delhi: Oxford University Press.

Kriger, Robert and Abebe Zegeye, eds. 2001. *Culture in the New South Africa*. Cape Town: Kwela Books.

Lenin, Ilyich Ulyanov. 1974. *Selected Works*. London: Progress Publishers.

Lukács, Georg. 1976. *The Historical Novel*. Harmondsworth: Penguin.

Malinowski, Bronislaw. 1948. *Magic, Science and Religion*. New York: The Free Press.

Marx, Karl. 1986. *Capital: A Critique of Political Economy*. Volume 1. London: Penguin in Association with New Left Books.

Marx, Karl and Friedrich Engels. 1974 [1848]. *The Communist Manifesto*. Harmondsworth: Penguin.

Meer, Fatima and Hassim Seedat, eds. 1996. *The South African Gandhi: An Abstract of the Speeches and Writings of M.K. Gandhi, 1893–1914*. Durban: Madiba Press.

Namboodiripad, E. M. S. 2005. *The Frontline Years*. Delhi: LeftWord Press.

Nandy, Ashish. 1983. *The Intimate Enemy: Loss and Recovery of Self under Colonialism*. Delhi: Oxford University Press.

Nietzsche, Friedrich. 1985. *Twilight of the Idols/The Anti-Christ*. Harmondsworth: Penguin Books.

Rathbone, John Paul. 2014. 'Lunch with the FT: Roberto Mangabeira Unger'. *Financial Times*, 3 October 2014. https://www.ft.com/content/73226246-48a7-11e4-9d04-00144feab7de.

Samassékou, Adama. 2017. *Humanitude, or How to Quench the Thirst for Humanity*. Paris: International Council for Philosophy and the Human Sciences.

Sitas, Ari. 2007. *The Ethic of Reconciliation*. Durban: Madiba Press.

Sitas, Ari. 2011. 'Beyond the Mandela Decade: The Ethic of Reconciliation'. *Current Sociology* 59 (5): 571–589. doi: 10.1177/0011392111408666.

Slovo, Joe. 1990. 'Has Socialism Failed?' *South African Labour Bulletin* 14 (6): 11–28. https://www.sahistory.org.za/sites/default/files/Has%20Socialism%20Failed%20by%20Joe%20Slovo.pdf.

Smith, Adam. 1974. *The Wealth of Nations*. London: Pelican.

Stedman Jones, Gareth. 1977. *Western Marxism: A Critical Reader*. London: New Left Books.

Sundar, Nandini. 2016. *The Burning Forest*. New Delhi: Juggernaut Press.

Thompson, Edward Palmer. 1978. *The Poverty of Theory*. London: Merlin Press.

Von Kotze, Astrid. 1985. *Organise and Act: The Workers' Theatre Movement in Natal*. Durban: Culture and Working Life Publications.

Wallerstein, Immanuel. 1979. *The Capitalist World-Economy*. Cambridge: Cambridge University Press.

AFTERWORD

AMRITA PANDE, RUCHI CHATURVEDI AND SHARI DAYA

In the opening pages of this volume, we reflected on the context from which the book emerged. We invoked, with Stuart Hall, the idea of 'postcolonial time' (Hall 1996, 242), to theorise the reality that the contributors to this book have inherited and inhabit, one that is marked by the spectre of 'university apartheid' as well as efforts to transcend it. University apartheid, as Teresa Barnes (2019, 3) has mobilised the term, refers not only to segregation in staffing and admission but also to perceptions and attitudes about the differential worth of some lives and cultures over others. Those understandings shaped practices in the past and remain with us today in various ways in South African higher education.

Within that context, the University of Cape Town (UCT) is the site from which we write. By its own account, UCT is shaped by legacies of 'systemic demographic inequalities' that are made worse by 'a culture of bullying' (UCT 2019, 81).[1] The university as 'a crucible of converging pressures', and as a place that has fomented 'pain and division', also contributed to the death by suicide of one of its luminaries, Professor Bongani Mayosi, in 2018 (Huisman 2020). UCT students and staff have sought to resist mistreatment and university apartheid in the past, and they seek to undo it today. This book is about the ongoing work of unmaking and remaking, which many of the university's academics are carrying out through their everyday teaching, research and learning.

In a postcolonial time of pain, division and converging pressures, as well as opportunities to undo the past and forge a better future, *what* do we, as academics in the humanities and social sciences in South African universities, teach? *How* do we teach? What have we learned through teaching, both from one another and from our students? How is that learning proceeding, and where do we hope it can take us? This book has attempted to address these questions from the vantage point of a few UCT academics, mainly based in the social sciences and humanities, all of whom are seeking to build on past resistances while attending to the recent calls for decolonisation by Fallist and similar movements.

The place and time in which our contributors hope to dwell is one of greater epistemic justice. Achieving this requires an interrogation of the embedded distinctions between the knower and known in our curricula and classrooms. This book takes a multiscalar approach to this interrogation, addressing disciplinary developments as well as pedagogical practices within institutional and classroom spaces. In the first part, the authors imagined and designed an inventive crossing of disciplinary, linguistic and national boundaries. Nomusa Makhubu describes movement across such boundaries in different aesthetic practices and art collectives as 'itinerant interventions'. These interventions allow the possibility of decentred and decommodified learning. The contributions by Rike Sitas and Shari Daya offer more such transgressions of spatial and disciplinary boundaries in 'Southerning' our theoretical and pedagogical imaginations. First, Rike Sitas explores how artistic practice could become the conduit for accessing 'the very human and emotional negotiations' that individuals and publics engage in as they take on everyday inequalities and injustices, both large and small. Reflections on these humanising artistic practices belong in a geography classroom as much as in an art history one. Next, Shari Daya and Rike Sitas' co-authored chapter on teaching urban studies through fiction and film shows us how an interdisciplinary curriculum and classroom might be created so that students do not, for instance, experience postcolonial cities such as Lagos and Nairobi only as places of deprivation and deficiency, but also as places where just imaginaries can be iterated through narrative and visual texts. In the final chapter of part I, Athambile Masola turns to multilingual and visual archives as transgressive methodological and pedagogical ways to recover Black womxn's voices in the curriculum and classroom.

In the increasingly neoliberal higher education sector where the university seeks to 'monetise' its brand, how should we respond to the call for itinerant, decommodified and transgressive learning across borders? Can these tensions be reconciled? *Should* they be reconciled? Inhabiting postcolonial times, we suggest, is about grappling with such questions. It is also about understanding how post-apartheid South Africa and other postcolonial states reckon with predicaments that seem irreconcilable. Further, it is about contending with the challenges that we face in these places, without holding up Western modernity and rationality as the normative models. In part II of the book, contributors who put forth new modes of teaching within the humanities and law, including Koni Benson, Kerusha Govender, Jameelah Omar, Shose Kessi and Hal Cooper, seek to do precisely that. In their research and teaching, these contributors mobilise the archives of everyday life, social and political thought, as well as debates about the present and pasts of their disciplines, in ways that enable students to redefine and theorise the meanings, possibilities and impossibilities of a good life, equality, justice and freedom, in their own contexts.

The last section of the book, focused on institutional history and spaces, connects these tensions to possibilities for reconciliation. Lungisile Ntsebeza speaks with Sepideh Azari about the fraught history and critical presence of the Centre for African Studies at UCT. Kealeboga Mase Ramaru similarly explores the histories and politics that have shaped UCT's African Gender Institute. Underlying the attempts to undo stubborn epistemic inequities, within and beyond the institution, lies the necessity of forging what Ari Sitas, in the final chapter, terms 'a non-derogatory ethic'. A genuinely just curriculum would closely study both the violent entanglements of past and present, and the processes that can bring about genuine reciprocity.

Through these contributions, we chronicle the history of UCT in an attempt to situate current debates around decolonisation within the spaces inhabited by the editors and contributors to this volume. We demonstrate that, along with higher education institutions across the world, UCT is witnessing a 'paradigm shift' where the need to rethink curricula and pedagogies is acute. We highlight the need to acknowledge the (productive) paradox that the institution now celebrated as the 'birthplace of Fallism' also has a troubling history of complicity in colonialism and apartheid. These past and contemporary injustices are thrown into relief as UCT embraces the 'decolonial turn' and attempts to spearhead several initiatives towards a more socially just environment for learning (Morreira 2021).

The Covid-19 pandemic swept across the nation and the globe before many of the initiatives outlined in this volume could find firm grounding. Universities were shut down as part of the national lockdown. Across the world, nations closed their borders to protect their citizens from spreading the virus. Once again, a crisis brought into sharp relief contestations over knowledge and power. It also brought to the fore what Sabelo Ndlovu-Gatsheni (2020, 368) labels the 'inadequacy of normal-times thinking and theorizing when applied to exceptional moments'. As the world economic systems went 'out of joint' in some respects, bringing to a halt what we all held as normal, so did the university education system. But not for long.

At UCT, management strategised to retain some semblance of business as usual, moving the academic project to an online mode and tackling the 'digital divide' with a plan to distribute laptops and data to students in need. So-called Emergency Remote Teaching (ERT) and Physically Distant Learning (PDL) were implemented. These decisions did not go unchallenged. There were calls from several departments and the Black Academic Caucus (BAC) to avoid making a hasty move to online learning, and instead to pause, engage with the enormity of the moment, strategise collectively at the national level, rethink our curricula, and learn the new technologies and alternative pedagogies required to 'best deliver a socially just curriculum building on the momentum generated by the intellectual movements that were developed post-2015' (BAC Letter to Executive, 20 March 2020).[2]

While management was applauded for its swift response in providing access to online resources, the so-called digital divide was recognised as just one aspect of the inequality among our students. Those critical of the decision to continue business as usual emphasised that the majority of our students did not have home environments that were conducive to remote work. They worried about the 'psychological effects' of the pandemic, the increasing burden of care responsibilities at home and work, the disproportionate burden of which fell on womxn (students and staff alike). But as universities scrambled to jump on the 'blended learning' bandwagon, these discussions were all too often sidestepped. On the one hand, the pandemic became a mirror for many past and contemporary injustices; on the other, it made visible the many paradoxes of the academy attempting to embrace epistemically and socially just learning while simultaneously wanting to monetise an unexpected, pandemic-driven push into a digital milieu (Sayed and Singh 2020). As we inhabit the pandemic-induced 'new normal', we must keep at the core what might well be the biggest challenge of postcolonial times – reimagining a higher education sector which does not see students and staff as disposable, and which can live by 'a non-derogatory ethic', especially in times of crisis.

NOTES

1   These legacies are, for instance, recorded in the findings of the university's most recent inclusivity survey (UCT 2019).

2   Not in the public online record but a copy can be obtained from the editors.

REFERENCES

Barnes, Teresa. 2019. *Uprooting University Apartheid in South Africa: From Liberalism to Decolonization*. Oxford: Routledge.

Hall, Stuart. 1996. 'When Was "The Post-Colonial"? Thinking at the Limit'. In *The Post-Colonial Question: Common Skies, Divided Horizons*, edited by Iain Chambers and Lidia Curti, 242–260. London: Routledge.

Huisman, Biénne. 2020. 'Professor Suicide: Bongani Mayosi Faced Animosity from Students and Colleagues, while UCT Failed to Support Him as His Health Faltered'. *Daily Maverick*, 26 June 2020. https://www.dailymaverick.co.za/article/2020-06-26-bongani-mayosi-faced-animosity-from-students-and-colleagues-while-uct-failed-to-support-him-as-his-health-faltered-report/.

Morreira, Shannon. 2021. 'Pandemic Pedagogy: Assessing the Online Implementation of a Decolonial Curriculum'. 7th International Conference on Higher Education Advances (HEAd'21), 22–23 June 2021, Universitat Politècnica de València, València, Spain.

Ndlovu-Gatsheni, Sabelo J. 2020. 'Geopolitics of Power and Knowledge in the Covid-19 Pandemic: Decolonial Reflections on a Global Crisis'. *Journal of Developing Societies* 36 (4): 366–389.

Sayed, Yusuf and Marcina Singh. 2020. 'Evidence and Education Policy Making in South Africa during Covid-19: Promises, Researchers and Policy Makers in an Age of Unpredictability'. *Southern African Review of Education* 26 (1): 20–39. https://hdl.handle.net/10520/ejc-sare-v26-n1-a3.

UCT (University of Cape Town). 2019. 'UCT Staff Inclusivity Survey. Findings from the Staff Inclusivity Survey'. 20 December 2019. https://www.news.uct.ac.za/images/userfiles/downloads/media/UCT_Inclusivity_Report_2019.pdf.

CONTRIBUTORS

Sepideh Azari was, at the time of writing her contribution to this volume, a doctoral candidate in the Department of Sociology at the University of Cape Town. Her research looked at the role of the natural and social sciences in the construction of 'the native' in South African scholarship between 1920 and 1940, focusing on an exploration of the epistemic formations and academic traditions of the University of Cape Town.

Koni Benson is a historian, organiser and educator. She is a senior lecturer in the Department of History at the University of the Western Cape, South Africa. Her research is on collective interventions in histories of contested development, and the mobilisation, demobilisation and remobilisation of struggle history in southern Africa's past and present.

Ruchi Chaturvedi is a senior lecturer in the Department of Sociology, University of Cape Town. Her teaching and research focuses on cultures of democracy, popular politics and violence in postcolonial contexts, particularly majoritarianism, Hindu nationalism and interparty violence in South India. She is currently researching the violent 1980s period in Natal, South Africa, to understand how cultural organisers and womxn political activists navigated that fraught landscape.

Hal Cooper completed his Honours in the Department of Psychology at the University of Cape Town and has an MA in social justice and education from University College London. His professional experience has largely been in the education and development non-profit sector, with extensive work being carried out with migrants and refugees in Sicily. He is currently an MSc student in evidence-based social intervention and policy evaluation at the University of Oxford.

Shari Daya is a senior lecturer in human geography in the Department of Environmental and Geographical Science at the University of Cape Town. Her academic background is in literary studies and cultural geography. Her work explores questions of material culture, identity, and ethical relations in cities of the global South. Her work is positioned at the intersection of literary studies and social science, reflecting her combined interests in narrative theory and methodology on the one hand, and in social and cultural analysis on the other.

Kerusha Govender completed her Honours in the Department of Historical Studies at the University of Cape Town. Her research interests revolve around the political nature of the historical narrative of South Africa's precolonial, colonial and apartheid periods, and what kinds of stories are left out. She is especially interested in diasporic communities, particularly Indians, and how they have been assimilated in South Africa.

Shose Kessi is a professor in the Department of Psychology and dean of the Faculty of Humanities at the University of Cape Town. Her research and teaching revolve around decolonial, feminist and pan-African psychologies. She is also a co-founder and the first chairperson of the UCT Black Academic Caucus.

Nomusa Makhubu is an associate professor of art history in the Faculty of Humanities, University of Cape Town. In 2018, she founded Creative Knowledge Resources – a platform for documenting socially engaged art practices. Her current research focuses on African popular culture, photography, interventionism, performance art and socially engaged art.

Athambile Masola is a lecturer in the Department of Historical Studies at the University of Cape Town. An award-winning poet who writes in isiXhosa, Masola's academic research and writing revolve around Black womxn's historiography, life writing, and intellectual history from the nineteenth and twentieth centuries.

Lungisile Ntsebeza is emeritus professor of African studies and sociology in the Centre for African Studies at the University of Cape Town. His research interests are in the field of the political economy of land in Africa. He also focuses on African studies, with specific reference to the University of Cape Town.

Jameelah Omar is an associate professor in the Department of Public Law at the University of Cape Town. She lectures criminal procedure, criminal law and an elective on criminal justice and the Constitution in the LLB programme, and a course on sexual offences in the LLM programme. Her research focuses on procedure and substantive criminal law, especially sexual offences. She also works on issues of state responses to dissent through her work on protest law and civil disobedience.

Amrita Pande is a professor in the Department of Sociology at the University of Cape Town. Her research focuses on the intersection of globalisation and the intimate with a particular focus on reproductive labour and new reproductive technologies. She is also an educator-performer touring the world with a performance lecture series, 'Made in India: Notes from a Baby Farm', based on her ethnographic work on surrogacy. She is currently writing her next monograph on the 'global fertility flows' of eggs, sperm, embryos and wombs, connecting the world in unexpected ways.

Kealeboga Mase Ramaru is a feminist organiser based in Cape Town, South Africa. She is the democracy and social justice programme manager at the Cape Town office of the Heinrich Böll Foundation. She previously held positions as a junior research fellow at the African Gender Institute at the University of Cape Town (UCT), innovation manager at the DG Murray Trust, and deputy head of the Equal Education Western Cape office. Her organising ranges through various thematic areas such as sexual and reproductive health rights, SOGIESC organising, social justice education and feminist leadership. She is also the co-founder and convenor of the Queer Feminist Film Festival (#QFFF) and is currently a Master's candidate in gender studies at UCT.

Ari Sitas is an emeritus professor of sociology at the University of Cape Town. An eminent poet, dramatist and renowned sociologist, his research and writings range from the fields of labour studies, ethics and international relations, to shared cultural histories of Asia and Africa.

Rike Sitas is an urban researcher and creative practitioner based at the African Centre for Cities at the University of Cape Town. She is responsible for a wide range of interdisciplinary and collaborative research projects and is currently working on urban arts, culture and heritage through 'Whose Heritage Matters', 'Power Talks' and 'Heritopolis', and on urban and technological interfaces through projects such as 'Young and Online in African Cities', 'African Cities Lab' and 'Platform Politics and Silicon Savannahs'.

INDEX